ALAN BALL

PLAYING EXTRA TIME

Alan Ball was born on 12 May 1945 in Farnworth, Bolton. He played seventy-three times for England, winning the World Cup in 1966. He won the League Championship in 1969/1970. On entering management, Ball had spells as player/manager at Blackpool, Portsmouth, Stoke City, Southampton and Manchester City.

ALAN BALL

PLAYING EXTRA TIME

with James Mossop

PAN BOOKS

First published 2004 by Sidgwick & Jackson

First published in paperback 2005 by by Pan Books

This edition published 2007 by Pan Books
an imprint of Pan Macmillan Ltd
Pan Macmillan, 20 New Wharf Road, London N1 9RR
Basingstoke and Oxford
Associated companies throughout the world
www.panmacmillan.com

ISBN 978-0-230-76857-4

1 3 5 7 9 8 6 4 2

A CIP catalogue record for this book is available from
the British Library.

Typeset by SetSystems Ltd, Saffron Walden, Essex

Printed and bound by CPI Group (UK) Ltd, Croydon, CR0 4YY

Visit **www.panmacmillan.com** to read more about all our books and to buy
them. You will also find features, author interviews and news of any author
events, and you can sign up for e-newsletters so that you're always first to hear
about our new releases.

To my wonderful wife, Lesley,
my three children and my three grandchildren,
without whom I would not have
achieved anything.

CONTENTS

INTRODUCTION

It was a dark, dank afternoon in early March 2001 but everything in my life felt sunny. I had been playing in a charity golf day in Surrey and was driving home to our Hampshire village of Warsash with the radio playing, happily immersed in my own contentment. I had finished with football, the game that had always been the passion of my life. In the solitude of the car the memories flew from starting out at Blackpool to playing for England, Everton, Arsenal, and Southampton and in America. Playing the game was my life. When I moved into management I lived the game with the same fervour, but nothing could match the tingle of lacing your boots before running out to face the opposition.

That was all behind me but life away from the game meant that I had so much to enjoy, surrounded by the closeness and warmth of my family. Lesley, the only girl I have ever loved, was the bedrock and leader of everything the Balls did. There were our three grown-up children, Mandy, Keely and Jimmy, and our precious grandson, Louie. There has always been a powerful sense of togetherness within the Ball family.

Then the mobile phone rang, jolting me out of my reverie. It was Lesley and I knew instantly that there was a problem. It was a call that was to change our lives. Mandy, our eldest daughter was due for a biopsy on a small lump she had found in her breast. Weirdly, that very same day, Lesley had felt a pain in her own groin but had thought nothing of it.

It was the beginning of the biggest fight, the most enormous challenge of our lives. I was to learn that my daughter had breast cancer and soon after that Lesley was suffering from the ovarian version of this horrible disease.

When I set off for golf that day I knew that Mandy was going for the results of her biopsy. We had talked it through the week before and although we knew how serious it could be, we had convinced ourselves that at her age, thirty-two, it was much more likely to be something less grave. Not long before she had given birth to Louie. I told her that ninety-nine times out of a hundred there would be no problems.

The phone call changed everything. I heard Lesley say: 'Alan, we've got a problem. They think it's cancer.' She said much more and so, probably, did I but I didn't hear any more. I was in the kind of trance that is shock.

Before that call I had always considered myself a lucky lad. I had played football at the top end, seventy-two caps for England and eighteen seasons at the highest club level.

Memories of winning the 1966 World Cup with such a grand set of lads always made me smile. I had experienced the highs and lows of football club management and now thought that I could look forward to a relaxed, comfortable time with my family.

After the call I was frantic, wanting to rush home but at the same time dreading arriving. It was difficult to take in what was happening. What could happen to Mandy? Would we lose our darling daughter? What had we done to deserve something like this coming into our lives?

I thought of all the good times with my mam and dad, Alan senior, who had been my mentor, inspiration, teacher, everything to me. I thought of the tough times when clubs such as Bolton and Wolves rejected me because I was too small and I realized the past meant nothing compared to the way I felt at that moment as I drove like a madman down the M3 to get to my family.

In my whirl of thoughts I remembered how I had coped with losing my father and then my mother. There was the loss of Lesley's mother and father that we had got through. But this was my daughter, my little girl. How does anyone handle that?

I drove straight to Mandy's house to find a heartbroken young couple with their baby boy and my wife with a look of horror on her face. It was the start of years of helplessness because, although we didn't know it at the time, cancerous cells were beginning to multiply in Lesley as well.

At fifty-six, I was the head of the family and suppos-edly the strongest, but it didn't always feel like that. All I could do was try to reassure everyone that it would turn out OK and pray that I would be proved right.

That day back in March, Lesley had gone to the

hospital with Mandy. She later told me what had happened. They thought they were just going to hear the results of the biopsy, but the doctor called Mandy in for an ultrasound scan while Lesley waited with little Louie. When Mandy came back to them she was even more subdued than she had been earlier. She said she had been told to wait.

They sat in the waiting room, trying hard to be light-hearted with the nurses and the other women who were there, but it wasn't really working. Everyone had gone by the time the doctor called Mandy back. The staff, the nurses, the doctor and even the women carers were understanding and friendly. Their expertise at helping everyone was marvellous.

Lesley was advised to wait. She wanted to go in with her and said to the nurse in a pleading voice: 'Please don't let them tell my daughter anything bad.' It was probably a futile request but the nurse gave her a gentle smile that was meant to be reassuring.

A few long minutes later Lesley turned around to see Mandy standing there with a look of absolute shock on her face. They had told her that the lump in her breast was the wrong shape. It should have been oval but it was round. There was no need for words. They tried to hold back their tears and embraced. Louie was not old enough to know what was going on. Mandy had been told to go to the breast clinic. It was a horrid day, cold and raining, and the clinic was at the top of a steep hill. The full impact had hit Mandy. She was shaking, with Lesley trying to push the pram with one hand and the other around Mandy's shoulders. As they trundled along, wondering what to expect, Mandy turned to Lesley and said: 'Mum, will you stop smoking now please.' Lesley has never had another cigarette from that moment.

They sat in the room for what seemed like an age. They were both crying but trying to be brave for each other's sake. The doctor told Mandy in a way that was both sympathetic and matter of fact that the lump was malignant and would have to be removed. He said she could wait a week and have it done under general anaesthetic, or they could do it that afternoon under a local one. The decision was instant. She had it done that day.

The doctor told us later that they had removed the lump but had to be sure of a clear perimeter of tissue. They felt they had achieved ninety per cent but wanted her to go back three weeks later for another operation. In that one they took the other ten per cent of clear tissue and found that the disease had not spread to the lymph nodes. That was the best news we could have had. We were not elated but the relief was enormous.

Mandy still had to face six arduous and debilitating sessions of chemotherapy and Lesley accompanied her to every one. Chemo is not nice. The side effects can cause nausea, headaches, weight changes, hair loss, acne and all sorts of unpleasantness. Mandy was stoical throughout.

In an instant, the family became obsessed with cancer. We studied websites and read books, trying to absorb as much knowledge as we could about the disease, and making sure that Mandy was getting the right treatment. Lesley was consumed with her research.

At that time I was unaware that Les had felt that pain in her groin. She said nothing and we went off to Spain for a holiday, Lesley and me, Mandy, Dave her husband and Louie.

Only later did I learn that Lesley was feeling quite unwell with the pain getting worse. I suppose, for Mandy's sake, she kept it to herself. We had a restful time on holiday but when we returned she went to the doctor, who prescribed antibiotics. But there was no change.

Unknown to me Lesley booked herself an appointment at the Nuffield Hospital for a pelvic scan on 3 May, less than two months after our daughter's tumour was removed. The radiologist scanned the results and told her the same day that he suspected something was amiss and advised her to see a gynaecologist.

That year there were two consecutive Bank Holidays, which meant she could not get an appointment until Wednesday, 16 May. Long before these traumatic events were to fall on us I had promised to play in the Robert Winsor Charity Golf Tournament in Majorca and was due to leave that afternoon.

'I am not going,' I said. 'They can manage without me and I would like to be here with all that is going on.'

Typical Lesley, she said: 'Don't be silly. You can't let him down at short notice. Dave and I will look after Mandy and you'll be back on Saturday anyway.'

I cannot believe even now that Lesley kept secret all the things that were happening to her. I went off to Majorca not suspecting for a moment that she was ill as well. The consultant had actually told her that there might be a serious problem and that he should perform a hysterectomy. They had arranged for the operation to take place on Friday, 18 May. God knows how she felt that night but by next morning she had decided how to handle the issue without giving us, the kids and me, any reason to worry.

She phoned us all and said she had been to see the doctor. She said to me: 'Don't worry, Alan. It's fibroids that have to be removed and luckily the surgeon can operate tomorrow.'

I didn't know what to think. I did not, at that time, suspect anything more serious but it was a worry. As I flew home on the Friday all sorts of anxieties passed through my mind before I concluded that I could not, dare not contemplate anything more serious. Life could not be that cruel. Could it?

Before I arrived at the hospital she had been told that it was ovarian cancer. She eventually told me the whole story that evening. She would have to have chemo, like Mandy, and the treatment would start a few weeks later.

I could not take it in. I was devastated. From that moment to this, I have faced the hardest battle of my life. I can't win it because I can't take it on board. I can't say: 'Give some of that to me, let me have it, let me help out.' All I can do now is try to win the battle of support, which I constantly think is not enough.

The fight goes on.

Alan Ball
February 2004

1

INSPIRATIONS

One afternoon after I came home from school in Oswestry I went out, as I always did, to kick a ball against a wall, trapping it, firing it back, catching the rebound on my instep and sometimes taking it on my chest. Nothing could come between me and this romance with a ball. Unfortunately I was wearing new sandals my mother had just bought. They were supposed to last two summers. But then I was only ten years old.

By the time I had finished a sole was hanging off. I knew I would be in trouble. My mother let rip about the state of the footwear and promised full retribution from my dad when he returned home. A fearful sense of foreboding enveloped me, trebling when I heard his key in the lock. As my mother delivered her critical report, holding a slipper aloft and saying something like 'Look what he's done now', my dad inspected the damage and suddenly reacted as if he had found gold dust. 'It's all right,' he said. 'It's his left foot.'

For days he had been on at me to use my left foot as he drove me towards the talent he never quite had as a footballer himself. My father was Alan Ball Senior, a man who was my mentor, coach, adviser, critic, psychologist, disciplinarian and caring father, and who drove me on in the way Richard Williams coaxed and harried his daughters, Venus and Serena, to become the world's greatest women tennis players.

Dad wanted everything for me that he never had himself. He was a lower league, journeyman player who managed at that level and had stints in charge of Preston North End and Halifax. His highest achievement as a player was making it to Birmingham Reserves. People have told me he was an uncompromising wing half with no great pace.

It seems that as soon as I came along, born in my maternal grandmother's house, 2 Brookhouse Avenue, Farnworth, Lancashire, during Victory in Europe Week on 12 May 1945, all he ever wanted was for me to be a footballer because of his love of the game. I never met anyone as fanatical about football as my dad.

Sense of family unity was also important. All the generations remained close and that is something I cherish today, though as a youngster growing up it is something you take for granted.

My first memories are of football grounds, the pervasive, liniment smell of dressing-rooms. Southport was the earliest memory. Dad used to take me there on the train. He was playing for them but my first memorable Christmas present was a Newcastle shirt. I have no idea why, except that he probably got it cheap. I lived in it.

Out on the Rec at Farnworth after school there were

those thirty-a-side matches and if you weren't sharp, being there five minutes after the school bell ended lessons for the day, you didn't get a game. It was rough cinders and the occasional patch of grass. When I was nine we moved to Oswestry, where my father was player-manager as well as running a pub, the King's Head, on the High Street. I was bright enough at school and passed the eleven-plus but it was football all the way – although I was not always successful at first because of my very small size. I was picked for the cross-country team and swam for Shropshire juniors, but found myself ignored at football until later on, when I began captaining teams.

There was boxing, too. One day a man called Jock Shaw came into the pub. He was a boxing coach at Park Hall Army Camp and set up a little gym in a loft we had out the back. I went there for boxing lessons. I remember them vividly. I loved it. Boxing toughened me up, prepared me for the likes of Tommy Smith, Norman Hunter, Nobby Stiles and various European and inter-national hatchet men. It meant I could look after myself and somehow helped my footwork on the football pitch, but while I ran and swam for the town teams, I was left on the outside looking in as other lads went off to play football with Oswestry Boys.

All the time my father was encouraging me. He could be hard. I had a paper round because you never had any money in those days. You had to earn it. I remember going to him one day and asking for a bike. He answered with a firm 'no' so I said I would save up and buy one myself. He just said: 'You are not having a bike. You'll run with that bag on your back and the faster you run the lighter it will become and the fitter you will be.'

Once my father realized I had the ability he slowly but surely started to put the foundations of my career in place. From twelve years of age upwards I was never a teenager doing the normal teenage things. I was being channelled towards a career without really knowing it. My first pair of boots were Pocock Continentals. I pestered my mam, begging for them. She saved up and took me with her to buy them one morning. I cannot describe the pride and joy I felt in those boots. Until the day I finished playing I looked after my boots.

I knew I was better at football than the others in the playground, although the teachers just looked at my size and that was against me from the start. Then, sadly, my grandfather became ill and Dad moved the family back to Farnworth to a pub called the Rose and Crown. He was my father's father, whom I adored. He had a very bad lung complaint, emphysema. His death devastated my dad.

The pub was 500 yards from Farnworth Grammar School and as soon as I was there I was captaining the school team. But there were knocks to come . . .

Although I was small and light I had determination in every pore and a level of skill that belied my size; this was recognized by the sports master at Farnworth Grammar School, Mr John Dickinson. I captained Farnworth and Worsley Boys and was sent for a trial with Lancashire Boys at The Rookery, Southport. I had also been playing against the big teams such as Manchester Boys and Salford Boys. Mr Dickinson had put my name forward for the trial. Under him, our school won the prestigious Daily Dispatch Shield.

The prospect of playing for the county really excited me. We were a good, decent side. I was getting goals and I was captaining them. As I went off to Southport on the train, thrilled that a big opportunity had come my way, I imagined myself convincing everybody that I had a talent. Absolute despair followed.

After fifteen minutes of feeling comfortable on the ball, knowing I was as fit as a flea and really enjoying myself, I was pulled off. I stood around until half time feeling only desolation as it dawned on me that I would probably hear no more from them. I went home a troubled soul, knowing there was no point in staying. Dad was disappointed for me but his philosophy was that they were looking for big lads.

He rallied me when I got back to the warmth of the Farnworth hearth. I remember his words clearly. He said: 'Don't worry. You've got all the ability in the world and you will grow. It's not all about size and power. They've got big, strong lads but look at Bryan Douglas and Dennis Stevens.'

Douglas was a small, slight winger with Blackburn Rovers and England. Stevens was my idol at Bolton Wanderers and when my dad said I could be a Dennis Stevens type of player, my ambition, which had been dented a few hours earlier, was renewed. He also said I could play for his team, Ashton United, as a schoolboy in the Lancashire Combination. Starting out with them as a fourteen-year-old was more than an experience.

There were some gnarled old professionals in that league and I remember a big left back playing for Hyde United trying to kick me over the stand in a Cheshire Cup match. It was a shock to the system when he growled: 'If that comes near me, lad, I'll snap thee in half.'

In many ways it was a matter-of-fact situation. I took it all in my stride, trying to learn all the time. Fortunately there were no clashes with school fixtures and I played just a handful of matches for them, though I learned plenty about the intensity of professional football even if my fellow teammates were bricklayers, electricians or van drivers in their day jobs.

It was the hardest league to play in and my dad, who could be described as a lovable rogue on occasion, fell foul of the authorities when rumours grew that this schoolboy footballer was being paid. The Lancashire FA, presumably on the advice of the Football Association, decided it was time to inspect the club's books. The outcome was that we were summoned to an inquiry in Manchester where we hadn't a legal leg to stand on. Dad had been paying me seven shillings for playing and Tuesday and Thursday training night and keeping five bob for himself. The club was fined a nominal amount and told to behave in future.

Nothing happened with Lancashire Boys. It seemed I was to have no future in football so I applied to Tillotson's, the local newspaper group who owned the *Bolton*

Evening News. I fancied being a sports journalist eventually but nothing came of that. I was still playing for the Farnworth Boys when a fellow called George Noakes introduced himself as a scout from Wolves. He invited me to visit Wolves every Saturday morning for training and trials and so on, and then at every half-term or school holiday. Another wonderful chance, it seemed, was opening up in front of me, although I knew I would be in trouble at Farnworth Grammar because the school team played every Saturday morning.

Dad went up to the school to tell them that I was moving on from that, arguing that Wolves was a wonderful opportunity. Mr Dickinson, the master who had pushed me towards the Lancashire Schools trial, was very understanding and may have been a frustrated footballer himself, but the headmaster did not see it that way. I dug in my heels. With my dad's support I said I would definitely be going to Wolverhampton and if they didn't like it I would just tell lies, saying that I was going to a wedding or whatever. I think Dad wrote my script!

My dad was engineering my future. Every night we had an hour against the wall with the tennis ball. Then he would produce a bigger ball and whether it was rain, snow or hail we would go straight to it before he had his tea. I had to be ready and waiting. Working with the ball was more important than homework. His dogma was always the same: 'The ball has to be your pal. You have to master it.'

Wolves was a dream place. Every half-term was a fantastic time. They were the team of the generation,

15

managed by Stan Cullis with players such as Billy Wright, Johnny Hancocks and Eddie Clamp. I was still something of a tot but the ball was my pal. I had gone from schoolboy football to the real thing. Everything about the place produced a tingle of excitement.

The training at Castle Croft area was fantastic and I was alongside names such as Barrie Stobart, Terry Wharton and Fred Goodwin. I was with them in an arranged practice match on this bowling green of a pitch. I played well, I was comfortable and I was so chuffed that I could handle myself, a boy among men.

Even sweeping the corridors was a thrill. This was for me; this was the life I wanted. I could not see myself settling for anything else. Eddie Clamp's mother had a boarding house and I stayed with her. Stobart lived there, and a little Scottish centre forward called Johnny Watt.

At the ground I loved watching the big stars come in. They would pat me on the head and say things like 'Hello, little fella' or 'Hello, young Bally, how's it going?' I got to know them all. I remember Roy Swinburne coming in one day and saying 'How you doing, little man? Are you enjoying yourself?' Of course I was, even just being there, doing the menial jobs, and playing head tennis with the lads in the gym in the afternoon. I was in my element. There weren't enough hours in the day for me. I never wanted it to get dark. It was my first feel of professional football. It was magnificent and I wanted it. But I was also anxious. I needed to be told if I was to be kept on for a final year before I left school. I knew another year visiting Wolves would cause problems at school.

Disappointment was just around the corner. A letter arrived saying thank you but that they would not be taking me any further. It was signed by Stan Cullis but it clearly expressed the view of the coaches who had seen me. It was all about size and strength. I was mentally down again asking myself the question: Where do I go from here? As usual my dad was sympathetic. He said he knew someone at Bolton Wanderers and would ask if I could train with them on Tuesday and Thursday evenings. It was also my last year at school and Dad, perhaps beginning to think that I might not make it as a player after all, began to focus on school. He reminded me it was my last year and that GCE examinations were important.

'You've got to graft this year,' he said. 'These GCEs are very important to your life. I got none because my brains were in my boots.' I tried my best but my heart remained in football. Mum was always in the background. She kept the house and family in perfect harmony but Dad was the one who cracked the whip and made all the decisions.

The invitation to train with Bolton came through and I played occasional games for the A and B teams and felt comfortable on the ball. Again I was facing rejection. I had left school and was waiting for my examination results when I thought it was time to seek out the Bolton manager, an old martinet called Bill Ridding, to see if there was any chance of a football apprenticeship at Burnden Park, where they played in those days.

I remember the usual words such as 'small' and 'frail', and then the words that truly shattered my hopes: 'The only apprenticeship you'll get, lad, is as an apprentice jockey,' said Ridding. The hurt was grievous. In our group were Ernie Machin, Carl Davenport and Gordon Taylor, who went on to become the chairman of the Professional Footballers' Association, as well as me. Taylor was the only one retained. Taylor now jokes in his after-dinner speeches: 'That's how much they knew at Bolton. They let Ernie Machin and Alan Ball go and they kept me.'

At the time Bolton were a big, strong, physical team. Francis Lee was in our dressing room but he had made the first team early among such hard, fit men as Tommy Banks, Roy Hartle, Nat Lofthouse and so on. I was out of it and going nowhere. My father, for once, was as disbelieving as I was unhappy. He said I should write to more clubs and go with him joinering. He had moved on from being a publican but he remained a character. He used to say that he could sell Zubes (cough tablets) in summer and ice cubes to Eskimos in winter.

I wrote to a couple of clubs more in hope than in expectation and soon after was surprised to receive a letter with a Blackpool postmark on the envelope. I opened it half expecting to read a brush-off from Blackpool Football Club. It was an invitation to a Saturday morning trial. It was like Christmas and birthday presents had all arrived at the same time. I could not wait. I would have walked to

Blackpool but there was a 7.30 a.m. bus that Saturday morning; as it meandered on what seemed a long and winding road through Bolton, Chorley, Preston and finally Squires Gate, Blackpool, I knew that in reality I was going to play for my life.

That was my attitude as I stripped to play with these strangers. I was going well and hoping that I was creating the right impression when, just after half-time, I was told to leave the pitch. Someone else was coming on and deep in my heart I felt the old familiar sense of failure. Ron Suart, the Blackpool manager, was approaching me, and I waited for the dreaded 'too small' verdict. I think he said: 'From what I have seen, son, you've got ability and I am going to give you a chance on the ground staff.'

Those words tailed into an emotional blur, as did the bus journey home. My life was just beginning and there were some sage words from my father. He listened to my excited version of the day's events and just said: 'You are a lucky lad. You just don't get chances like that. Now, remember this, you are sixteen and at seventeen they have to decide whether to sign you as a pro. So, you've got a year in which to make sure they have to sign you as a pro. You won't get that if you go out drinking and mess with girlfriends and all that stuff. You have to make sacrifices. You have to want it so badly that nothing else matters. Don't throw this chance away.'

The club found some wonderful digs for me with Mrs Mawson at 2 Levens Grove, Blackpool. My fellow lodgers were Emlyn Hughes, who went on to play for Liverpool and England, a clever wing half called Johnny Green, and

Hughie Fisher, who later became my teammate at Southampton. Quite a happy coincidence for two England
captains to emerge from that little house, although Emlyn
arrived some time after me.

On the pitch, either playing or in training, my mind
was like lightning but I needed my feet to keep up. I
knew I had to find an initial burst. Again, I turned to my
father and he had the solution. He told me to buy a pair
of sprinters' spikes and to learn how to pick up my feet
properly. He said if I did 100 sprints a week I would
quicken and he was spot on. I practised away from
people, when the training pitch was empty, because I did
not want anyone to see me doing this extra work. I didn't
want the others to know that I was aware of my short-
comings.

My father was driving me on, pursuing his philosophy
of complete fitness, and saying: 'You've got to be better
than anyone else. Your passing, your control, your technique, it's all terrific. All of that will make up for your
lack of size because your heart is big enough. There are
seven days a week and you have to have six in and one
out. Five in and two out, no. Four in and three out and
you will never be a player so don't even think of going
the other way.' His philosophy on complete fitness never
wavered.

He knew that in me he had somebody who really
wanted to learn. He had some simple ways of putting
things, reminding me that if I was in bed by 10 p.m.
there would be another midfielder somewhere out until
11 p.m. so I was nicking an hour on him. He was so

dedicated to getting me to the top that he never left a thing undone. He put things in my head and when I reflected on them I always had to agree that he was spot on with his knowledge, wisdom and sheer common sense.

I did go out with the boys from the digs but was always back by nine. At first I commuted to home in Farnworth. Ray Parry, an established first teamer who lived in Blackpool, would drive me back and forth before I saved enough to buy my first car, a second-hand Triumph Herald.

As a ground staff boy I worked on the pitch under Harry Cummings. He was a fabulous character who had his own way of dealing with young miscreants who dared to give him cheek or, as we often did in summer, staged little fights with the hoses used to water the pitch. He caught us one day and blamed me. Impudently I asked him what he was going to do about it.

Two days later he shouted across to me: 'You, come with me.' I thought he was going to put me inside painting or scrubbing. I followed him and he took me down the side of the grandstand on the way out of Bloomfield Road, where we came around the corner and stopped in front of the biggest, smelliest heap of manure you could ever imagine. He just said something like 'There's the wheelbarrow and there's the spade so get on with it.' For a week he had me spreading the stuff, putting a dark brown carpet all over the pitch. His revenge was good and proper, and expertly timed. I never gave him lip again. It was all part of the wonderful experience of being at a football club, no matter how lowly my station.

I was also impetuous in my desire to succeed. I wanted more than ground staff and apprenticeship status. My determination began to get me in trouble. I was invited to train with the first team on one occasion and was so frantic in my lust for recognition that I got into a fight with a senior player called Barrie Martin, who followed his 'Who are you?' with a thump. I could not get through to anyone just how desperate I was not to be rejected ever again in my life.

Improvements in my game were happening all the time and suddenly, pre-season, I was playing in a practice match alongside Stanley Matthews, who was later to be knighted in recognition of his footballing genius. As a revered veteran he was choosing his games, only playing a handful a season, but I was the boy in charge of his boots. They were handmade Co-op boots, the lightest I had ever felt or seen. They only lasted a couple of games and he always trained in them.

He was a god to us all and I gave those boots such tender and loving care – although come Christmas he never gave me a tip. Later people told me he was one of the tightest men you would ever meet. As far as I was concerned, he was a wonderful man.

I incurred his wrath one day when I hit the ball inside the fullback for him to run on to. It was the pass you tried to hit all day with the winger making ground to take it in his stride. Matthews just stood on the spot, shaking his head, watching the ball run towards the corner while pointing to his feet.

I said: 'If it's on inside the fullback you chase it and get there.'

I was an angry, unknown teenager. Ron Suart pulled me off straightaway and in the dressing room afterwards Stanley, after grumbling about the cheeky little so and so, said to me: 'You do not talk to me like that.'

As soon as I arrived home that night I told my dad how perplexed I was; how could I be chastised when I had said the right thing? He agreed with me, but said when playing with Stanley Matthews, I should get the ball to his feet. It was a massive lesson for me but indicative of the kind of person I was becoming. I didn't care for reputations. I was going to walk through everybody to get where I wanted to be.

Even then I needed a huge stroke of luck. On a Thursday morning before the start of the 1962–3 season Blackpool were preparing for one of the most formidable of fixtures, Liverpool away. I had played well in the reserves the previous season and was ready to resume where I had left off, except that on this particular Saturday I was to be involved with the A team.

Even when Matthews reported injured I assumed that Mandy Hill would step in; then he was hurt in training and Ron Suart pulled me out of what was the club's third string and into the first team. I was just seventeen years and three months old and had become a full-time professional on my seventeenth birthday. Suart simply took me to one side at the training ground and told me I would be making my debut at Anfield. Liverpool had just been promoted and I realized I would be up against one of the game's most experienced hard men in Ronnie Moran. Bill Shankly was in charge of Liverpool, embarking on a spell of unprecedented success that made him into a true legend in his own lifetime.

There were 57,000 people in the ground. Previously a few hundred folk had been the biggest attendance at any match I had played in. Strangely, I wasn't nervous. I was loving it. I shuffled down the steps towards the pitch and looked across at Moran, who appeared to be everything I had expected – old, craggy and dangerous. I like to tell the story that as we lined up he handed me a piece of paper and on it I read 'Liverpool Royal Infirmary, Evening Menu'. I thought to myself, this is going to be some debut. It was. We won 2–1, and the further the game went, the more I enjoyed myself. Over the years I have seen people freeze in such situations. You either love it or hate it, and I revelled in the tense importance of the occasion. I remember looking around, taking in the Kop in all its high-octave urgency. It was a beautiful sunny day. Perhaps there were some nerves at the very beginning, but I was confident in my feet. I knew that if I could get the ball I would have a good game. I always maintained throughout my career that with a bit of possession and a little luck I would always play well.

Jimmy Armfield was playing behind me. He simply talked me into areas when we didn't have the ball, and I knew that when I was in possession I should drag the ball inside so that he could make the overlap run on the outside. He was brilliant at that. Ray Charnley and Ray Parry scored for us that day. It was a great win and it was the beginning of Anfield being a lucky ground for me throughout my career.

I went home a happy lad, riding down the East Lancs Road with one of my mates. I didn't have a car so I cadged a lift. Once home I waited for my dad to come in from managing Ashton United and I said to him: 'Dad, I was great today.'

At that point the happiest day of my life was interrupted when he gave me what he felt was an appropriate rollicking: 'Don't come here telling me you've made it after one game,' he said. 'Who do you think you are? You can call yourself a player when you have twenty first-team games under your belt this season, not one game. It's when you go in day after day and the manager and the players know what to expect of you that you are a good player. That takes time and experience.'

Those words blew away any cockiness. One minute I was revelling in the instant memories of Anfield on my seven pounds ten shillings a week, and the next moment the man I loved most in the entire world was hammering me. He was right, of course. I played two or three more matches and then went out, playing half a dozen times that season, but returned to the side at the start of the 1963–4 season and stayed in.

It was a good team with a fine spirit fostered by the likes of Roy Gratrix, Jimmy Armfield and Barrie Martin, the lad who first slapped me down as a kid when he thought I was a bit uppity. Ray Parry was a wise bird who taught me many things. One piece of advice was invaluable in matters away from the game. He said you had to look like a footballer. It was never a sin to be skint, he used to say, but it was a sin to look skint. I've always tried to look smart ever since he stressed the importance of clothing and looking the part. He only had to tell me once because I was a sponge soaking up all the advice and information I could find. I would always take it on board because when professionals who had experienced great careers told you things, you listened. Ray was my guiding light in those early months of first-team football.

Then there was a player who came down from Scotland, Pat Quinn. He had the brain of a fox, a stealthy player who came to Blackpool from Hibs. I learned so much from him in the year before I made the World Cup squad. He taught me about what he called 'the yard' on the pitch: change your body, change the picture, change your angle and open your body.

I picked up things from him all the time, and from the others who didn't realize that I was picking their brains, urgently seeking to know everything about the game. At the same time I was getting myself in trouble because I was cheeky. I was disrespectful to opponents I should have bowed to.

There were two incidents in my first full season, 1963–4. We played Manchester United at Blackpool and I provoked the incident with the great Denis Law that saw us both sent off. As I moved alongside him during a passage of play I said, 'You're finished, you're old, step aside.' Next time the ball came between us he came in late; we got up and we both lost it. We were off. When they took our previous into consideration he was suspended for nine weeks and I got seven. He was blazing mad with me. I felt shocked but I couldn't say anything then. We were together at a dinner in Aberdeen in 2003 and he was on his feet, eyebrows raised, pointing his finger at me and wagging it, saying: 'He's there. Sent off at Blackpool. Cheeky little bastard.'

It was just ding-dong every time I played against him. You knew what you were going to get from Denis and hopefully everyone knew what they were going to get from me, including him.

The day after President John F. Kennedy was assassinated in Dallas in November 1963 we played at Fulham and I scored my first hat-trick before getting involved in some fighting which meant a sending off. Again.

I was sitting in the dressing room on my own trying to come to terms with events when the Fulham chairman, Tommy Trinder, who was a well-known music-hall comedian, came in, put his arm around me and said: 'That was one of the most fantastic performances I've seen from a young man, but don't do stupid things like that again.'

Shocking, really. Nineteen years of age and sent off in a First Division game. It was all part of my make-up then. I wanted to tell people that I was so fiery because nobody was ever going to take away this wonderful thing that I had, this life in football.

All the time I had the closeness of my family for support. Grandparents and parents were wonderful. The family unit was as tight as a clenched fist, but liberally sprinkled with humour. When I was at school in Oswestry, my father's dad, Jimmy, used to meet me at the gates at the end of lessons. He would always have a tennis ball and as we wandered back towards the pub through the park and along the main road, he would throw the ball and I would trap it. He was a joiner by trade and it was an immensely sad day when he died at the age of fifty-four.

Then my mum's dad took over the football. He was a pit man, a real character who had been a miner all of his life. Norman Duckworth was his name. He made me laugh almost every time he spoke. He bred budgies and had the almost statutory coal miner's whippet. I was in the tin bath in front of the fire one night and this was how the conversation went.

Me: 'All right, Grandad?'

Him: 'Aye, had a hard shift today but t'whippet's done all right. Done 100 yards fast. We'll win on Sunday. She did 100 yards in four seconds.' (They used to race whippets at the pit-head every Sunday.)

Me: 'That were fast, Grandad.'

Him: 'Aye. She fell down t'mine shaft.' Everybody laughed.

As a bit of a treat, when I was just getting my first wage packets as a fully fledged professional at Blackpool, I took him to Old Trafford to see Manchester United in a night match. Soon the wind was blowing the rain in on us. He removed his flat cap and tucked it in his raincoat pocket. I advised him to put it back on or he might catch a cold. He looked at me and said: 'Nay, son, I'm not watching the telly tonight in a wet cap.'

A lifetime at Agecroft Colliery had left several marks. During his time there he was injured when he was trapped between two of the wheeled tubs they used to move the coal around. He had to wear a kind of corset. He would crouch for ages at home, often in the dark, because that was how he spent his shifts in the pit.

He never learned to drive and remained a good, old-fashioned, down-to-earth man; happy smoking his Woodbines and watching me play. Every holiday was at the miners' home, either Blackpool or Babbacombe, near Torquay. When we won the championship at Everton in 1970 everybody was invited up to the boardroom with their families. Grandad Duckworth came too, flat cap, string bag and all.

John Moores was the all-powerful owner of Littlewoods pools and mail order business, and chairman of the club. I introduced Grandad to him and he said straight out: 'My name's Norman Duckworth. Who are thee? Are thou't pools man? I've done them pools every week and I've never had a penny yet.'

I was cracked up but Moores took to him instantly and he was invited to the boardroom at every home game. He was given a glass of champagne on one early occasion and all but spat it out, saying it tasted like detergent.

When I was living in London and playing for Arsenal

in 1973, Lesley and the kids went away for a short holiday leaving me at home with our Great Dane dog and Grandad, who was visiting. While I was training, leaving Grandad at home with the dog, he decided to go to the shops for some provisions because he quite enjoyed cooking. When I let myself in I found Grandad sitting on one of our matching Chesterfield chairs and the dog on the other, just looking at each other.

Grandad explained: 'I'm staring this bugger out and he won't beat me. He wouldn't let me into the house until I fed him three bloody pounds of lard through the letter box.' He never realized he was truly a naturally funny man. He died of the 'miner's disease' silicosis.

Family ties have continued to be important to our family. Where we live now our three children, Mandy, Keely and Jimmy, are within fifteen minutes of us and we have some wonderful Sunday lunches at home with them, their partners and our grandchildren. We laugh, and although Lesley's illness makes her tired they are always gatherings to cherish. Our marriage has been one of the strongest imaginable and all three of our kids know and appreciate the values of loyalty and honour in their own marriages.

I was at Blackpool when I first met Lesley. I was giving my sister Carolyn a lift to the stables where she used to ride her pony and Lesley was there helping out. I had my first car then, a second-hand Triumph Herald that I had bought with my bonuses.

Lesley was bright, very pretty and expressive. I was a sixteen-year-old apprentice footballer and she was fourteen. I have adored her ever since. I probably made the first move by asking her to meet me in the local coffee bar. Then we went to the cinema quite often but perhaps the defining period came when we went on holiday for the first time.

There has been laughter in our lives ever since, but at no time more than when we talk about the first holiday we had together, driving through France. Blind leading the blind springs to mind.

We were either brave or foolish. We had paid for our tickets but, as one of the Goons said on another occasion, money was so low you had to stoop to pick it up! We were two kids driving in a foreign country without a clue as to the language, the habits, France itself. Our spending money was the sixty pounds we had won at Bolton greyhounds. We were hardly off the ferry when we stopped for a meal and took a far heftier slice out of our spending money than we had anticipated. We eked out the funds as best we could but the money eventually ran out. We drove back purse and pocket empty, and almost sick with hunger. Driving to the north of France during the night we managed to buy two tomatoes, a piece of bread and a bottle of pop.

We were mad with craving to get back to the ferry or to anywhere we might get something to eat. We stopped at 4 a.m. at a village water fountain to clean our teeth and discovered that the bottle of pop had blown up in the back of the car.

As we drove on to the ferry Lesley could stand the pangs of hunger no longer. She was struggling to go on.

We were the second car for the very first ferry that morning and started a conversation with the couple in the car ahead of us. We owned up, and told them we were starving and had no money except the seven pounds it would take for the petrol to get us home. We went to the restaurant, ordered full English breakfasts and couldn't pay. We borrowed the money from our saviours and paid them back through the post when we got home.

Experiences such as that emphasize the meaning of togetherness. I had met Lesley's parents, Jack and Hilda Newton, and got along with them fine. Jack was a barber and Lesley wasn't keen on me referring to him as 'Scalper Jack'. They were always supportive and enhanced the prevailing sense of family values.

Playing professional football was all I ever wanted to do and soon life became even better. I was a regular in the first team after my opening in-and-out season, scoring goals and setting up chances for others, when I received an invitation to go for trials with the England Under-23 squad. In my fertile imagination I could immediately see a row of caps in a trophy cabinet the family would have to buy. I was just approaching my eighteenth birthday and I knew I was good. I believed that if I was given the opportunity I would take it and never be dislodged from the team. I was devastated, mentally bruised, when I was rejected again and they chose David Pleat ahead of me. I knew at that point that I was never going to be a right-winger. It was 1963. I was not wanted and the old hurt was back with me.

My form in the Blackpool side continued to improve. My dad kept on reassuring me that my international time would come. I felt that way, too, realizing that only hard graft and dedication would get me to where I wanted to be. It worked because between 4 November 1964 and 3 November 1965 I played in eight Under-23 internationals with the team winning three, drawing four and losing one. I scored the third goal in the 5–1 win over Rumania at Coventry and the first goal in the 3–0 win over France at Norwich, and was sent off in the 0–0 draw with Austria in Vienna. In my frustration I was deemed to have thrown the ball at the referee.

Tommy Smith, the Liverpool hard man with whom I had many a tussle in our league matches, was a regular in the Under-23 shirt and was just as uncompromising in England white as he was in Liverpool red. The England manager Alf Ramsey, later to be knighted after England's 1966 World Cup win, was in regular attendance at these Under-23 matches and it later transpired that he liked what he saw.

All the time I was enjoying Blackpool. I was not given a specific, tactical job. I was just allowed to blossom and flourish. I was quick and nimble and had the ability to go past defenders. Ron Suart was a lovely man who encouraged me to enjoy my football and to make things happen. I had a marvellous rapport with the fans and the freedom of the pitch.

There were constant references in the newspapers linking me with big-money transfers to the big city clubs.

I was not fazed. I was a boy enjoying himself although other clubs were winning cups and championships. In my young and enthusiastic mind I simply wanted to play First Division football with Blackpool.

2

ENGLAND AND I EXPECT

As a boy I had the dream. In the teenage years that dream became desire, and before my twentieth birthday the fulfilment of everything arrived. I played for England. I was nineteen years old and the youngest member of the World Cup squad. In three years I had gone from being rejected by Bolton Wanderers to playing for England. Lottery, football pools, winning horse races . . . nothing could ever compare with winning that first, blue velvet cap with three lions and the braiding and the golden tassle that went with pulling on the white shirt deep in the stadium in Belgrade on 9 May 1965. I was amid such company as Bobby Moore, Jack Charlton, Gordon Banks, George Eastham and Nobby Stiles. We drew with Yugo-slavia 1–1, with a goal from Barry Bridges.

That was the first of seventy-two occasions, but there had been something of a curtain raiser to my full inter-national tour. As usual my progress had been punctuated by disappointment. One moment I was elated, like the time I was chosen to tour with the Under-23 team in 1964, when I had barely established myself in the First Division with Blackpool. It was a stunning moment when

I opened the envelope from the Football Association inviting me to join the tour of Hungary, Israel and Turkey.

When we arrived in Hungary I just stood and marvelled at the famous Nep Stadium. My dad and grandad had told me all about the 'magical Magyars' with Ferenc Puskas, Nandor Hidegkuti, Zoltan Czibor, Sandor Kocsis and the rest of that wonderful team. They revolutionized the game and caused an enormous amount of grave head scratching when they beat England 7–1 at home and 6–3 at Wembley in 1953–4.

The atmosphere was intoxicating without the need for alcohol but my old angst was soon to return. The Under-23 manager was a dour Scot who managed Sheffield United. He was a quiet man who was cautious in the extreme, so that some of the journalists used to mimic him in private with their sayings of John Harris, such as: 'I believe it's going to rain . . . off the record.'

To be ignored for all three matches was not funny and I was impatient. I wanted to play but I came home to Blackpool without having kicked a ball in action. At the start of the 1964 season I was still playing well and made my Under-23 debut against Wales at Wrexham on 4 November 1964. We won 3–2 and an international career was born. That was the start of my Under-23 grooming when I had eight caps and two goals.

The following summer, with everybody starting with the hot flushes of World Cup fever, I went on the full England tour to Yugoslavia, West Germany and Sweden.

Only my wildest dreams made me think I might be

playing because in May and early June I had played on tour with the Under-23 side and managed to get myself sent off for throwing the ball at the Hungarian referee in a 0–0 draw in Vienna. I imagined that Alf Ramsey just wanted me in a full international environment to have a look at me, although I reckoned he knew all there was to know. I was correct in that assumption, because on the day before the Yugoslavia match I saw him coming towards me in a way that suggested he was about to open a conversation. That, I knew, was rare for him. He simply said: 'I think it is about time you made your debut for your country, young man, don't you?'

I can't remember my response but my unspoken thoughts were probably something like, 'too right'. The England team the following day was Banks, Cohen, Wilson, Stiles, Charlton J., Moore, Paine, Greaves, Bridges, Ball and Connelly. It meant that I had fulfilled my promise to my dad, made after I had been rejected by Bolton, that I would play for England before I was twenty. When I rang home my dad, as usual, said he had never doubted I would make it. Mam, as always, was in the background, but came to the phone to tell me she was proud of me.

Any nerves disappeared as soon as I was on the pitch, which seemed bigger than most. I was comfortable. I enjoyed it and felt I played a decent role in the draw. Next stop, three days later, was Nuremburg in West Germany. As usual, I was anxious to hear who was in the team because while I never had a moment's self-doubt on the pitch, I would inevitably be anxious off it, waiting for the team announcement. It was a slightly experimental team. Alf kept the same defence, the one that saw him through the following year's World Cup, but brought in Mick Jones, Derek Temple and George Eastham for Jimmy Greaves, Barry Bridges and John Connelly.

Eastham played with me in the middle of the pitch and it was like taking a lesson from a professor. I played my part all right but I learned more about passing and movement at international level than I had ever imagined before. Pat Quinn at Blackpool had taught me about passing and making angles, but George took me to another platform as we beat the Germans 1–0 with a goal from Terry Paine. Just watching George was an education in itself. He talked to me throughout the game and I watched his body shape and the way he approached the ball or the way he stood as the ball came to him. He was never square; always half cock so that he could get his passes off. It was something I gratefully picked up from him and that became a feature of my game. He was terrific that day and I have often wondered since why he never won more that his nineteen caps.

The third match on that tour, against Sweden in Gothenburg, brought a 2–1 win and I scored my first of eight international goals, with John Connelly, restored to the side, scoring the other.

We were on our way and I began to accept that I could call myself an established international player – not that my father would have approved of such self-confidence. Although Alf had almost certainly decided on his World

Cup defence he continued to tinker with midfield and attack.

I missed the matches against Wales, Austria and Northern Ireland in the autumn of 1965 and was back with the Under-23 side at that time, helping them defeat France 3–0 at Carrow Road where, although I say it myself, I had a blinder, and after that I was back with the full squad from 1965 to May 1975. The build-up to the summer of 1966 was intriguing. We had some good results, but when we defeated West Germany 1–0 at Wembley on 23 February with a goal from Nobby Stiles we were booed off the field. I remember Alf remarking that if it had been the World Cup final there would have been no jeering. I never forgot those perceptive words.

Then came more anxiety. Alf named his twenty-seven-man World Cup squad, which had to be whittled down to twenty-two. It was the most traumatic time in my early life. I smile now when I see Sven Goran Eriksson taking the players, wives and kids off to Dubai for a sunshine break, just as I smiled at pictures of the England squad preparing for the 1998 World Cup at La Manga with Paul Gascoigne trashing his room after being told he would not be going to France.

We had a pre-tournament camp, too, at Lilleshall in the Midlands, where luxury was a word that hadn't been invented. On the way and during our stay I was acutely aware that five players were going to receive the dreaded message: not wanted. I made my decision. I would not be one of them. If there were to be any races, any challenges, nobody would beat me. I had to stay in that squad whatever it took. All the time the guiding voice of Alan Ball Senior was supporting me on the phone.

Alf had an interesting panel of coaches and medical men with him. They were a carefully selected bunch, able to cover every aspect of preparation. There was Harold Shepherdson from Middlesbrough, Les Cocker from Leeds, Wilf McGuinness from Manchester United, Dr Neil Phillips from Middlesbrough and Billy Taylor from Manchester City. Alf and his team covered every aspect of the game. Tactics, technique, team building, teamwork, fitness and diet were all involved, and it seemed like many other things as well. I had difficulty sleeping at night because of my insecurity. I would lie awake in the dormitory, telling myself that I was doing fine but that I had to be even better, quicker and stronger the next day. On the Wednesday we had a match and I took a knock. It hurt and any other time I would probably have gone off for some treatment, but if I left the pitch now for the physios to see to me I would not be able to show Alf what I could do. I put up with the pain and had a decent game. Then Friday dawned and Alf was to announce his twenty-two.

He sat us all down in a room, twenty-seven of us, all wondering who would draw the blank cards, as it were. Typical Alf, he made a serious preamble, thanking us all for being there and saying that he would name the twenty-two and that the others would be on standby in case of injuries. He said the names he was about to announce would go forward to represent England in the

World Cup and they would be delivered in alphabetical order.

He cleared his throat and the first name was Alan Ball. I cannot remember another word of that meeting. I simply could not wait for it to break up so that I could go and telephone my dad. I admit now that I was so selfish that I didn't even think about commiserating with the five who faced the thumbs down, Johnny Byrne, Bobby Tambling, Keith Newton, Gordon Milne and Peter Thompson.

All week I had been thinking about how horrible it would be to feel that sense of rejection so close to being on the biggest stage of your life. My whole life was consumed with thoughts of the World Cup. It was with me morning, noon and night. I would be thinking about Wembley and names such as Pele and Eusebio when I was washing my hands. I could be looking at the television but not seeing the picture because my mind had drifted towards the twin towers of the old stadium.

When I called my dad he was, as usual, delighted but managed to conceal it with a reminder that there was more to be enjoyed than just being in the squad. 'Great,' he said. 'Now you've got to get into the team.' That was typical of him. Whatever I achieved there was always another mountain to be scaled. Don't get cocky, and all that. He was right, of course, because he was saying that if I didn't get a game I would be doubly disappointed.

We all went home that weekend and I did commiserate with the lads who would not be rejoining us when we linked up again for pre-tournament matches in Finland,

Norway, Denmark and Poland. We won all four, scoring twelve goals and conceding one. The win against Norway, which ended 6–1 in Oslo, brought a four-goal haul for Jimmy Greaves. I sat that match out as Alf continued trying different permutations with his front five.

Before that he had played me as a striker alongside Joe Baker against Spain in Madrid. When Alf had a role in mind he always consulted the player first and so he came to me. There was no real point. I would have played anywhere for England but he asked me and I jumped at the idea. I had played inside forward for Blackpool and I knew what was required even if, at five feet six inches, I was not from the mould of classic strikers.

We ran out into that hugely impressive Bernabeu Stadium with Alf's instructions singing in my head. We were to play everything in to feet with everybody joining in and that way, with our touch, it should work.

We were up against two Spaniards in their central defence and sure enough our passing skills made them desperately unhappy and frustrated because we beat them 2–1 with goals from Joe and Roger Hunt. I was certainly feisty in those days, regarding every game as a matter of going to war against the opposition. The Spanish papers called me the 'poison shrimp'.

Our successful build-up to the World Cup followed that, with Alf making his profound statement that England could win the Jules Rimet Trophy. Some people chose to pooh-pooh the notion but we believed him to a man. Getting together immediately before the tournament was emotional. It was exciting, expectant, daunting. This was the big one. We stayed at the Hendon Hall Hotel in north London. The television was full of the great teams flying in to Heathrow and Manchester. The preliminaries, including interviews with the press, radio and television, dragged on. We were itching to get started. The opening match was against Uruguay at Wembley on 11 July. The kick-off could not come soon enough.

We were becoming slightly weary of the long haul to the training facilities at the Bank of England ground at Roehampton, which meant a coach journey often taking an hour and a half from north to south-west London around the dreaded, crowded North Circular Road. One day we suggested that Bobby Charlton, who usually acted as our spokesman, have a word with Alf about perhaps switching to somewhere closer. Alf said he would think about it. The bus had nudged a couple of miles further in what seemed like fifteen minutes when he turned around and said: 'I've thought about it and we're going to continue with Roehampton.' That was it. Nobody ever argued with Alf though I never found him difficult to get along with.

Alf was the person who polished me as a player. I have always been a quick learner and he added several dimensions to my thinking. There was a perfect example of Alf's dressing room manner when he came up to me at half-time in a match between the Football League and the Scottish League at Hampden Park, Glasgow. We were winning 1–0 and I could see him walking towards me. I thought I'd had a good half and he was coming to praise me. I was wondering what he might say. He sat down beside me in that quiet way of his and asked: 'Do you think Bobby Moore can pass the ball?'

It seemed a strange question and I replied that of course he could, adding that he was one of the best passers of the ball in the English game.

He then said: 'Why do you keep going back and taking the ball off him?' Mmm, I thought, and he added: 'If he can pass it to you fifteen yards further up the pitch then you are much nearer to the opposition and the danger area where you can pass it through people, so let Bobby pass it to you. There is no need for you to go and take the ball from him.'

It was wonderful advice and I never went back to take the ball off Mooro (that was his nickname) again. I realized while Alf was speaking that he wanted me in positions where I could deliver the passes that would hurt our opponents. It was such wisdom that made me a proper international player: it is speed of thought and instant control of the ball that are the true essentials of a player at that level.

Alf was studious and knowledgeable, and knew exactly what he wanted from his players. He read their personalities. He never wavered in his convictions of how the team should play. Anyone who saw or read about his Ipswich Town players who won the First Division Championship in 1962 will be aware of the small-town side that had no big names but came with a style of playing that opponents could not fathom. Their withdrawn left-winger, Jimmy Leadbetter, took up positions deep on the left that allowed him to link up with midfield. Opponents never knew where to find him. The Ipswich tactics that brought success were the result of Alf's advanced thinking.

He also, often unwittingly, provided the squad with a barrel of laughs. His innate stubbornness frequently provided the smiles. You did as he said even when it came to the squad going to the cinema. He would tell us he had heard about this good film and that we would go as a group to see it. Invariably it was a cowboy film because he liked Westerns. I am sure that underneath he was laughing at us because he probably realized we would rather have a pint or a game of cards.

There was one occasion when we were going off to play on a close season tour where the summer weather would be hotter than England and none of us was fond of the heavy worsted suits from Simpson's of Piccadilly we had been given to wear. We decided to send Bobby Charlton again with a request for more lightweight attire.

Alf gathered us around him before training the next day and said: 'Bobby, I have thought about the situation with the suits and we'll have the ones from Simpson's of Piccadilly, I think.'

On another occasion we were having the post-match banquet at Wembley after one of the home internationals and at the end Alf approached Bobby Moore and said: 'Robert, I think we ought to go.'

Bobby pleaded to be allowed to order one more round. Permission was granted and we sat around chatting away and drinking our beers until Moore told Alf that we were all ready to leave for the hotel. Alf heard him, pulled over a waiter and ordered a large brandy for himself, while we had to wait for him to finish it. That was Alf's way of making sure you were in no doubt who was in charge of everything. It was also an example of his unique sense of humour.

He was an intensely loyal man. If you put in the effort for him on the pitch he would pick you. When we were doing it right we always said it was harder to get out of his team than to get in it. Nobody took anything for granted. There was his famous riposte while we were rushing for the cars after one midweek international when we all had to be at our clubs the following day. Martin Peters was just ahead of me and he turned and said: 'Goodbye, lads, 'bye, Alf, see you next time.' To which Alf replied: 'You might.'

I was going to say the same as Martin but quickly changed to saying something like: 'Goodbye, and thanks a lot, Alf.'

Once the World Cup started we had all the glorious palaver of the opening ceremony and then the match against Uruguay. Everybody in the squad wanted to be in the team. By now, after all the pre-tournament matches and beyond, the back six were picking themselves. Thankfully I was among the front five, as was Jimmy Greaves and John Connelly. Everyone at Wembley and watching on television had been geared up for a football carnival. They were let down. It was a typical opening World Cup game, with caution as the byword. A defeat would have been a great blow. We tried, but they were masters at getting the goalless draw and that was how it ended. It just petered out into a really tame match with very few chances, and I realized as we walked off that I had taken part in a very poor match that neither the spectators nor I had particularly enjoyed.

All the headlines the next day reinforced the view that it had been a miserable evening, but I did not agree with the prevailing view. It was that England would not win the World Cup, that nothing had changed and that the team was little short of a bundle of rubbish. The theme kept running for three days until the next match against Mexico at Wembley. I began to worry because Alf was clearly looking for something different and left me out along with John Connelly in favour of Terry Paine and Martin Peters. I thought I had blown my chances when the team came out and won 2–0 with goals from Bobby Charlton and Roger Hunt. The team had played particularly well. The show was back on the road, and so were the favourable headlines and the encouragement of the country's supporters.

Next up was the third group match against France at Wembley. This time Ian Callaghan came in on the right and we won 2–0 again, with Roger Hunt scoring twice. England had qualified for a quarter-final match against Argentina, who had finished second to West Germany in Group II.

By now the country was in the middle of World Cup fever but I was miserable. I was a moping, walking nightmare around the place. I had played one game,

England had won the other two in the group and I was completely out of the picture, I thought, because Paine and Callaghan had played in the two wins wearing the shirt I had hoped would be mine. I concluded there was no way I could get back in. I trained hard because I wanted to keep myself fit. I was always involved in the tactical things, but had resigned myself to watching the quarter-final from the side of the pitch on the seats behind Alf, Shepherdson, Cocker and Taylor and son, when Alf came up to me.

His opening words were: 'How are you, young man?' Alf was not one of those managers with whom you banged on the door and launched a one-man protest demanding explanations why you were not in the chosen eleven. You were expected to accept his decisions and get on with life without disruption or mood changes. I found it difficult to hide the latter at times.

I told him as politely as I could that I was a little disappointed. I said I was feeling low because I thought I had played reasonably well in the opening match.

He listened and said: 'I don't see why you should be low, young man, because you've got a job to do tomorrow. You will play on the right side of midfield. They've got a very good left back who likes to attack but he won't be able to attack you.'

Suddenly I was happy again. The Argentine's name was Marzolini, and he was renowned as an outstanding, world-class player, yet Alf clearly thought that between Paine, Callaghan and Ball, I was the man to fight Señor Marzolini. This was right up my street. The tougher matches, those in which you were expecting a scrap or a row, were made for me. I loved them. I was ready for anything. Nobody could intimidate me, and as we walked down the tunnel that day at Wembley I felt as proud and confident as I had ever done. This one was a fight all the way through. The team, as a whole, did not touch the heights I had been forced to watch against Mexico and France, but we were now in the knock-out stages of sudden death. My personal duel with Marzolini was something to be enjoyed in retrospect.

Overall the game was a dog-fight. It must have been poor for the spectators and it was looking like another goalless draw when, with the only decent bit of football played all afternoon, we scored the goal that put us into the semi-final. Martin Peters curled the ball in at the near post and Geoff Hurst, who had drifted out of his space, came back in and leaped to glance the ball into the bottom corner thirteen minutes from time.

We battled our way home from there. I reckoned I had done my job keeping tabs on Marzolini. I had stopped his effectiveness. He was a player who liked to get forward and in other matches he had been the springboard of many of their attacks. There was an unhealthy, spoiling cynicism about the Argies though. They were reckless and undisciplined and had little regard for either the laws of the game or the rules of normal behaviour. They knew all the tricks and tried them all. If you went down they came to help you up and that was just the way it looked to the ground. But no, they were pulling hair, tweaking ears and pinching chests.

It was a horrible way to play football but Alf had warned us, even if he did get into trouble for calling them animals, which they were. He had warned us about the nasty pieces of work we would be playing against. Rattin was probably the biggest culprit of a bad bunch.

The referee, Kreitlin, was as busy as anyone putting Argentine names into his book. Rattin was sent off before half-time but refused to go. It took eight minutes of arguing to get him to leave the field of play and then he strolled slowly along the touchline on his way to the dressing room, pausing to run the corner flag through his fingers.

The sadness of it all was that they were a good side. They had talent. If they had stayed at eleven men and played their football we would have had a very difficult time trying to beat them. They had been secretive and hidden from the outside world throughout almost all their time in England and we were not sorry to see them go.

England were much more open. We were at our hotel and everybody knew it. We were not hidden behind mansion walls and driving around with blacked-out windows. We were part of the people. We were the Englishman's football team. We were approachable. People could touch us. For example, the night before the World Cup final we went to the cinema in Hendon and as we walked in the people in there gave us a fantastic reception. Walking back to the hotel there were people in cars tooting their horns. It gave us a great lift. We were representing them. We were ordinary lads as they were. The only difference was that we had been blessed with the gift of being good at football. We were walking shoulder to shoulder through the streets with the people. I am not sure that today's players would or could do that.

Anyway, the semi-final against Portugal was on the horizon. It was a match to anticipate with relish. We knew they would try to beat us by playing the purest football, unlike Argentina, and in Eusebio they had one of the stars of the great game. He was a mercurial figure, brought up in Mozambique. He had natural flair for scoring goals and when he had the ball at his feet he was rarely dispossessed.

Approaching the semi-final we were full of confidence. We had not conceded a goal, every one of us was playing well, as were the Portuguese, and Wembley witnessed an exhibition of flowing passes, good goals and a truly masterful performance from Nobby Stiles, who snuffed out the threat of the living legend Eusebio. His was the man-marking role and he did it to perfection. There should be someone like Nobby in every club side. He was magnificent. He never gave Eusebio a kick, so that he hardly saw the ball clearly until his penalty late on and by then we were two up with a brace from Bobby Charlton.

We were a goal up after half an hour when Ray Wilson slipped the ball through to Roger Hunt. The Portuguese goalkeeper, Pereira, managed to block the shot, but Bobby was swooping in to rifle the rebound. It was tight, but with eleven minutes to go Geoff Hurst powerfully broke out of a tackle near the right-hand post and cut the ball back for Bobby to pull the trigger for his second. Eusebio's penalty came after Jack Charlton had fisted out a header from Jose Torres.

We were worth our win. Our football flowed and I knew from the way the team had worked together that I would be in the team that played in the final at Wembley on Saturday, 30 July 1966. It was the day of all days in the history of English football. The scene in the dressing room after the 2–1 semi-final win over Portugal was wild. Euphoric seems too tame a word. The place was packed with officials, media; it was open house, with everyone so thrilled that we had made it to the final.

It was not yet time for the players to start partying. We went back to the Hendon Hall Hotel that night, straight from the dressing room. It was still after 11 p.m. when we arrived back. Alf insisted, quite rightly, that we stick together. We were allowed two beers each, had sandwiches and then went to bed.

It was as simple as that. Supporters and officials may have been cavorting around the West End but we were tucked up in bed. Whether many of us were sleeping is a different matter because there was always the inevitable habit of playing the game over and over again in your head.

Nobby was my roommate and had been over the time we had been with England. He had one ritual that never changed. As a Roman Catholic he had to find a church on match day and slipped out early, always waking me up on his return while I pretended to still be asleep. When he left for church that Saturday morning neither of us knew if I would be in the team. The defence, which included Nobby, was as usual untouchable.

When Nobby came in from church expecting to find me asleep I asked him how things had gone and he laughed to see me awake. I told him then that he had driven me mad every single match day, getting up and making a noise early in the morning. He thought I might have heard if I was playing.

Jimmy Greaves was the player holding things up. Jimmy had taken a nasty gash on his shin during the match against the French. The wound would not heal. It was almost down to the bone and as it kept opening the doctor, Neil Phillips, kept stitching it. In the end he became worried and said he was not stitching it any more. He felt that with the stitches continually bursting he would have to leave it to heal naturally, totally. As everyone waited for Jimmy's fitness to be decided, because it was 100 per cent certain that if he had been fit he would have been in the team, there were worries for four of us. If Jimmy came in, who would make way from the front five who had played against Portugal? Obviously Bobby Charlton was a fixture, which meant there were doubts about myself, as well as about Roger Hunt, Martin Peters and Geoff Hurst. Alf left it as late as he could that Saturday morning before deciding that he could not risk Jimmy breaking down. There were no substitutes in those days. It was Saturday morning and Alf just tugged me after breakfast and told me I would be playing for England in the World Cup Final.

My time with Nobby was always fun. He was unbelievably untidy and not the prettiest sight first thing in the morning. But we were so proud and happy to be part of the World Cup thing. We were enthusiastic; almost pinching ourselves to make sure we were dealing in reality. After church Nobby went back to bed and I said I would go and see Jim Terris, the Adidas representative whose boots we wore.

For wearing the company's boots we were to receive £1,000 a man in cash. Imagine that – I was just twenty-one, playing for England and carrying £2,000 upstairs for wearing Adidas boots. I would have bought my own but this was different. I walked into the room and Nobby was still lying in his bed as I tossed all the notes so that they came down all over the place like confetti. The World Cup Final against West Germany was only hours away. We laughed like kids. The build-up to the match was already on television with cameras outside the hotel. They had caught Nobby walking back from church.

Again, I had to ring my dad in Farnworth. He had called the night before and said that if I wasn't picked he probably could not afford to come to watch the match. He was a bit old-fashioned that way but he was soon filling his old Morris Minor with petrol.

The rise in tension came gradually. We went through all our usual routines. We had been through quite a lot together by now, so collectively but privately we were making sure our minds were right. We knew what was expected of us, but it was only when I climbed into the coach for the short journey to Wembley that the enormity of the occasion began to kick in. As we drove away people were banging on the sides of the coach. There were supporters dressed in red, white and blue along the route. There were messages and banners, one of which read: 'NOBBY FOR PRIME MINISTER'.

Trying to get into Wembley through the crowds was difficult despite a police escort of outriders. I was almost overcome by this wonderful glow the atmosphere created. It wasn't nerves but it was a strengthening of the resolve that I must not let these people down. Defeat was unthinkable. It may have crossed the minds of the older players but I never considered the possibility or what the reaction might have been. I never said a word to anyone on that journey to the stadium. I was happy to be alone with my thoughts. I knew it was my day. My legs felt good. Everything about me felt right. Whether it was to do with those mystical things called biorhythms I don't know, but I sensed that everything was going to come right for me on that day.

Even in the dressing room for an hour beforehand I was quiet. I tried not to fill my mind with anything other than the thoughts that there was a match to be won. In the tunnel before we marched out there was the inevitable nervousness, but I was always in control. Then the noise as we entered the arena alongside the Germans hit me. This was special. I thought briefly of my parents and my sister up in the stands. Lesley would be with the other wives, fiancées and girlfriends somewhere behind the royal box. I searched for them briefly but it was impossible, and soon I closed out everything except the match and the concentration that would be required.

I made a couple of mistakes, but overall everything went right for me all the way through. I knew my role and as the game went on I became stronger. It was an incredible game of highs and lows. It was also pure theatre of the most dramatic kind. Germany led after thirteen minutes, when Ray Wilson, quite out of character, headed weakly down to Haller, who scored. Wilson, in character, went on to give a towering display at left back. We equalized six minutes later when Geoff Hurst met Bobby Moore's free kick to head past Tilkowski.

It was all ebb-and-flow football. Gordon Banks made an astonishing double save from Overath and then we went ahead. I took a corner kick, Hurst had a shot half-cleared, the ball was bobbing about and Peters forced it home from point-blank range. Surely we had the game won.

The supporters were celebrating with a minute to go and then Weber scored his heartbreaking equalizer. It had sprung from a shocking decision by the Swiss referee to award the free kick in the first place.

Heartbreaking but not soul destroying. It was a hot day, everyone was shattered but there was extra time to be played. I was definitely among the shell-shocked. Alf was not one of them. He said calmly and coldly: 'You've won it once, now go out and win it again. And stand up. Don't let those Germans think you are tired.'

Then he went to every player individually and when

he came to me he just said something like: 'Attack, attack, every time you attack.' I was up for it all right and the first chance I got I hit a swirling shot that was heading for the roof of the net until Tilkowski tipped it over. It gave me a big lift and I felt I was well and truly on my way to something special. The Germans had a man-to-man marking system and I was up against Karl-Heinz Schnellinger, who was regarded as one of the best defenders in world football. I had him on toast. I was up against him all afternoon and I just kept grinning at him, then going past him and hurting the rest of their defence with my passes and crosses. I wanted the ball all the time. I knew I could have played all day. It was everything I had been brought up for, with my father, the cross-country running, the boxing, the fitness and the stamina. A man once said to my dad long before the World Cup that I was just a runner on the pitch. I remember my dad telling him that it was a special ability and it showed up in that last half hour.

I could have gone on until nightfall. It was just wonderful at that age, twenty-one. I suppose I was like an Olympic runner who knows he is going to win. His legs feel good and mine felt good all through the game and into extra time. I was running again when I made the cross that Geoff Hurst thundered against the German crossbar and dropped down, and the Russian linesman pointed to the middle signalling a goal. He could not have been sure whether it was over the line or not. I couldn't and I was twenty-five yards closer than him. But I saw Roger Hunt's reaction. He turned away elated when, as a natural predator, he would have made sure the ball was in if there had been any doubt. He is the one who has convinced me that it was a goal. There was a hiatus that lasted for what seemed like minutes. The referee, Gottfried Dienst, talked to the linesman and they concluded that it was a goal. The Germans still don't believe it to this day. Then, of course, Geoff Hurst made it 4–2, running on to a pass from Bobby Moore who was just as cultured in the one hundred and twentieth minute as he had been in the first. As Bobby was carefully plotting his pass there were some of us just willing him to boot the ball into Row Z.

It was over. England had won the World Cup. I learned later that Lesley had fainted when the Germans had equalized in normal time. She and the other women had been on their feet in premature celebration when Weber delivered his hammer blow. She had never fainted before and has never done so since. It was that kind of a day. My dad, the inspiration of everything I did, could not conceal his exhilaration but he left the stadium immediately afterwards because he had to fly to Ireland for a coaching job he never landed!

Down on the pitch in those seconds after the final whistle I could not help thinking to myself, we've done it. I am a member of the best team in the world. I was close to Big Jack and he was down on his knees, really emotional. His brother Bobby was crying. Mind you, Bobby was always crying. Little Ray Wilson, who I had always marked down as a toughie, had also lost it, and then it struck me that these were the older guys.

They had realized the enormity of what had been achieved. I was all for getting down to the West End to do some partying, being naive. I found out much later in my career the toughness of football, and it was only later that I began to understand why the older ones were wiped out.

Bobby Moore accepted the trophy from the Queen and we danced around Wembley carrying him and it. We jigged and skipped – well, Nobby and I did as the young ones – and the whole country joined in the party. All my dreams were fulfilled that afternoon and although I cared mainly about what Alf and my peers thought about me, I did enjoy one paragraph which I read in a review of the 1966 final. It talked about 'England being inspired by the splendid control, tireless running and subtle passing of the electrified Ball'.

Of course I enjoyed that but it had been a monumental squad effort all the way through. Each character in the final eleven was different but they were all great men. Sadly, we lost Bobby Moore to cancer, but the rest of us are as bonded today as we were all those years ago.

Although we were very different and from all parts of the country, Alf wanted us to be like a family and that was what he got. We all got along famously with a lot of humour involved. Gordon Banks's version of humour was deadpan and occasionally wicked. He was a perfectionist in training and I recall us refusing to fire shots at him after one session. He always wanted extra work and required players to stay behind to fire shots at him to give him some serious practice. He would never let anything in so finally we told him he was shattering our confidence. Next time he asked us to stay behind we just walked off, leaving him on his own. It was probably as a result of this dedication that he became the best English goalkeeper of all time. He had plenty of games and practice sessions where he was just unbeatable.

George Cohen and I operated on the same, right side of the team. You would rightly expect us to be totally different, with me a broad northerner and him the sharp cockney. But I loved and adored him and still do. He is excellent with his self-deprecating humour, and whenever we meet now at any functions he always introduces me as 'Alan Ball, the best right winger I ever played in front of.' George loved getting forward, but he also had a knack of whacking the ball into the crowd so hard if danger loomed that we joked that the spectators down our side of the pitch were issued with gumshields. He was as strong as a bull and when I think back to the quarter-final match against Argentina I realize why Alf brought me back. He knew that, together, we would bottle up that entire side of the pitch. George was not the greatest passer of the ball, but he was a powerhouse. Nobody ever went past him, nobody could beat him for pace, but when he went off on his runs we never quite knew where the ball was going to end up, which is why he was often in front of me.

Ray Wilson was a complete contrast. He was sharp. As they used to say in the north, he could catch pigeons. He was a droll Yorkshireman but always friendly, always pleased to see you and very close to Bobby Charlton.

They shared rooms on international match occasions. I went to Everton straight after the World Cup and on my debut at Fulham I scored the winner. As we were running back for the restart Ray said something that remains very special to me to this day. He said: 'You deserve everything you get in football, son.'

No winger ever got the better of George Cohen or Ray Wilson in my experience. Nobby Stiles was on his own in every sense and we all loved him like a little brother. If ever a player justified that terrace song 'There's only one . . .' it was Nobby. Funny and accident-prone, but loveable and a terrific player. Ask Eusebio. Whenever I played against Nobby in club football you might have been forgiven for thinking that World War III had broken out, but once the game was over and once his teeth were back in we were in each other's embrace. Nobby never tried anything he knew he might not complete. He was never a chancer but played to the limits he knew existed. There was nothing fancy about him but he was one of those players who would die for the cause. If you told him to sit tight or mark someone, he would do it. He was content to be there, breaking up attacks and giving you the ball as if inviting you to peel off and do something great. It was as if he was saying: 'There you are; there's the ball, you go off and be a star, you create and score fabulous goals. You can have all the praise. This is my job; you can rely on me to do this. Go on, I'll help you to be a good player.' He was a very special player with a vice-like tackle.

My relationship with Jack Charlton has always been

rich. I love the man dearly. He is one of sport's towering figures in more ways than one, but I used to wind him up unmercifully to the point where he would clip me around the ear. At five-a-side matches when the two captains had to pick their men I used to wink at the lads to make sure that Jack was always the last to be picked, giving the impression that nobody wanted him. He used to protest: 'What about me?' Nobody took any notice and one day he twigged what was happening and chased me all over the pitch to give me a slap. Another stunt also backfired on me with Jack. We had a yellow jersey that went to the worst player in those little matches. It was my job to go around and pick up the votes and I would say, regardless of the count: 'And the winner of the yellow jersey today is . . . Jack Charlton.' He would lose his temper and be after me again.

There is a wonderful story of how Jack, picked for his first international match at the age of thirty, asked Alf one day why he had been chosen. The reply was typically withering but slightly tongue in cheek when Alf said: 'I don't always choose the best players, Jack.'

Jack could be contentious at team meetings. He was never afraid to speak his mind and I think Alf quietly admired him for that. His instructions to Jack were simple. He told him he was powerful in the air and that was a strength. He was to be the dominant force in the centre of defence. He had to be positive in the tackle, he had to attack the ball in the air, he had to boss the centre forward and he had to remember, said Alf, that he had a man with a brain alongside him. Jack and Alf occasionally had their differences but they tolerated each other out of a mutual respect and there was no doubt that the big man was crucial to England's success. He could be so contrary that when Adidas and Puma were vying for the boot deal he said he would engage both and wear one boot on either foot.

Bobby Moore, that 'brain' alongside him, became my best friend in football. When I first met him as a young lad going to join up with the England squad I was in awe of him. I had always been amazed at his coolness and vision on the pitch and his uncanny ability to play himself out of trouble. He was also a handsome, worldly-wise figure who knew his way about town. On one of my first international visits to London, when I didn't have to rush back north the following day and they were going out into the town, I asked him if I could go with him.

He just turned around and got hold of the back of his jacket and told me to take hold of it. We went into London. I was wide-eyed and would have been completely lost on my own. It was the beginning of a wonderful friendship that led to some dazzling nights out and some wonderful footballing experiences. He was the most decent and proud man you could ever wish to meet. For some reason he took to me, although anyone might have thought on meeting us separately that we would have nothing in common.

His performances in the World Cup matches were absolute essays of skill, calmness and leadership; Moore did not know the meaning of the word panic. The more intense the pressure, the cooler he seemed to be. He had one of those footballing minds that was a yard ahead of everyone else. He put the rest of the players at ease. He was the best defender, the best reader of the play, a superlative captain. He would have been officer material in the military world.

There were many occasions when I roomed with him and that experience gave me another insight. I thought I was a tidy person but he was just immaculate. He used to carry his own little travelling iron. His handkerchiefs had to be ironed and there were times when I saw him running the iron over his money. He put his trousers under the mattress on the bed. It took him twenty minutes to get ready for bed because everything had to be spot on. In a way it was just like the way he played football. Everything had to be just right.

In many ways he reminded me of one of my first sartorial influences, Ray Parry, at Blackpool. He taught me the value of smartness and the wisdom of buying good clothes. Bobby Moore's attitudes stuck with me and I learned so much about dressing well from him. He was always immaculate, from the time he got up until he went to bed.

He was also one of the most generous of men. He would be first to the bar ordering the drinks and invariably he would be the last to leave after several invigorating lagers. He could laugh at himself and he could play a devilish prank. One of his favourite stunts was to drop his trousers at the bar at some stage during a session just for a laugh to mildly shock people.

There was an occasion after the World Cup and I had

joined Everton, when I was in London and needed some treatment before I joined up with England. Bobby suggested I go with him to the West Ham ground where their physiotherapist, Rob Jenkins, would see to me before we went off to link up with the squad.

I was sitting on the bench having some ultrasound on my ankle when Rob came in carrying a crate of lagers. I couldn't believe my eyes. Anything like that at Everton would have been impossible. It just couldn't have happened. Here I was at this friendly club in London and they were having drinks and chatting away as if they were in the pub. Bobby knew how intense I was and chuckled as he offered me a drink and I shied away as if he was passing me a black widow spider. They could not understand that this was not a Sunday morning routine at Everton for anybody going in for treatment. From there we went to the pub for the Sunday lunchtime session and then went to join England where he had three days of absolute preparation.

In Bobby's thinking, Sunday was his off time and was there to be enjoyed. After that it was down to business and, borrowing the words of a Carly Simon song, nobody did it better.

Roger Hunt remains one of the true gentlemen of our football times. Everyone had a decent word to say about him, and in many ways that was a reflection of the whole squad. We enjoyed each other's company. Our wives and girlfriends got along well and that kind of harmony must have helped us on the pitch.

Roger was a marvellously unselfish team player. We

fed the ball down the channels to him and he would chase it all day. He never stopped running. He'd go after the ball, galloping away into the corners. He would always try to turn a bad ball into a good one, and would go in fearlessly where it hurt. He scored crucial goals and made the decoy runs for others such as Bobby Charlton or Geoff Hurst to come through to execute the spectacular. If you wanted a golfing partner he was your man and even today, anything you involve him in, he is always there with his thanks. He retired from international football early, when some people thought he still had many caps to be won. He concentrated on his club football the way Alan Shearer, in recent times, left the England camp to prolong his club career with Newcastle. It is not something I could have done, but I respected Roger's decision.

The three points to the triangle of stars, who came to England from the West Ham academy, as we used to call it, were Moore, Geoff Hurst and Martin Peters, and they all reflected marvellously on Ron Greenwood, the man who had nurtured them and who later became the England manager himself. Geoff was funny, down to earth and simply brilliant as a late-developing goal scorer. Give him a chance and he would finish it for you with a goal. A World Cup Final hat-trick says it all. He was big and brave and strong, excellent at holding the ball in forward positions, waiting for the support to arrive. As a leader of the line he was as good as it gets.

Martin Peters was quiet, studious and according to Alf 'ten years ahead of his time'. Martin was the one player who struck a serious note. He was always concerned that things were being done the right way within the squad. He was immaculate in almost everything he did, which often made me think that West Ham must have had coaching or advice on how to dress and behave away from football. Martin had the ability to glide through games. If he wasn't involved in the first or second pass you could be sure that he would be involved somewhere, even if it was drifting towards the far post waiting for the final ball.

Bobby Charlton, who became Sir Bobby along with Sir Geoff Hurst and Sir Alf Ramsey – all their titles were deserved – was just Bobby. He had gifts to die for. He was basically a quiet man whose talking came from the magic of the boots – except, as already mentioned, when we needed a senior statesman to speak to Alf about some issue. Wherever you went in the world the foreign football fans knew everything about Bobby Charlton. He was our Pelé.

In a strange way we were all bonded by a rare togetherness and yet we were all different. Alf encouraged us to be together. We were allowed to have a couple of beers after matches as long as we were in the group. Naturally, some liked a beer more than others, but nobody took liberties as we were aware of our responsibilities as England players.

The biggest night for celebration came after the Jules Rimet Trophy was in England's custody. To ride on the coach to the Royal Garden Hotel, Kensington, where the official function was to take place, was an experience never to be forgotten. I was truly staggered by the people lining the pavements all the way, cheering and waving their balloons and flags. It rammed home to me just what this win meant to the country. Tens of thousands of people brought the traffic to a standstill.

With the Football Association in charge, there had to be an issue of annoyance. While there was a banquet for the players and officials, all the wives and girlfriends were shunted off into a room of their own for dinner. We hadn't seen each other for what seemed like weeks. Nobby's wife, Kay, often jokes about the present the wives each received at their place setting that night, which was a pair of scissors. As far as the players were concerned, we were just 'touch your cap' serfs to some of the powers in the game. It was: 'Hello, Ball, hello, Charlton.' It was as though they were stuck in the Dark Ages.

They paid us a bonus of £1,000 for winning that World Cup and we had to pay tax on it. I paid super tax that year, at the age of twenty-one, eighty per cent in the pound. I told my dad never to tell me to vote Labour again. I argued that I was being hammered for being successful.

We met the girls when the official business ended and the Labour Prime Minister of the day, Harold Wilson, went home, probably smiling to himself about England's win. We went off to Danny La Rue's club, where he gave us the best night of our lives. Within ten minutes of us arriving there was cake and champagne. Ronnie Corbett was the cabaret. He was extremely funny and the whole show and evening blended into a magical, rewarding event.

On the morning after the final we were front, back and middle page news. Television could not get enough of us. We were floating as if in some fantasy, but this was real. We did a television shoot with Eamonn Andrews and then we all went our separate ways – separated, but friends for life.

At that stage you yearn for a private moment to look at the medal on your own, to contemplate the career that had been so driven, so compelling and, for all the disappointments, so much fun. For my parents it was the ultimate moment of mam and dad pride. From that day there was always a replica Jules Rimet Trophy on display in the family home.

After the celebrations, Nobby and Kay went off to Ireland and Lesley and I drove home with the Connellys in our red Ford Zephyr. We stopped off at the Knutsford Services area on the M6 and I smiled to myself as I sat there eating egg and chips with a World Cup winners' medal in my pocket.

Mexico 1970 seemed a long way off.

3

TAKING OFF

While I was settled and happy at Blackpool and giddy from the success of the World Cup win, something sinister started to happen. The events that unfolded exposed my naivety. I kept receiving anonymous phone calls saying that Don Revie, the Leeds United manager, would like to meet me. The voice on the other end of the line said that Revie believed that Billy Bremner, Johnny Giles and Alan Ball would be the basis of a Leeds side that would go all the way to major honours. One day I drove to a bleak meeting place on the Saddleworth moors between Lancashire and Yorkshire and met him at a secret location. I listened to him. He had a firm north Yorkshire voice and a very persuasive tone. He told me he was desperate to sign me, that it was only a matter of time before I left Blackpool and that he wanted to look after me until the timing came right for a move. I told him I was happy at Blackpool, especially with the World Cup imminent.

I suspected that would not be the end of the matter but was not prepared for what happened next. About ten days after our meeting, there was a knock on the front door. Lesley answered it. It was a dark, rainy night and there was a man on the doorstep. He gave her an envelope and said, 'This is for Alan Ball.' Lesley took the envelope and we counted out £100 in notes.

It happened almost every Friday and all the man would say was, 'No names, no pack-drill, here is an investment.' I kept it for a long time. It was silly of us to even contemplate taking the money, and looking back I find it hard to imagine how unworldly we were. It was a way of Revie saying, 'Don't forget that when the time comes to move we will have looked after you.' It all came out in a High Court case involving Revie.

I didn't even tell my dad about the money because I am not sure how he would have reacted. Nor did I tell Ron Suart until he pulled me into the office one day. I had been given seven days off and Lesley and I went to the Lake District. This was, of course, long before mobile phones. I became restless after a few days and was itching to get back into training with my Blackpool mates.

Suart simply asked me where I had been because he had been trying to get hold of me. He told me there had been a board meeting that morning and that I had been sold. 'Sold!' I was incredulous. He said there were two clubs involved and it would be a British-record fee of £110,000. They had both offered that amount and I could take my pick. I guessed one was Leeds. The other was Everton. He guessed right when I said that I might want to speak to my dad, who was working as a foreman joiner for Bennett's of Warrington while being part-time manager of Nantwich Town.

Dad dropped what he was doing and took time off work and came home for a family summit. Making a decision did not take long. Everton, we knew about. We used to go to Goodison Park to watch a lot of their mid-week games if I was not involved with playing for Blackpool. I had told him about the envelopes from Leeds United. He was not impressed and quickly made up my mind for me when he said: 'I would advise you to go to Everton. It's the type of club for you. It's almost on the doorstep and they don't suffer fools.'

Revie heard about the Everton interest and was on the phone again, almost frantic in his efforts to persuade me to go to Elland Road, but the Balls were not for turning. It was sad leaving Blackpool because I have always believed in loyalty, and the club, especially Ron Suart, had given me the chance when I was desperate and they had allowed me to blossom.

I drove my dad to Everton to meet the manager, Harry Catterick. There were no agents in those days. Everything flowed easily. I was joining a massive club; my wages were more than I had ever imagined. The hardest part was having to ring Revie to tell him of my decision. He was not happy but he never mentioned it again when he later became manager of England while I was still in the international team.

Early days at Everton were not simple, especially those first training sessions. There is a pecking order in football dressing rooms and you have to find your place. At Blackpool I was an international player and although I arrived at Everton having helped England win the World

Cup just a couple of weeks earlier I was still the young new boy. I looked around and everywhere there were famous faces and tall reputations – Roy Vernon, Alex Young, Fred Pickering, Alex Scott, Ray Wilson, Dennis Stevens, Brian Labone, Jimmy Gabriel and Gordon West. The only players I knew were Ray Wilson, my England colleague, and Gordon West, who had been our goal-keeper at Blackpool. I have always had confidence in my ability but as I took everything in, the feeling was over-whelmingly daunting.

They were household names at one of the biggest clubs in the land. I sensed some initial jealousy. I had come for big money and I was surely going to take someone's place in the first team. There was a toughness about the place and initially little of the camaraderie I had enjoyed at Blackpool. Everyone was jostling for positions. There was a dog-eat-dog atmosphere. The smiles were not forthcoming and I knew I had a scrap on my hands.

I sat next to Dennis Stevens, a player I had admired greatly when he was playing at Bolton Wanderers. He remembered me as a youngster who had not made it at Burnden Park, where Bolton used to play before they moved to their impressive Reebok Stadium. Dennis was careful with his money and he gave me some quiet advice when he said: 'I don't know what contract you are on but make sure you march those little green soldiers up to the bank and leave them there.'

When I arrived home I told my dad that the welcome mat had not been laid out and that I had not felt comfortable. As usual he had the right response when he said I would soon be accepted as one of them if my play was helping to bring in the bonuses. The non-triers are the ones who get nailed. He instilled in me that respect had to be earned and could never be taken for granted.

But my life was changing in other ways. In May 1967, Lesley and I were married, and we knew that as long as we were together we would be happy. We would raise a family and happiness would prevail. I never had a doubt about that.

All the time I was getting an insight into management. Ron Suart had been a lovely man; Catterick ruled by fear. I never saw him in a track suit and the same applied when I went to Arsenal at the end of 1971, while Lawrie McMenemy at Southampton was the best manager any player could have worked under. He may not have been a fantastic football thinker but he allowed me to find my own way while planting thoughts in my head the way Malcolm Allison apparently did with the likes of Colin Bell and Mike Summerbee in their Manchester City days. They still revere him.

Thus, at Everton, I was on my own in many ways and the smiling man who signed me, Catterick, turned out to be the toughest boss of all. The dressing room was tough and the manager was a fearful dictator.

He was very hard but after a couple of years of barking and sniping, the fear evaporated. As soon as he realized as much he moved people on, but he did bring together a telepathic midfield trinity of which I was such a part – Kendall, Ball and Harvey. To this day I cannot visit Merseyside without someone wanting to talk about the part we played in Everton's successes in the seventies, when we won the League championship. Howard Kendall, a native of the north-east, came from Preston North End; Colin Harvey was a local lad and while Catterick had the nous to put us together we sorted ourselves out on the pitch. All the knowledge of how the game should be played came from my father.

We were fit. We became mates. We were competitive in training but in matches instinct and understanding took over. We could have found each other in the dark. Howard had a 'good engine'. He could pass the ball long or short and he had a masterful tackle. He was a good talker on the pitch, plotting the course of a match, using his vision, and it was a shame that with so many top midfield players in the country, he never won an England cap.

Colin was as fit as a flea, a powerful tackler and a strong runner. We all had football brains. We were creative. No one could mark us. Opposing teams tried all kinds of tactics to stop us but if they had handcuffed gorillas to us we would have run them to death. If they wanted to play football we would match them at that. If they wanted a fight, we fought them.

Colin was the quietest of the three and I am delighted to see people giving him some kind of credit for bringing Wayne Rooney through the Everton junior ranks. When Kendall, Ball and Harvey were together we played purely off-the-cuff football. The improvisations were inspired.

We were far from a three-man team. Gordon West was a fantastic goalkeeper and a one-off character. There was no funnier sight than seeing an Everton fan run to give him a handbag, which he would hang on his arm and strut around his goalmouth like an imitation catwalk model. He was also an avid stamp collector, which set him aside from most footballers.

Brian Labone, our captain, was a born leader of men. He galvanized us as a team off the pitch as well as on it. Before the majority of away games, when we would travel by train from Lime Street, he used to make sure that the whole team went to a Chinese restaurant near the station, where we all ate a massive meal together before catching the afternoon Intercity express. He was always working toward team spirit and achieved it 110 per cent.

Tommy Wright, the fullback who played for England and was in the 1970 World Cup squad, was another inimitable lad, a typical Scouser who liked a drink. I remember going into the Bellefield training ground one day and spotted a lad sitting by the door, which was locked because the physiotherapist, Norman Borrowdale, hadn't arrived. The lad turned out to be Tommy, who had three or four empty beer bottles around him and clearly somebody had dropped him off for treatment for an injury. In reality, when he played, there was no one fitter. He was just imbued with part of the Liverpool weekend culture.

We had big John Hurst at the back alongside Brian Labone, Labby as we always called him. Labby would go for everything and Hursty, the wonderful foil, would read the game expertly and pick up anything loose. Alex

Young, Golden Vision, was very special on the ball. He and his wife, Nancy, became very good friends.

Joe Royle came into the side as a youngster and gave us another dimension as he developed into a superb striker. We usually played out football on the ground, a genuine passing game, but if we were in any kind of trouble we would launch the ball into the penalty area for Joe to make something of it. He was a regular goal-scorer. Then there was Johnny Morrissey on the left. Pound for pound he was as good as you could get. I used to love playing with him. I could drift over to his side and play one-twos with him all day. He was a brave, strong winger, which was not the norm. Members of the wing fraternity were supposed to be light and timid. Johnny was the opposite. He would munch people. His best trick was giving the ball to the fullback and then sorting him out.

We had young Jimmy Husband on the right, showing his great pace and knack of scoring vital goals. Then there was Ernie Hunt, who had come to us from Swindon complete with his rich, evocative West Country accent. He was an incorrigible practical joker. Ernie, Howard and I used to live near each other in Formby and would share the driving to training. At one time we used to pass a group of Scouse workers who were digging a hole at the side of the road. They were Liverpudlians and they had spotted us which meant, naturally, that we would be the targets of their good-natured stick. Going and coming back, they were waiting for us and gave us plenty.

Ernie planned his revenge. On Fridays, the physio

Norman Borrowdale used to bring us fresh eggs, and we would each buy a box. On the way home we approached the hole and could just see the tops of the shovels with the Scousers hidden and working away in the bottom. Ernie told me to stop the car. He got out with the carton of eggs and proceeded to bombard them. They were trapped. The yolk was on them and by the time they were able to scramble out of the hole we were in the car and away.

One day when I went to pick him up he got into my car wearing a gorilla suit under his raincoat. We were on our way into training when he spotted a fellow sweeping the road. He told me to pull over and began asking the man for directions to Southport Zoo. As he started to tell us, Ernie jumped out of the car in his gorilla suit and began to chase the poor bloke down the road. Cars were stopping, people were laughing. It was incredibly funny.

He would be driving down fashionable Lord Street in Southport when he would come across a pedestrian crossing which gave him the opportunity to wave people across with a huge gorilla's hand. He bought three Sergeant Bilko hats and insisted on Howard, him and me wearing them when we went out for a meal with our wives. We walked down Lord Street in them one day.

Lesley and I took him to a frightfully posh party one night, and halfway through there was a scream with an upper-crust voice calling out, 'Oh, my God.' He had left a realistic plastic dog dropping on the carpet in the middle of the lounge as well as severed fingers in the salad. It was all part of the tremendous fun we had on Merseyside.

No one can deny that success came to Everton under Catterick's stewardship but there were times when it seemed we were playing well despite him and not because of him. He never took a training session. He never imparted any footballing philosophy to think about. He had problems with one-to-one relationships. He was strong when it came to lashing out the big stick and you always knew when it was coming because you could hear him pounding down the Bellefield corridor in his heavy brogues after you had been beaten on the previous Saturday. The lads would be sitting there like naughty schoolboys waiting for the headmaster to arrive to administer the appropriate punishment. I think that he was shy underneath. He wanted to be friends later in life and there were times when I felt sorry for him.

For all that, I loved my time on Merseyside. I had a great understanding with the supporters. I had married Lesley, I was playing for England and once the senior players realized I could handle myself and that I could play a bit and enjoyed a laugh, everything was fine.

I had joined Everton on a Monday morning ahead of a Saturday match at Fulham. I had quickly become friendly with Jimmy Gabriel, an old Everton stalwart, and on the Friday night we were staying at the Russell Hotel, a favourite overnight stay for northern teams in those days. Jimmy suggested an evening stroll. I was excited. I was on an all-time high, a World Cup winner ready to make his debut for a great club after a record transfer. Jimmy was banging on, extolling the praises of the club, telling me how much the supporters would love me and so on. I liked Jimmy. He was a passionately enthusiastic Scot who played with his heart.

As we were walking along with the conversation bubbling, he suddenly turned into the doorway of a pub and said: 'Come on, I'll buy you a pint.' To say I was taken aback hardly describes my response. I told him I didn't drink. Going into a pub on a Friday night was an absolute taboo. Still, I followed him in, knowing it was all wrong. He had a pint of shandy and I had a lemonade as he continued to tell me about Everton and Merseyside as if I had joined an amazing fantasy club. All the time we were in there I was terrified that somebody from the club would walk in. Just being in a pub, in the smoky atmosphere, was bad enough even if I wasn't taking alcohol.

No one spotted us and I went to sleep dreaming on Jimmy's words and the prospects of my career at this wonderful Everton. The magic lingered because next day with my England World Cup winner, George Cohen, in the Fulham team as well as Ray Wilson and me in Everton blue there was all the fuss and commotion of intense media interest.

It was a beautiful day and there could have been no better ground than Craven Cottage for me to make my debut. It was on the same turf that I scored that memorable hat-trick for Blackpool. We won 1–0 and I scored the winner fifteen minutes from the end. In the dressing room afterwards I was thinking that at any moment I would wake up and realize it was all a dream. The journey back to Lime Street Station told me otherwise.

Our compartment was invaded by supporters and I seemed to be singled out for happy, friendly, mobbing.

The supporters had apparently taken to me instantly and scoring the winning goal away from home on debut is, I guess, a significant marker. Even more significantly, in Merseyside terms, where the Everton–Liverpool rivalry is as amiable as it is intense, came the 'derby' match at home. I was about to experience why such a fuss is made about these fixtures played on grounds separated by Stanley Park. The noise from the packed crowd as we ran out was staggering. Manchester United at home had been deafening but this had an extra edge to it. I remember looking up at the Goodison Park clock in the corner of the ground. It was three o'clock and there were no nerves. I was loving every moment of it as if this was my stage. I had a fear of nobody and I knew that this was what I wanted for the rest of my life. The image of that famous old clock will never leave me because when I looked at it again it was twelve minutes past three and I had scored two goals. The whole place was jumping. I was comfortable on the ball and making runs to support the others. We won 3–1 and while the Liverpool supporters would have gone away saddened but never angry, that could not be said for the feeling that had developed on the pitch.

As were heading into tunnel at the end, our fullback Sandy Brown was giving Ron Yeats a piece of his mind. Yeats reacted and pushed Sandy down the steps all the way to the bottom. There was a huge kerfuffle with players pushing and shoving. I just stood back and watched. I had never seen anything like it before. All that and I was the new kid who had scored three goals in two games and we were right up there in the league. After the match I collected Lesley and we drove to Blackpool to see all the lads I had been unable to say farewell to, still in awe of the players I had joined. What a start!

I knew I was on my way to proving myself in their company, especially to Fred Pickering, who had told me in his typical forthright Lancashire way that I might not even get into the team. I wanted to show them that I would scrap for them, earn them their bonuses, join in any of their fights, because that was the way I had been brought up. I was raised to respect authority and to have a deep work ethic when it came to training and playing. I had a pride in being the last one off the training pitch, always wanting to give more.

I also saw how some of the players reacted to the manager's methods. Roy Vernon would be smoking before and after training. Alex Young, the man the fans called the Golden Vision, had abundant ability but he did things his own way. Fred Pickering was a big, strong lad but he could be very stubborn. For the five years I was at Everton I never quite got over the shock of the way the Catterick regime was run. Not once was there an encouraging arm around my shoulder. It was all discipline and fear. Wilf Dixon joined the club as a trainer but he was a fitness fanatic rather than a coach.

I could talk to him but most of the time I had to work things out for myself, or listen to my dad. It was only when I joined up with England that I was learning anything tactically. As I grew older I began to stand up to Catterick more. I never understood why the training-ground gates were always shut. He used to watch us arrive from his little turret of an office that looked out over the car-park entrance and training ground. We had to sign in like factory workers and he would never listen to excuses. An accident blocking the East Lancs Road was no reason for being a few minutes late. We won the First Division championship in 1970 and lost an FA Cup Final to West Brom but, typical of the way the manager operated, he began to break up the team when we were in our mid- to late twenties.

The 1968 final was a match everyone expected us to win. We had beaten Leeds in the semi final at Old Trafford, a match I didn't play in because of injury, and Johnny Morrissey took over as penalty taker to score the winner from the spot. With that out of the way there seemed no reason why we shouldn't have been climbing those famous steps up to the Royal Box at the end of the final. After all, we had beaten West Brom 6–2 on their own ground, the Hawthorns, in the league, with me scoring four goals in a match for the first time in my life. We also saw them off at home, 5–1. I scored three on that day to make it seven goals from two games. As you can imagine I was rather looking forward to the final.

I have never played in a more one-sided game in my life. We were shooting in for ninety minutes but just couldn't score. Then Jeff Astle got a freak chance when the ball came back to him off Ray Wilson's backside and he put it away to give them a 1–0 win. It was a perfect example of how crazy football can be. Our play from box to box was simply fantastic but we couldn't finish. I knew that was the closest I would ever come to winning an FA Cup Final.

I resented the fact that Catterick never taught me anything. I needed a coach, a Malcolm Allison type, who could extend and expand my mind. Someone to make me think about breaking down tight defences, perhaps, but it never happened.

We did have our fun, of course. Alex Young introduced me to horse-racing and I have been a fan of the turf and a lover of horses ever since. We had become friendly with Barry Hills, who was assistant trainer to John Oxley before he set up on his own. Alex and I bought the first horse he ever trained on his own. It was called Daxal and was utterly useless. Since then Barry has trained some very fine horses and has won many of the sport's big races including the 1,000 Guineas, St Leger and Prix de l'Arc de Triomphe.

Living close to our training ground was the legendary Bill Shankly, who was as amusing and as effervescent as Catterick was dour. One day I was sent off for a mis-timed tackle on Ian Callaghan, who was Shankly's winger at Liverpool. A couple of days later Shanks called me up and said he disagreed with the sending off and that he was prepared to travel to London to the Football Association hearing to support me. A Subutteo table was laid out and Shanks was asked to give his version of events using the miniature players. As he shuffled them around he said: 'There was a scuffle on the far side where there was a slightly mistimed tackle by Mr Ball here. I spoke to my player afterwards and he said it had not been a dangerous tackle.'

The referee asked: 'Mr Shankly, from where did you see this incident?'

Shanks: 'From the dug-out.'

Referee: 'With all due respect this happened right in the far corner of Goodison Park from where you were. You were a long way from the incident with a linesman also in your way.'

Shanks thought for a minute, trapped, but produced a reply that had me stifling a chuckle: 'Aye, but as soon as I saw the incident developing I threw the linesman to the floor to get a better view.'

He made me smile after one of the low points in all my gripping derby experiences. In our championship year, 1969–70, Liverpool came to Goodison Park and defeated us 3–0. It was a hiding, leaving a feeling of desolation that would linger until the next time for the supporters. I felt for them because I knew what it meant to the blue half of the city. As we left the field that day he was waiting for us, shaking our hands with a 'well done, son, well done, wee man' and so on. Shake his hand and keep walking was the only way to deal with it.

We still had to go to Anfield with a handful of games to the end of the season. A win would have us within touching distance of the trophy. We did it with goals from Joe Royle and Alan Whittle. The championship was virtually ours and the champagne flowed. We could not help querying the whereabouts of the notably absent

Shanks. True to form, he impishly poked his head round the dressing-room door and said: 'Three–nil at Goodison, two–nil at Anfield, you are beaten three–two on aggregate in any competition in the world.' With a smile, he was gone. We won the title comfortably, losing only five matches out of forty-one. We were a very special side with no weaknesses and Catterick broke it up too easily.

My memories of Merseyside are mainly fond ones, although there is another example of the fear factor invoked by Catterick. After our first baby, Mandy, was born in 1968 she developed complications one morning. In today's world a footballer, or anyone for that matter, would stay with his wife and child. I had to go into training. I dared not call the club to tell them about my problems. It was only after training that I heard that Lesley and the baby were back in hospital. The neighbours had organized everything.

Lesley's pregnancy was the inspiration for a dart of Scouse humour. Her condition had been mentioned in the *Liverpool Echo* and I recall the moment when I went to take a corner. As I backed off towards the crowd, a wag shouted: 'I don't know who's in labour, Bally, you or the missus.'

I loved it. You couldn't hide. You could never kid those supporters. All they asked was that when you pulled on the blue shirt you did it justice. As my dad always said, give them 100 per cent and the rest will be a doddle.

There was an FA Cup quarter-final match against Liverpool one Saturday night with a full house at Goodison and an equally packed Anfield watching the match unfold on the big screen. It was a windy, horrible night with a game howling up the River Mersey, but we won. It was one of those to-and-fro matches and then, in the second half, the ball was played through the middle. Gordon Milne was shepherding it back to Tommy Lawrence. Something in my mind told me to take a gamble as they might just leave it to each other.

They did. It ran at an angle and the wind was threatening to take it out of play but I managed to get on the right side of it. They could only watch as it dipped into the far corner of the net and I wheeled away. The fans were going barmy as we celebrated. Evertonians danced the night away.

The story goes that Jimmy Tarbuck, great comedian himself and a renowned Liverpool supporter, was seen leaving Anfield close to tears after watching the match on the screen, when somebody tapped him on the shoulder and cracked: 'Don't be upset, Jim. It's only a film.'

Jimmy calls me 'the fox' because he says I always played with the cunning of a fox against Liverpool.

It was just another cameo of wonderful days in a city that will always be a part of me, deep in my heart. We had some memorable matches even if we did go out of two major competitions in three days, the European Cup against Panathinaikos of Greece in the quarter final and beaten 2–1 in the FA Cup semi-final by Liverpool towards the end of the 1970–1 season. I was out for two months with a pelvic injury in that season and became worried about my career, especially when it was realized that I was doing the wrong rehabilitation.

For the first time I felt fallible. I sensed that Catterick was anxious to change things and I left the following season. The transfer to Arsenal came as a shock.

4

MEXICO WAY

For four years wherever I went and wherever England played we carried the standard as World Cup winners. Respect was everywhere and rightly so. In that context we went off to Mexico for the next World Cup in 1970 feeling good about our chances and ourselves. We had heard about the rejuvenation of Brazil with Pelé back to his best. We knew the usual suspects, West Germany, France, Italy and inevitably the host nation, would all fancy their chances. But in the intervening years we had lost only four of thirty-four full international matches.

Some people felt that the squad Sir Alf Ramsey flew out with was perhaps stronger than the 'boys of '66'. The nucleus of that side remained with eight of us in the squad, Gordon Banks, Nobby Stiles, Jack and Bobby Charlton, Bobby Moore, Geoff Hurst, Martin Peters and myself. The additions looked good. George Cohen and Ray Wilson had given way to Keith Newton and Terry Cooper at full back, and Francis Lee probably benefited most from Roger Hunt's decision to retire from international football. There were plenty of contenders for the role of winners four years on. Jack Charlton, though he was in the squad, sat through most of the matches, with my old Everton pal, Brian Labone, lining up against Moore and Alan Mullery taking over Nobby's role. Banging away on the fringes trying to get a game were people such as Peter Bonetti, Emlyn Hughes, Peter Osgood, Jeff Astle, Colin Bell, Tommy Wright, Allan Clarke, Norman Hunter and so on. The only players not to get onto the pitch at some stage were Nobby, Hughes and Alex Stepney.

Before the greatest football festival of old began to unfold, Sir Alf had a plan. He made us train at altitude in Mexico, and then had us flown down to Colombia and Ecuador to play international matches against those countries in conditions similar to the ones we might expect in Mexico. As it happened when we played Colombia in Bogotá at 7,500 feet above sea level it was relatively cool and the pitch was very wet after heavy rain. We won comfortably enough. I managed a goal in the 4−0 win with Martin Peters (two) and Bobby Charlton getting the others.

No problem; we were almost ready to move on to play Ecuador in Quito. We had a few hours to kill and as we were at the best hotel in the city, El Tequendama, that was no hardship. Bobby Moore and Bobby Charlton drifted into the jewellery shop where I had earlier had a nose around myself. Bobby Charlton was looking for a present for his wife, Norma.

I was just meandering about when I sensed that there was something of a commotion going on. There were raised voices and someone from the shop was clearly confronting Moore. As the rest of us were ushered away the police arrived and Sir Alf was there and I could tell there were accusations and denials flying about. The two Bobbys who had been in the shop together made statements, and by this time we were ready to leave for the airport to fly to Quito for the second warm-up friendly against Ecuador before going on to our Mexican base in Guadalajara. The word had gone around that Bobby Moore had been accused of stealing a bracelet from the hotel shop. We kept it to ourselves so that the journalists travelling with us did not find out for ages that something was amiss.

Sir Alf was a worried man, as we all were. We knew that as world champions we were not the most popular people to be in South America. We also knew that the charge against Bobby Moore was completely false. There could never, ever conceivably be any chance that Bobby would have done that. We saw it as a plot to destabilize us, perhaps to damage our confidence. Bobby was a colossal presence in our team and that only emphasized my belief that they had tried to snare him with a set-up. We had to leave him behind with the British Chargé d'Affaires in Bogotá. A couple of FA men stayed behind as well. Bobby Charlton offered to remain in Bogotá to keep Moore company but that was not seen as a good idea.

We defeated Ecuador 2–0 at an even higher altitude, where the air was thinner and the ball moved faster. That was a serious test of stamina and fitness. We were over 9,000 feet above sea level. The lads not in the first team played a match immediately before us. I knew it was going to be torture when I spoke to Tommy Wright as he was coming in after playing. I asked him if it was hard and he couldn't speak. He tried to, but there were all these white flecks around his mouth and he just kept swallowing. His eyes were rolling. When we played it was as if I suddenly felt I knew what an asthma attack must be like. We couldn't breathe. Alan Mullery was the shouter, always telling people where to be and where to go, but in this atmosphere all that came out was a gurgle.

It was in Quito that Sir Alf had to trim his squad from twenty-eight to twenty-two, always a terrible time for the manager and those being cut adrift. Out went Peter Shilton, Bob McNab, Ralph Coates, Brian Kidd, David Sadler and Peter Thompson. All six were invited to stay and travel as members of the party, but they were out of the squad. At the time I could not understand why Sadler and Thompson were the only ones who decided to stay.

After beating Ecuador we took the flight to Guadalajara, managing a storm delay at Panama City on the way. By the time we arrived in Mexico the entire world knew of Moore's plight.

The airport was heaving with television crews, photographers and reporters. There were FIFA officials and British Embassy people and the hundreds of rubbernecks that are attracted to such occasions. The local paper described us as arriving as drunks and thieves. They may have been influenced by the sight of Jeff Astle who, because of his fear of flying, had taken that extra drink to try to calm himself.

Maybe the local media were indignant because of Sir Alf's dismissive way with them, but that was Alf. He was entitled to be more downbeat than usual because his captain and natural leader, the cornerstone of his attempt to retain the Jules Rimet trophy, was under house arrest in Bogotá with a shop assistant saying he had taken a £625 bracelet. Her main evidence was that she had seen him lingering over the cabinet.

Four days after his arrest and four days before the opening match, Moore was released. When he arrived in Guadalajara he had neither trained nor slept but, completely in character, he returned with all his usual dignity and swept straight into the preparations as though nothing had happened. Once Bobby indicated that it had been a set-up, nothing was said and we put the incident behind us. We got down to the hard work and one day we had a visitor to the training ground, João Saldanha, the previous manager of Brazil. He told us he had endured the exact same experience at the same hotel in Bogotá. Little wonder the Colombians never pushed the case against Bobby.

There was plenty of anti-English feeling. The Mexican people had set against us. They knew all the tricks. The newspapers carried vicious cartoons but our mood was one of upbeat solidarity and that was emphasized when we lined up as a guard of honour to welcome Moore to the Hilton Hotel. He had missed five days of training, but looked as though not even five minutes had been taken out of his schedule. He was as calm as anyone when the Mexicans began parading around the hotel at all hours of the night trying to keep us awake. Most of the lads changed rooms but they failed to make life unhappy because this was the World Cup, the big one, again, and we were ready to do our duty.

That involved Group Three matches against Brazil, Czechoslovakia and Rumania with the top two to go through to the quarter-finals. The days were sweltering, the sun intense. I kept meaning to fry an egg on the pavement but never got around to it. Guadalajara was at 5,200 feet and we were to play our games at the Jalisco Stadium, where the heat would be ferocious. We felt, however, that the medical men had done everything right by us in our preparation with regard to dehydration and so on. It worked perfectly in that first match which, to be honest, was not as uncomfortable as it might have been. The rain was coming down when, with twenty-five minutes to go we scored the goal that counted, to our delight and that of the estimated 3,000 English fans in the stadium.

Before the game Rumania's star forward, Dumitrache, had been predicting that he would score two against us. At the final whistle I could not resist sticking two fingers up and saying to him: 'Where's your two then, pally?' He just shrugged. I could be irritating at times!

Brazil beat Czechoslovakia 4–1 with a majestic performance that had people whistling through their teeth, and Rumania beat Czechoslovakia 2–1, which brought us to the crunch, that midday kick–off against Brazil. The heat was burning at that time with the sun at its zenith, so that a suspended microphone over the middle of the pitch cast a small shadow over the centre circle. It was ninety-eight degrees Fahrenheit. Again, we were well prepared. I was covered in sunblock, I wore my socks very long and we had special aertex shirts. We were learning about our bodies – about water intake, salt and blood counts. Sir Alf made one of his memorable speeches. 'Would you give gold away?' he asked, somewhat mysteriously. Before anyone could answer he added: 'Well, the ball is gold today. Don't give it away and you will defeat these Brazilians. If you give it away in this heat you might not get it back.'

We kept it; we took the play to them and matched them in every department. Don't forget they were subsequently regarded as the best football team of all time. It was just a wonderful match to play in and I have only one grouse. I will maintain until the day I die that Tostao elbowed me in the face just as I was about to nick the ball from him. He turned back on to his right foot and crossed the ball. It went straight to Pelé. With Brian Labone facing him and Terry Cooper straining to get across, Pelé decided against a shot and elected to slide the ball almost gently at an angle for Jairzinho. Cooper lost his footing as he went for a last-ditch interception and Jairzinho hammered his cross shot high into the net with his right foot. I don't want to sound grudging but there should have been a free kick awarded against Tostao.

We were not done. We may have been tired but we came back for more. You could not play flat out in those conditions. I had to adapt my game and played in bursts. Even then, for all our fine preparation, we were losing anything from seven to ten pounds in weight in ninety minutes. I managed to bounce an effort onto the Brazilian bar with the goalkeeper, Felix, beaten. We were beaten but unbowed and Bobby Charlton made a remark that really summed up this terrific match between two skilful, committed teams when he said after watching a film of the game: 'You could take that film and use it for coaching. That is what the game at the top is all about. There was everything in there, all the skills and techniques, all the tactical control, the lot. There was some very special stuff played out there.'

There was also what could fairly be described as the save of the century when Gordon Banks defied gravity to flick away a header from Pelé. The great man himself had shouted 'Goal' as soon as the ball left his forehead, according to Alan Mullery, who was not far away.

We left that game undaunted, knowing that we had the team capable of retaining the trophy. Brazil defeated Rumania 1–0, which meant they topped the group. Plenty of folk were indulging in the mathematics of the situation as we went forward to our final group match, but the bottom line was that we must not lose. Brazil could relax. If we lost by a goal, points and goal difference would put us absolutely level with Rumania and lots would have to be drawn. If we lost by two goals then Rumania would go through. Sir Alf decided to rest some players and introduce recruits. He must have been feeling confident. Keith Newton came back after injury, Jack Charlton replaced Brian Labone, and Colin Bell took over from me, while Clarke and Astle replaced Lee and

Hurst. The Czechs made several changes and emerged looking bright and constructive, which was worrying.

We were not at our best. These things happen from time to time; days when everything you try just seems not to come off. Thankfully, we scored after forty-eight minutes, when Colin Bell was fouled in the area and Allan Clarke despatched the penalty. I went on twelve minutes later in place of Bobby Charlton, whose appearance took him level with Billy Wright's record 105 full-capped appearances for England.

We were through to face West Germany in a quarter-final in León, a town at higher altitude than Guadalajara at the end of 150 miles of dusty desert and mountain road. A rougher ride was to follow. León had been the Germans' 'home' ground during their Group Four exploits and the critics were quick to point out that in progressing to the quarter-final stage they had scored ten goals to our two.

We had conceded only one, Jairzinho's goal for Brazil, and Banksy rightly deserved much praise for the two clean sheets out of three, but soon we had a problem. He had complained to one or two people about feeling unwell on the evening before our match with West Germany. I knew he would be desperate to play, but when one of the other lads reported that he had seen Gordon looking terrible and leaning on the arm of Dr Neil Phillips around breakfast time I began to realize that no matter how keen Gordon was it was looking as though we would have to play without him.

It was late on, just before we left for the ground, that

Sir Alf announced that The Cat, Peter Bonetti, would be playing. We all regarded him as an outstanding goal-keeper, but it was a shame because the very sight of Gordon Banks's name on a team sheet was usually enough to intimidate the opposition. The German players had nothing but respect for him and his absence was a serious blow. It seemed he had been afflicted with stomach trouble known by visitors to Mexico as Montezuma's Revenge. On the subcontinent they call it Delhi Belly, but it was not a laughing matter and it was really galling when we recalled the preparations we had made to protect ourselves from such illness – no salads, no ice, only bottled water and so on.

We were brilliant for an hour. I was enjoying my personal little duel with Overath and enjoying being irritatingly waspish again. The Germans didn't like it but in those days I had little respect for reputations. We took the lead after thirty-five minutes through Alan Mullery with a well-worked goal as he rounded off a move he had started in our half of the field. Early in the second half we scored again through Martin Peters. Surely, at 2–0, we were on our way to the semi-final. Looking back I believe we subconsciously took our feet off the pedals. We also hit the wall physically. Sir Alf made two substitutions, with Colin Bell and Norman Hunter, two strong boys full of running, replacing Bobby Charlton and Martin Peters with the score at 2–1. I could see Sir Alf's thinking. Bobby had played three hard games in a week covering acres, as had Martin, another long-distance runner. The plan was for the two substitutes and me to shore up the middle of the park. With Colin Bell running all over the place and Norman in his 'none shall pass' mood I looked at them as two wise substitutions with a semi-final only three days away.

Then things started to go wrong. They put on a flying winger, Grabowski, and he began to cause us problems, although with twenty-two minutes left we looked home, if not comfortably. Then everything started to slip. Franz Beckenbauer, who had started moving forward fluently, tried a shot that slipped under The Cat and into the net. It should have been a simple, everyday save but he missed it, 2–1. At that point Bobby Charlton went off and Colin Bell came on. After eighty minutes Peters went off and Hunter came on but the German surge continued. A back-header by Uwe Seeler, who was just knocking it in the general area of the goal mouth, went in because The Cat was caught in no man's land and we were staring at extra time.

There was to be no repeat of Wembley 1966. Some of our lads were wilting in the intense heat and with eleven minutes to go Gerd Muller, unhindered, was hooking the ball past a transfixed England goalkeeper. We tried to get it back. We worked ourselves to a sweat-soaked standstill, but we could not get the goal. It has to be admitted that they were better than us in extra time. We could not raise ourselves to the pitch as we had before. I never thought we would lose. The score flashed around the world. We had lost 3–2 in extra time after squandering a 2–0 lead.

In the final moments I knew it was slipping away from

us. Some of our lads were tiring. Their legs were heavy, their lungs burning, their shirts soaked. We tried everything, but fate was taking an inevitable course.

Back in the dressing room it seemed like twenty minutes before anyone spoke. Everyone was just bewildered by the turn of events. How could it happen? How could we lose after being 2–0 up? It hurt because we felt we could win the World Cup and become immortalized in English sporting history. Sir Alf was devastated. As ever he tried not to show his emotion, but we knew how badly he felt. He restrained himself with words like disappointment and said we would have to think about what had happened and learn from it.

We went back to the hotel somehow hoping to wake up from the nightmare. The night before at some weird nocturnal hour back home my dad phoned me and told me to 'go out and die for England'. He knew I didn't really need to be told this because that was my way of operating in every match. It hadn't worked. I am not sure if the disappointment has ever eased but back at the hotel, with a few beers on the lawn beside the pool, we had a bit of a wake that produced a false charge of cheerfulness. Three of the lads and their wives had gone straight off to Acapulco immediately after the quarter-final. I could not have done that. I had to be a part of the whole experience until we left the plane at Heathrow.

There was an amusing moment the following morning on the long coach trip from León to Mexico City. Tommy Wright lapsed into tears, and as he was crying Sir Alf came up to him and put a sympathetic, fatherly arm around him, saying: 'Don't be too upset, young man. You've got plenty of time. There's another World Cup coming up in four years' time and you're young enough to be in that.'

There was a pause, and then Tommy delivered his reply and his reason for being upset. 'There's no beer left on the bus,' he said.

It was a long and torturous trip back, but it made me all the more determined to never lose a match like that again. Again, I vowed to myself that whatever happened I would give everything I had, every last breath and heartbeat, to get what I wanted for my country and for myself. Qualifying matches for the 1974 World Cup in West Germany would soon be on us. I would be a senior player by then and I wanted to play my part in taking revenge for the disappointment of León.

We failed to make it to the finals, which was a blow to everyone and cost Sir Alf his job. The two qualifying matches against Poland were our undoing when we lost 2–0 in Chorzow and drew 1–1 at Wembley. I was out of order in Poland when I reacted as one of their players tried to put his boot into Martin Peters's face. The old red mists came over me and I leapt at him and put both hands around his throat and tried to wrestle him to the ground. I was off. There was no arguing. Sir Alf gave me a thorough roasting after that and all I could do was apologize to him and the rest of the lads. Maybe I was frustrated because we were not playing well. Bobby Moore did not have one of his better nights, and when the Poles came to Wembley we were both watching from the bench carrying injuries. I had damaged my knee ligaments playing for Arsenal. This was the night the Polish goalkeeper Jan Tomaszewski made a name for himself with some unbelievable saves. Brian Clough famously referred to him as a clown. Some clown!

We were out. A wonderful era was coming to a close. Sir Alf was sacked on 1 May 1974 with very little in the way of thanks from the Football Association. The country had knighted him in gratitude for all he had done on behalf of sport and national morale, but he just left Lancaster Gate quietly, having been paid very modestly during his years in charge.

It left a huge gap as far as I was concerned. I was hovering around the thirty mark. Don Revie came in and I knew there was history between us after my reluctance to play his transfer game when I was a lad at Blackpool and he was managing Leeds United. To be fair, he seemed to hold no grudge and I captained England six times for him, winning three, drawing three. High among my memories was that night in March 1975 when we defeated West Germany 2–0 at Wembley. With Alan Hudson, Malcolm Macdonald and myself rampant we absolutely blitzed them, but Revie never played the three of us in the same side again. Supermac had a purple patch for England, scoring all the goals in a 5–0 win over Cyprus at Wembley two months later.

My time was running out, though I did not see this coming, and my last game for England was the 5–1 win over Scotland at Wembley on 24 May 1975. At the time I was feeling good about my play. My form had not dipped and I had struck up a good relationship with young Gerry Francis, who had come into the side. We were playing some superb football in the middle of the pitch. There seemed to be plenty of international football to look forward to.

Then one day, unheralded and totally unexpected, a letter from Revie dropped through the letter box. It was unsigned, thanking me for what I had done for England, telling me that he had decided that Gerry Francis would be captaining England and wishing me all the best in the future. I was gobsmacked. What disappointed me was that he didn't even speak to me either man to man or on the telephone. It was just a letter that he did not have the courtesy to sign. I had been his captain, I had worn the shirt seventy-two times and here I was being tossed aside like a piece of flotsam. I drew satisfaction from my record over the years and the fact that I had regained my international place after twice breaking my leg.

Maybe I was too experienced in the ways of the world for him. Looking back I think I know of one or two things that might have annoyed him. He had the squad staying at West Lodge Park Hotel in north London and in the afternoons, when there was nothing on the official team agenda, it seemed a good idea to go along to my friend Bernie Winters's house, which was not very far away. Bernie was a regular visitor to Arsenal and I often met him on nights out in London. I had struck up a good friendship with Alan Hudson and took him along to Bernie's, where we drank tea and chatted to while away the time. Players were often looking for things to do and

I was quite open about it, but I am sure Revie got it into his head that we were going to Bernie's for two reasons: to drink something stronger than tea and to indulge in some serious gambling using Bernie's telephone. When I told Bernie this he said he wanted to make sure that the record was straightened and wrote to the Football Association, setting out the reality of our cups of tea.

On another occasion the squad was called together in summer. Some of us had come back from our holidays and we were not training. As one of the oldest and most experienced members of the squad I asked if it was all right for us to go out for a drink in the evening. Revie imposed a midnight curfew. The White Hart was the Arsenal local in Southgate. It was just down the road and some of us went out. He did not take kindly to that move and made some noises about my lack of discipline. I told him they were grown men and that I could have made the excuse that I was rounding them up. Les Cocker was waiting for me when I got back.

Revie felt we had abused the curfew, something imposed on most squads, and had posted his trusty lieutenant, Cocker, to wait up like a timekeeper. Les had been with me a long time and I think he was probably trying to find an excuse for me. It appeared I had to carry the can for some lads missing the curfew because I, as captain, should have taken the responsibility of whipping them in.

I was disappointed with the way my international career ended, but it had lasted a long time with all those caps and soon I was ready for the next chapters of my life.

5

FAREWELL EVERTON

Back at Everton for the start of the 1970–1 season there was much to look forward to. We were the Football League champions with a title to defend. We were in the European Cup and running at the top of our form with a team that almost picked itself. The disappointment of Mexico 1970 soon abated and domestic hostilities resumed.

Somehow we never quite found the magic of the previous season and crashed out of two major competitions in three days in 1971, losing our European Cup quarter-final to the Greeks of Panathinaikos and knocked out of the FA Cup at the semi-final stage by our old rivals, Liverpool, on the neutral territory of Old Trafford, 2–1.

I was out for two months in the early part of the season because of a pelvic injury. I fought my way back but became worried for my future career when it was discovered that I was doing the wrong rehabilitation. I was travelling to Manchester for injections on a regular basis over six weeks and for the first time I began to feel fallible. I had been right on top of my game when I kicked off the new season in August, but the injury dragged me down. I tried to play through the discomfort, which was silly and meant I could only give sixty-five per cent of myself some of the time.

I was just getting my fitness and form back and celebrating the birth of our second daughter, Keely, at Hope Hospital, Salford, on 17 December 1971 when I went into training. We had moved back to Worsley to be nearer our parents. With a new baby and my form back I was contentment itself.

Then I received a surprise. On my way in to training I was intercepted by the physiotherapist, Norman Borrowdale, who said: 'The gaffer [Harry Catterick] wants to see you upstairs in his office.' I wondered why. I knocked on the door and went in, and Catterick motioned me to sit down. Then he just looked at me and said coldly: 'We have had an incredible bid for you. It is a British record transfer of £220,000 from a top side. Their manager is in that room down the corridor. I suggest you go and speak to him.'

I was flabbergasted. No way, was my immediate thought. I asked Catterick: 'Why? I don't want to go. Why are you selling me? I am your captain. I am twenty-seven years of age. I am playing for England. I am playing well and you want to sell me. I just can't understand that.'

He said: 'It's business, son. I am doubling my money. I've had you for six years. I am making a profit on you and I have had an awful lot out of you. Football's business, son.'

I told Catterick straightaway that I didn't want to speak to anyone. I was more than happy playing for Everton; Keely was just two days old and the last thing I needed was disruption. Everything in my life was comfortably in order.

He said I should speak to my dad and handed me the phone. I rang him and told him what had happened, that the board had accepted the bid from Arsenal, and asked what I should do. Before going home I had a word with Bertie Mee, who was aware of my reluctance. I agreed to travel to London taking my dad with me, the following day to talk to him about the move, terms and so on. It was clear that Catterick wanted me out.

When I told my dad that Arsenal were the buying club he said there was no bigger club than the Gunners, who had achieved the League and Cup double the previous season, 1970–1. He told me to head for home as soon as I could. Once there he was focused in his own way, saying, first of all, that he could probably fix something that would keep me in the area. He didn't relish the thought of me moving down south.

He rang Manchester United and Manchester City straightaway, telling first Frank O'Farrell and then Malcolm Allison that Arsenal had been on for me and that I did not like the idea of moving to London.

O'Farrell, the United manager, said he had been playing David Sadler in midfield and he was doing a good job, so that there was little interest. Allison said he would speak to the board and see what they might be prepared to offer. Suddenly the intrigue piled in. It seemed that

United were having second thoughts and had arranged for someone to be at Euston Station to let us know they were still interested.

Arsenal got wind of this and as the train pulled in to Watford Junction, the last stop before the London terminus, Euston, the Arsenal secretary, Ken Friar, was on the platform looking out for us and telling us to leave the train as he would drive us to Highbury. Had I managed to get to Euston and met the United representative I might have jumped back on the train and returned to Manchester.

That didn't happen and soon I was listening as Bertie Mee and Friar talked about finances, bonuses, performance incentives, living accommodation and so on. I realized that the basic wage of about £250 a week sounded fabulous and much more than I was on at Everton. I was treated with courtesy and understanding every inch of the way. Dad made an excuse to leave and phoned Malcolm Allison at City to tell him what I had been offered. Malcolm said there was no way City could compete.

I was leaving the north. Dad and I went back on the train, had a bottle of champagne and laughed all the way home. I had the standard ten per cent of the £220,000 fee and a three-year option.

On the ride home there was much to reflect on. Turbulent days, fun-filled days, international days and those early days when I had to stand my ground or drown in a dressing room awash with mean spirits and strong wills. I fought with our fullback, Keith Newton, at Leeds one day. He played the ball across our penalty area and Billy Bremner came in and scored. We were going for the title that year and his mistake meant that Leeds inched closer to us. I hit him on the pitch and had another go afterwards. Yes, we played for England together and were good pals, but that's the way I was. I couldn't be doing with mistakes. You had to win.

My reputation as the inflammable redhead was growing in those prime Everton days. No one was allowed to get the better of me. That inbred determination to be the best was never far from the surface. On one occasion I was having a brilliant game at Tottenham and was going to turn Cyril Knowles on the line when he dived in too late. It was my first bad injury. We were wearing white socks and in a second mine was crimson as the blood flowed from a gash that needed fourteen stitches. I believe I was in some kind of shock; the way people sometimes are when they have seen a bad accident.

Dave Mackay was also playing for Tottenham that day and he had belted me early on. It was his typical just-letting-you-know kind of introduction. It was like being hit by a tank. He was the hardest man I ever played against but his tackle was fine, while Cyril had been too late. I knew Cyril was wrong and I said, publicly, that they should leave it to me for justice to be seen to be done. We had Spurs back at Goodison the following Wednesday.

I played with heavy padding around the stitches but was still in tremendous pain. I lined up at outside right, telling Howard Kendall to go into the middle where I usually played. Cyril was at left back. The crowd knew, the referee knew, what I was up to; I even said to Cyril: 'I'll die for you tonight.'

I had told Howard I was looking for revenge. I caught Cyril a beauty. I let him play the ball and then I just went right through him and waved him off. He left the pitch. The Tottenham players and their people on the bench were ranting at me. I was booked. I had waited for my opportunity and afterwards I explained: 'Nobody hurts Alan Ball because until I stop playing I will hurt them back.' It was the law of the jungle in those days. Sometimes you have to wait a long time to get them back.

I had twice-yearly wars with Trevor Hockey. My battles with my World Cup roommate, Nobby Stiles, and the feud I had with Billy Bremner, never abated. We would go at each other non-stop because you were allowed to in those days. I used to joke with referee Clive 'Book it' Thomas, asking him to book me before the kick-off so that we could get it over and done with. He would see Nobby and me having the usual ding-dong and after a while he would run by and say: 'Have you two sorted it out yet?' There was no real animosity, just two players who would not let the other get on top.

I remember Everton beating Manchester United 5–0 at Goodison early one season and I won the duel hands down. At the end I put my arm around Nobby as we walked off and suggested he didn't play against people like me very often. He was blazing, but in the return fixture they gave us a similar beating.

Denis Law, George Best and Bobby Charlton were at

the peak of their amazing powers. I used to tell them that if they fancied having a go against me they did so at their peril. I would be around for a long time. It was the arrogance of youth on my part. When I look back now I am surprised that I had the audacity.

One of the several things that disturb me about the game now is the way it has become intensely tribal. There is hate around the grounds, and all this shirt kissing by the players in celebration of a goal is nonsense. We were much more loyal to our clubs than the majority of present-day players are. The clubs sold us rather than us walking away from them. The fans were the important people and you had to earn their respect, too. The crowd clapped you at the end; you didn't clap them, as happens now.

Thankfully, the Everton fans admired the way I played for them but there were still some scallywags along the way. As my father said when I joined: 'Don't try and kid them. Just put sweat on your shirt, occasionally spill a bit of blood and they will love you.'

The day after we won the First Division championship by nine points from Leeds United in May 1970 Lesley and I were at home in our lovely detached house recovering from the champagne of the night before. A van pulled up outside, no number plate and no markings. Three lads emerged and opened the van doors revealing rolls of cloth, carpets and suit lengths. 'Take your pick, Bally lad,' one of them said. I declined gracefully.

John Moores, chairman of Everton and a partner in Littlewoods Pools, had an enormous estate not far away.

One day at the club he asked about our garden and I just happened to say that it was so sandy there was little we could do with it. He said he would send somebody round but we thought no more about it.

Lesley and I were sitting at home again, quite happy with our modest little lawn and flower border, when we spotted a man in a deerstalker and plus fours, accompanied by an Airedale terrier, walking down the road. We were smiling at his appearance when he turned into our drive. He announced himself as the Moores' head gardener and said that he would be looking after us on a weekly basis. He did a marvellous job. We had a garden that could have won prizes.

I always had a good relationship with the chairman; Mr John as we always called him. He came to sit beside me one day at the club and asked how I was faring. I said I was very well, thank you. He leaned closer and whispered: 'You aren't taking your corners as well as I would have liked. You've got to get that left foot alongside the ball.'

I always said: 'Yes, Mr John', 'All right, Mr John.' It seemed he was giving me corner-taking advice every time he came to sit with me, which was about twice a month. I didn't have the heart to tell him that I wasn't taking the corner kicks. But he was a wonderful man and remains among my joyful Everton memories.

Members of the Swinging Blue Jeans band lived just down the road, as did Mark Pender of the Searchers. They were our friends. My lifestyle was changing but I was having a good time on the pitch. In the 1966–7 season I scored eighteen goals from fifty-one appearances in all competitions. The following year it was twenty from forty and the season after that, eighteen from forty-nine. We started to go out after games, often to a nightclub called Toad Hall or the Kingsway Casino, both not far from our Formby home. It was at the casino that I met the manager, Terry Hussey, who was an Everton fan.

We became friends after a casino punter challenged me to a foot race. He had questioned the wisdom of my being seen drinking, an athlete and all that, even if it was after a match. I told him that whatever exercise he fancied tackling, I would be better than him. For a fiver we raced from the casino to the pier and back. We spent his fiver there and then, Terry acted as starter and he has become such a close friend that he now lives half a mile from our house in Warsash.

Life was galloping on and after moving back to Worsley I learned a very important lesson. Sometimes we get ahead of ourselves and my mistake was to imagine that I could become a successful businessman when I bought a filling station in Heaton. Friends and colleagues had been telling me that I should be investing for the future. Other players had put money into business interests.

I lost £10,000 in the venture by making the mistake of putting too much trust and faith in other people. I could have been made bankrupt, but I am proud of the fact that I repaid every penny of the debt.

Garage ownership was clearly not for me, but through that business I developed an interest in cars that were big, sporty, fashionable or American. I had an E–type Jaguar and then a huge American limousine that I drove to Epsom for the 1971 Derby, which was won by the great Mill Reef. We thought we were the bee's knees, me with a few quid in my pocket and Lesley looking fantastic in her miniskirt.

As we approached the entrance I could see the gateman eyeing Lesley in a way that did not suggest full approval. 'Sorry, Madam, I'm afraid you cannot come in as your attire does not reach the standard of dress required,' he said.

What? Short miniskirts and hot pants were not allowed, he insisted. I argued but he would not be moved, and it was clear that there was no point in sending for a higher authority. It was looking as though we would have to make a humble retreat and perhaps join the throng away from the stands where the standards applied, when Jimmy Tarbuck came into the picture.

He pleaded with the previously implacable official, Lesley lowered her skirt by a couple of inches and we were allowed in. Jimmy became a life-long pal and we were also very friendly with Bernie Winters as we began to enjoy the London scene.

It was not as easy at the Arsenal training ground or in the dressing room, but I had one final memory to sustain me in the first arduous months. It involved Bill Shankly, the Liverpool manager and one of football's most endearing characters. After I had returned from signing for Arsenal I took Lesley to one of our favourite restaurants, the Casserole in Worsley. We were talking about the prospect of living in London when the head waiter came to the table and said there was a phone call for me.

The old, familiar Scottish voice rasped that he had discovered where I was from my mother. He said: 'I know you got back at 3.30 this afternoon, son, because there was suddenly a thorn plucked from my side. I wish you all the best, son. You've been great on Merseyside.'

I was almost in tears, hearing those words from such a great, whimsical, passionate football man.

6

UNEASY GUNNER

Arriving in London to join the famous Arsenal in December 1971 was the very essence of excitement. I had been raised in an environment of laughter and dedication. I was a northern working class lad and you never lose your heritage. You never lose the feel for life, that determination to succeed, and although I was thrilled to be walking through the famous marble halls I was never the nicest person around a football club. I could never tolerate being second best. I was a horrid person in training. I expected people to be the same as me. I was a hard person to get on with because I had been thrown out too often in the early part of my footballing life and I never wanted that to happen again. Nothing would be allowed to stand in my way. If I was being selfish it was because memories of rejection as a youngster and my fight for recognition in those early Everton days were still with me.

My first two years at Arsenal were the hardest of my life. Nothing wrong with my debut at Nottingham Forest, where we drew one apiece with George Graham scoring the equalizer, but problems were just around the corner. It did not take me long to detect some initial resentment in the dressing room. The Arsenal players were a close-knit group who had just won the League and Cup double. The way they played, the tactics, were also foreign to me, playing from back right up to the front. Everything at Everton had been about passing football with me being the cog through the middle with Colin and Howard, making things happen, running the show. Suddenly I found myself dropping back to take the ball from Frank McLintock, Peter Simpson, Pat Rice and Bob McNab. Either that or the ball was flying from defence up to John Radford and Ray Kennedy, making midfield almost redundant except for chasing down whenever the opposition were in possession.

I was fighting for my football life almost from day one. I ranted, I argued. There were rows as I constantly asked why I had been bought. I told them the Arsenal way was wrong, that they would never succeed in Europe with such methods. I demanded change, saying they needed to play through people, through midfield.

They did not like my attitude. In their minds, here was this upstart who had come in for a record fee and was trying to single-handedly change their world; a world that had brought them fame and fortune as champions in both domestic competitions. I bickered and fought and felt isolated and alienated on the training ground. I moaned that there was no possession stuff, no crafted passing movements. It was all long balls forward. I have to admit that it did suit them, but there were a few changes made when Bobby Campbell took over the coaching from Steve Burtenshaw.

Frank McLintock played a huge part in turning things around to my way of thinking. I was always banging on about the need to have two ways of playing because other teams would soon cotton on and take the appropriate measures to counteract the known way. I preached the need to play the ball through me, through the middle, from where I could prompt more initiatives. Frank listened and I was extremely grateful to him. He is a strong character and the best, most forceful captain I have ever played under. He led by example. He also took up my cause, using the argument of the wisdom of having more options. Bobby Campbell, who had his own views on how the game should be played, listened, and as they began to play more through me I began to win the respect of the other players.

Events away from the stadium or the training ground at London Colney also had an adverse effect on my spirit. Soon after arriving in London and living in Palmers Green in rented accommodation, we lost our lovely black Labrador dog, Tosca. He was murdered in the vilest way imaginable. Lesley and I were having a few days break when the maid we had left in charge telephoned to say that Tosca was struggling with 'a problem'. It transpired that he had been snatched on the street and some deranged monster or monsters had wrapped a tight elastic band around his penis. When he was found, obviously distressed, the maid took him to the vet, who said it was too late to save him.

We loved that dog. He was part of the family, an ex-police dog. He was very trustworthy and clever, perhaps too clever for the police because when they were training him at Hutton, headquarters of the Lancashire Constabulary near Preston, he showed himself to have a mind of his own. He would sail through all the obedience tests but every now and again, perhaps when he had to run through a row of hoops, he would go around one of them and nobody could make him change. Maybe I recognized something of myself in him.

At that time, the police told us, there had been a spate of dog murders, including that of a dog belonging to Bernie Winters. The police were concerned that children might become victims of the cruel, deranged criminals who were perpetrating such outrageous and heinous deeds.

A couple of weeks after Tosca's murder we were due to move into our new house at Nazeing, just off the A10 road out of north London. It was around this time that I began to realize how much care Arsenal took in looking after their players. The club did, and probably still does, look after every need. All that is required of the footballer is that he pulls on his boots and plays as well as he possibly can.

All other matters, whether they be involving solicitors, accountants, bankers, estate agents or cars, are taken over by the club. When Lesley was having our baby, all the pre-natal and post-natal care was looked after by the club. Jimmy was born on 4 September 1975 at St Mary's Hospital, Paddington, where Princess Diana had her sons Prince William and Prince Harry.

Having taken Lesley to the hospital, I went home and

had no sooner arrived there when the phone rang from the hospital asking me to return. I wasn't one of those fathers who want to wait and watch but, clearly, something was happening. When I arrived the nurse told me to go straight in to see Lesley. The nurse said the baby had been born but would not tell me if it was a boy or a girl. I cannot describe how fantastic it was to see Lesley holding this tiny baby boy. James Alan, we called him, but he was Jimmy from that day on.

It is perhaps just as well that I was having this happy domestic distraction because my hands were full trying to find my place in the dressing-room pecking order, which was never going to be easy for a man with powerful opinions who thought he could change a successful, regimented collection of winners.

The demise of Tosca was only one of several unsettling events off the pitch at Highbury. A year after our 1971 arrival Lesley went down at the age of twenty-four with a condition that should go down in the *Guinness Book of Medical Records*, if such a thing exists. She had 196 gallstones. The pain she bore was indescribable, but that was only part of the intense hospital drama. In between the bouts of agony she had a miscarriage, a baby boy, as if to heighten the misery that was going on in her mind and body. On some occasions she was reduced to crawling around on her hands and knees, unable to stand up because of the torture. They had to give her pethidine, and these days she would be the first to admit that she was a complete mess. They were unable to operate until there was a break in these regular bouts of distress.

Once in hospital in Harlow they did the operation, blitzed the gallstones and we all waited for her to recover. At her age, and being as fit as the proverbial, we imagined she would be on her feet and away from the hospital in a couple of days. It didn't work that way. Instead of bouncing back as we all expected she began to go into a decline. Her mother took the two girls, Mandy and Keely, beautifully dressed, to see her, but came back to stagger me with the words: 'Alan, you've got to do something or she is going to be dead.'

Lesley told me later that she had spent hours just staring at the corner of the room without a care. She knew her mum and little daughters were there but scarcely noticed them. Her acknowledgement was a limp kind of nod before she lapsed into what appeared to be a fateful trance. This went on for days. She became weaker.

I knew I had to do something. The hospital was not moving to reverse her downward spiral. I rowed with the doctors and nurses, who seemed powerless to do anything apart from attaching tubes all over her. She could not eat or drink anything and it seemed to me that they thought she was just being wimpish or stupid. She tried to sip some tomato soup, but it came hurtling back up from her stomach in an instant. I was aware of medical etiquette but in sheer desperation I phoned Dr Sash, the Arsenal doctor.

The surgeon at the hospital was not happy with me for taking this route and 'the doc', as we always called him, reminded me that it was not the done thing for one medical man to comment on or interfere with another's work. However, he said he had a suspicion of what the problem might be and would speak to the hospital. I pleaded with them. I could see my wife dying in front of me.

The hospital doctor listened to Dr Sash and on his advice they took her down for an X-ray. From this they saw that her stomach wall had collapsed and folded over completely. This time the operation worked perfectly, but Lesley was anxious to get home because her mum was getting more and more exhausted running around after the two girls and she was also suffering from angina. She stayed one night after Lesley came out of hospital, so that Lesley was straight back into running the house and looking after the kids. She did that for about three months before I had to go up north for something and decided to bring back my mother to help with the girls and the housekeeping. Soon after dinner that night Lesley collapsed in the bathroom with the same symptoms that had been created by the gallstones. It was weird and frightening. Lesley was screaming. We had to get her to hospital, where they were worried. I was angry again, asking all sorts of searching questions and arguing with the doctors. The pain turned out to be some kind of phantom thing. Everyone concluded that the combination of Lesley's tiredness and relief had brought on the symptoms. There were no more gallstones, her stomach was fine and she was home again in two days.

Back at London Colney and Highbury, I was playing and training well and putting in an extra session in September 1975 when more drama hit the Ball household. Jimmy was about six weeks old when Lesley put Keely, who was three, into her little chair on top of the pram and went to collect Mandy from school. As they returned Mandy had a little friend with her and Lesley paused outside our house to talk to a neighbour who wanted a peek at little Jimmy. The two little girls bounded up the steps playfully, as infant schoolchildren do, when there was suddenly the sound of breaking glass, then silence, then a girl screaming. Lesley later relived the drama for me. It appeared that Mandy had fallen on the step and put her hand out to save herself, but had gone right through the plate glass on the door. She had severed the artery in her left arm. They could hear the blood pumping, spurting out and slapping onto the ground. Lesley let go of the pram containing Jimmy with Keely on top. Fortunately the neighbour caught it. Even more fortunate was the coincidence that both Lesley and the neighbour had read the same article about accidents in the home. They applied direct pressure, rather than a tourniquet, and probably saved Mandy's life.

The ambulance summoned to get them to the hospital managed to get lost. They could hear it in the distance and were just setting off for the hospital by car when it appeared around the corner. When I received the call I could not get to the hospital quickly enough. They were already performing an operation.

There was still some frustration in my footballing life and I started to live life off the pitch probably too fast for my own good in the early Seventies. I started to go for what were perceived as trendy clothes. I grew my hair longer and I started wearing beads, which was totally alien to anything I had previously believed in. Looking back, I have no idea what I was searching for, but my drinking increased and I started to stay out. Gambling took a hold. I was spending money and my sense of discipline disappeared until we were not far from being skint. I was earning good money and London captivated me. But it almost undid me as I went downhill.

I was rebelling against the way the team were playing but I was going the wrong way about it. I had my problems, but instead of getting my head down and working through them I was hitting the city more than I should have done.

When Arsenal trained at Highbury I would go into London for a long lunch at the Fox Club in Clarges Street and if we were at London Colney, which is near Elstree and further out of the city, I would head for the White Hart in Southgate, the Arsenal players' local.

Even when I was in the city, 'lunching' until six or seven, I would stop off at Southgate. Foolishly, you didn't worry about breathalysers and such in those days as long as you drove carefully. I was usually home by 9.30 or ten o'clock at night and then up for training again next morning before resuming where I had left off the day before. Can you imagine that routine today? It went on like that for years.

I had enjoyed – if that is the word – the flavour of horse racing with Alex Young during my Everton days but our horse, Daxal, was useless. At Arsenal we had a good horse called Go Go Gunner, which I shared with

Peter Marinello, Charlie George and Stan Flashman. He won races for us, kicking off at Newmarket. There was no doubt that I was hooked in those days. When I broke my leg in the last match of the season – Terry Venables sat on it by accident – in 1974 it provided the perfect opportunity to indulge in my passion for the sport of kings. I had a boot on my left foot, hired an automatic car and it was first stop Chester, where I stayed with Geoff Lewis who, three years earlier, had ridden one of the most famous horses of all time, Mill Reef, to win the Epsom Derby. Geoff rode Millsbomb to win at the Roodeye, as Chester's ancient course is quaintly called, but soon I was off to Newmarket to see our horse in a maiden race.

Lester Piggott, the greatest of them all, had been booked to ride, and as he came into the parade ring before the race he touched his hat in a doffing gesture to me. He may have recognized me from football pictures although I had met him before. I was embarrassed and told him to stop it and just tell me whether the horse was good enough to keep through the winter or should we send him to the sales. As the order came for the jockeys to mount he just turned to me and said: 'I'll win.' He had so much faith in his own skill. I went hobbling off to the bookies and had £60 at 13/8, which seemed a particularly skinny price for such a big field. He slooshed in, as they say. On another occasion I had a £200 bet which seemed as certain as a penalty kick and Lester won again. I rang him that night to thank him and say I would like to give him a present and asked what he would like.

He said Go Go Gunner was a nice horse; he wanted nothing by way of reward except to be on the horse for the following year. At the beginning of the next racing season I broke my leg again and was immediately back racing. I spoke to the trainer, Ian Walker, and we agreed that Go Go Gunner should run at York, the Ascot of the north, with Lester up. We finished third and Lester jumped off to admit that he had made a mess of the race and said he should have won. He advised us, however, to drop him a notch in class and then have a really decent bet. We did that and he raced at Windsor under Pat Eddery to win in a canter.

Go Go Gunner was a really good horse to us. We had great enjoyment in his company, and adored his strength, his pace and his courage. Eventually he went jumping where, sadly, he met his end. It was a great sadness to hear that he had died. He will always be remembered with fondness.

It seemed that I had acquired a reputation as a gambler and that was given as the reason for some of our financial insecurity. Gambling never sent us tumbling into money problems but our naivety did. We never worried, we spent without a thought and debts on the house were the main reason why we ran into trouble. There is no doubt that towards the end of my time at Arsenal we were struggling. Our car had become a modest green Volkswagen Polo. We also had a little, old brown mini.

We could still raise a laugh at the time, recalling the day I had returned from signing for Arsenal. Lesley had come out of hospital that day with Keely just a day old and we were in bed laughing our heads off because we had a three-year contract with a three-year option at £15,000. On reflection these days, it probably should have been more, but I had no agent to help me and I was just happy to sign for what amounted to £90,000 basic over six years. Agents have only become a part of football in the last fifteen or twenty years. There were one or two about earlier but they were not so much agents negotiating pay deals at clubs, but were more likely chasing endorsements for their men.

It was still top money in 1972. We were happy spenders. We spent on clothes; we ate out a lot and generally lived it up. We were regulars at the famous nightclub Tramp, entertaining people. We did not need an excuse to hit the town. Our visits to the West End were sustained over four or five years. After I had captained England for the first time against West Germany in 1975 I booked a table at Tramp. We didn't arrive until quite late but by the end of the night my table was packed with such names as Anne Bancroft, Mel Brooks, Marty Feldman, Alan Hudson, Bobby Moore and so on. I sat down next to Telly 'Kojak' Savalas and the champagne flowed. I paid for everything.

After all, I was captain of my country. We had an overdraft but no one worried; not even bank managers, although we were living beyond our means for a while. It wasn't as though we were going out and spending, say, £5,000 on a ring or buying a new Jaguar; the money just went on a high standard of living. We were in debt, but we weren't the kind of people who would ever 'welch' on anything. We were just silly spendthrifts, but I have absolutely no regrets about my time in London. It was a wonderful place to be and the scene was constantly exciting.

We made great friends, becoming very close to Bobby Moore and his first wife Tina. George Graham and Frank McLintock were close to us, both fabulous friends. We were at shows almost every Saturday. They were the best times of our lives until Terry Neill came to manage the club in August 1976.

I remember going home to Lesley and saying that it was time we took stock of our debts and our lives because, as I put it, 'I don't like this guy and he doesn't like me. We are not for each other.'

It began a chain of events that led from me captaining England to joining Southampton, who were in the Second Division, for £60,000 with my international career over. We had no money and no cars, and quickly downsized the house. At the end of the 1975–6 season I was allowed to go to South Africa to play a few games for Budgie Byrne's team, Hellenic. I was there for a few weeks and we had a great time. I played well and Hellenic won matches with a decent set of lads. Some nights I would be holed up in a hotel and invariably rang Lesley or she rang me. We were on the phone for ages. In the end the phone bill was as much as I earned over there and we had our phone cut off. I had a fantastic time, assured that I would have enough money to enjoy the last week and have plenty left over for Lesley. When I went with Budgie to see the main man, the situation changed. He said they had no money to give me. I was flabbergasted. I pointed out that I was on my way home having done a good job for him – the team were top of the league and in the semi-final of the Cup. I argued that I was going home to start the new season in England and needed to be paid. I was told I was not allowed to take money out of South Africa, which was a new rule as far as I was concerned, but that I could take krugerrands, which amounted to about £300. I had to smuggle them back in through Heathrow.

We eventually sold the krugerrands but typical of me, I kept thinking that there would be some more money coming to me from South Africa. That's the way I was and still think I am, always believing that someone's word is his bond.

I was no sooner back in the country, realizing that Terry Neill had taken over, when he called me in, as was his right. I will never forget the scene as I walked in through the marble halls to be confronted by this fellow in jeans and a denim shirt, the manager of the mighty Arsenal. He had a bit of a swagger about him, said it was good to see me back and asked if I was fit. He told me there were a couple of pre-season practice matches arranged in Switzerland and that he would see me on the training ground. I am usually deadly accurate with my first impressions; I realized straightaway that he was not my kind of person.

His training methods did not improve my perception of him as he talked to us like children – among us were experienced players who had been around the block a few times, such as Malcolm Macdonald, Graham Rix, Geordie Armstrong, Liam Brady and David O'Leary. One day ahead of our game against Young Boys of Berne Neill came in with a Subbuteo table under his arm and two bags in his hand. He put the table down and I realized very quickly that he was not talking my language when he put down two of the miniature players and said they were his guards, his centre backs. They were there, he said, to protect the whole of the defence as guardians.

I tried to catch Macdonald's eye and could hear Brady muttering 'oh dear' under his breath as Neill pulled out more of his little men and moved on to midfield, Brady and Ball territory. These, said Neill, were his snipers, who would be picking people off with their passes, here, there and everywhere. I was waiting for him to laugh at us as if he was having us on, but he continued the military theme when he played two up front and said they were the sharpshooters with their rifles on their knees. He said he liked his strikers, his sharpshooters, to shoot on sight. The lads tried to stifle their mirth. I attempted to make eye contact with Wilf Dixon, the trainer who had followed me from Blackpool to Everton and was now with Arsenal. He wouldn't look because I am sure he knew that this kind of hogwash would not work with me. Wilf had also been with Neill at Hull City and they had become friends. Wilf was not a tactician and whatever he thought about the malarkey going on in front of us he would never rock any boat.

I could not take it all in convincingly. I had come

through my battle with the club. Everything was played through me. I was the fulcrum. I was beginning to wonder what he would say next when he produced the other bag and suggested that we were probably wondering what it contained. He said it contained the opposition and emptied the bag on the other half of the table pitch to reveal a pile of yellow Indians. 'That's how you are going to treat every opposition – yellow Indians. We are the cowboys,' he said.

We won easily enough that night. Macdonald lived up to his 'Supermac' title. He would get the ball, set off on a run and score goals. He was uncomplicated, brave, quick and strong. I had a fine understanding with him and when we had a beer afterwards we both commented that we were going to have some fun under Mr Neill.

I had little respect for Neill after the cowboys and Indians fiasco, and it disappeared altogether after Peter Storey and I had been away on duty elsewhere on the Wednesday. He told us to have a lie-in on Thursday morning but to report for training in the afternoon. He had three bags of footballs placed at different areas of the edge of the penalty area and another behind the goal. He started lobbing the balls over the bar to us and we had to run on to them and smash them into the net, six apiece.

After a couple I told Peter to start missing so that we were hammering them high and wide. He never twigged that we were taking the mickey, even when he began rolling the balls from the side of the penalty area for us to side-foot into the net. I would love to know just what was in his mind that possessed him to put on such an exercise in which we didn't even break sweat — we were after all, two very experienced international players.

Don Revie had left me out of his England team after my last international, a 5–1 win over Scotland at Wembley in May 1975, and once Neill arrived and made his presence felt I knew I would soon be on my way, especially when he signed Alan Hudson. The story Hudson tells is that he was told by Neill that he wanted him to play alongside me because we had played together so well in the 2–0 win over the Germans in 1975.

I knew my cards were marked. Perhaps I had become too strong in the dressing room. I also had a contemptuous view of the manager, and as I have found to my cost if the dressing room isn't right and the main men do not respect you then you have to cut the head off the strongest man. Neill, sensing my feelings and my leadership among the players, had me walking out of the door to meet Southampton as Alan Hudson was walking in.

I was heading in the direction of some happy days under Lawrie McMenemy at Southampton, who did as much as anyone in the cause of clearing our debts. Arsenal had told me that Leeds, Bolton and Southampton were interested in signing me. I did not really fancy a move back north but I spoke to my old friend Jimmy Armfield, who was in charge at Leeds, and told him that before I did anything, I wanted to talk to Southampton.

Driving into Southampton I remember being impressed with the approach to the ground. Along a tree-lined avenue, past the common, turn right and there is The Dell. The club was on a high. They had won the FA Cup with a 1–0 win over Manchester United the previous season and things were happening. McMenemy spared nothing in selling me the virtues of the club. He said the place could be mine; he had some feisty youngsters who needed organizing as well as some good, older players, but that he was looking to the future. He got up and walked past me, locked the door and said words to the effect that I was not leaving until I had signed. He said that no matter what wages I was on at Arsenal he would, at the very least, match them, and he offered a three-year contract. It was all fine but I was bothered about a signing-on fee. I knew that if I could go home with a wedge of decent money I would be able to clear my debts and start again.

Lawrie said there would be no signing-on money and I quickly replied that I would not be signing if that was the situation. He must have heard about my high living because he said something like, 'With your record I am not giving you any signing-on money but go and find yourself a house up to £30,000.'

I went home to Lesley and asked her if she wanted the good news or the bad news. Before she could reply I said that the bad news meant there was no signing-on fee but the good news was that we could pick a house which would become ours after a certain length of time.

We went a bit over the top. Well, we would, wouldn't we? It was a gorgeous house in Chandlers Ford, a beautiful part of the city. It was probably the best thing we ever did and we were presented with the deeds after it had been bought.

The first game was away to Plymouth on an icy day. The pitch was frozen on one side. I was playing right-hand side and Mick Channon was just ahead of me. Plymouth bombarded us for fifteen minutes and I looked across at Mick with a kind of look that asked what the hell was going on. He just smiled and said, 'Welcome to Southampton.'

It was the prelude to some wonderfully happy times.

7

SAINTS (AND SINNERS)

When I dally along memory lane, my times at Southampton as player (1976–80 and 1981–2) and as manager (1994–5) provoke many a smile and a sense of achievement. When Lawrie McMenemy signed me from Arsenal he probably knew he was taking me into a world that I would need to come to terms with very rapidly. It is hard enough when you move, settling the kids into new schools, getting your house right, making sure your wife is happy, as well as training and settling in with so many new characters.

Lawrie believed in characters and he had his share at The Dell. He had footballers, mimics, know-alls and whimsies who added up to a collection of talented players although they were not far from the foot of the Second Division. My father, who had been consulted on every move I had made throughout a career of 600 First Division and Cup appearances with Bolton, Everton and Arsenal as well as seventy-two caps and two World Cups with England, was wild when I told him I had signed for Southampton. He said that dropping down a division was accepting second best when I could have gone to Leeds, a big club still in the big time. I told him I felt comfortable and that we would win promotion. He just said, in his own critical way, which I had become almost immune to as I grew older, that I was finished. Leeds had its attractions, but I had a feeling for Southampton. I admired the way Lawrie McMenemy ran the club. Hampshire was and still is a beautiful county and he was offering to put money into our new house.

I also had a belief that we could do well. Lawrie had told me that I could run the team from midfield and that eventually it would prove to be a wonderful end to my playing career. I looked around the dressing room and there was talent in abundance. He brought in Peter Wells as goalkeeper. Ted MacDougall, a proven goal scorer, was there along with such good and experienced names as Peter Osgood, Channon, Steve Williams, Jimmy McCalliog, Nicky Holmes, David Peach, Peter Rodrigues, Jim Steele and so on. There was young Steve Moran, and Lawrie added Chris Nicholl, David Armstrong and two Yugoslavs, Ivan Golac and Ivan Katalanic.

When Lawrie signed me just after Christmas 1976, a few months after Southampton had surprised everybody by winning the FA Cup, Southampton were fifth from bottom. We picked up. We started to gain confidence, rose to eighth and the following season were back in the big time, going up into second place. There were riotous scenes and parties everywhere after the last match, when we drew 0–0 with Tottenham.

We played some excellent football. I had carte blanche to run the middle of the park, and even in the dressing room I was given permission to control what was going on. There were some strong characters around and a pecking order, so once again I had to assert myself to gain their respect.

A lot of them were outstanding footballers who were getting on a bit and were not as enthusiastic about training as they might have been at an earlier age. This was where Lawrie McMenemy was a mastermind. He knew how to handle the barrack-room lawyers, the shop stewards, the ones who needed a cuddle and those who deserved chastising.

Lawrie's man management was one of his great strengths. He treated us like adults and showed a shrewd understanding of the way some of us were. After we had beaten Mansfield Town 2–1 to lie third in our promotion year we faced a fourth-round FA Cup second replay against Grimsby Town after two goalless draws. We were to play the decider on a neutral ground, Filbert Street, Leicester, on the Monday night following our Saturday game at Mansfield. By Sunday lunchtime we were a bit bored, so Ted MacDougall and I decided we would go for a sauna, which would not be complete, of course, without a bottle of champagne. We were nicely settled in when Lawrie's face appeared at the sauna window. He'd been out for a walk and was wearing his sheepskin. He opened the door. With any other team, having champagne in a sauna on the day before a match might have been a punishable offence, with the culprits being made to feel like naughty schoolboys. I asked Lawrie if he fancied a glass and he stepped inside for a cosy chat and a drop of bubbly, still in his big coat. All of a sudden, as often happens in saunas, his pores shot open and the sweat teemed off him. He left very hot but with a smile and we did the business for him next day with a 4–1 win.

He knew we would produce results for him but there was a lot of dressing-room debate as to how to go about it. Channon and I gelled superbly. MacDougall was hard to get along with but he was a terrific goal scorer and we knew how to get the best out of him. Lawrie was shrewd enough not to come into the dressing room on the stroke of half-time. He would wait five minutes until we had sorted out our arguments. By the time he came in there might have been three fights, four cups of tea thrown and an unholy shouting match. It was often as bad on the training pitch, with arguments raging about tactics. Lawrie was astute enough to allow us to get on with it, knowing that many of his players there were extremely capable of devising ways and means to defeat the opposition. Peter Osgood had played under Dave Sexton, one of the most highly regarded coaches in the game at Chelsea. Rodrigues and Nicholl had acute footballing knowledge and between us we sorted things out. The debates were not always pretty, but we got the job done and took Southampton back to the First Division.

We had an eight-match undefeated streak either side of Christmas, but did not hit the top until three matches from the end of the season. Draws against Orient away and Tottenham at home left us in second place and the parties began.

Lawrie very cleverly pulled off an exciting and unexpected coup when he persuaded Kevin Keegan to join the Saints on his return to England from S.V. Hamburg, where he had twice been European Footballer of the Year. It came as a complete surprise. There had been no newspaper leaks and people were astounded that he had chosen to move to The Dell. Lawrie's powers of persuasion were becoming legendary, but with Keegan's love of horses, shared by Channon and myself, it was not really such a surprise when you thought it through. He was anxious to set up a stud, Channon already had horses and they shared ownership a few times. I had played alongside Kevin on his debut for England against Wales and knew that Lawrie had pulled a master stroke in signing this all-action, jack-in-the-box type of player. Lawrie knew how to get them. It was a fabulous signing for the club, as were Joe Jordan and Frank Worthington. He was never apprehensive about signing the big names. He knew he could handle them. I have always admired him for that, and in bringing such excellent footballers he was giving the club several massive lifts one after another.

I had agreed to go to Vancouver Whitecaps in Canada for the summer while still on Southampton's books and I had accepted the player-manager's job at Blackpool so, in effect, I had three jobs at the same time. Blackpool agreed to my arrangement with the Canadians and I went off to join an ambitious set-up being run by the former Blackpool and England goalkeeper Tony Waiters, along with the ex-Arsenal fullback Bob McNab and a fellow called John Best. We won the soccer bowl and I was voted MVP (most valuable player) in the whole tournament.

I flew back early to join Blackpool as player-manager and had Ted MacDougall as my assistant.

There were some hilarious times in America, especially in 1978 when Philadelphia Fury, who had signed Osgood, invited me over. It was a brand-new franchised team run by people like the musicians Peter Frampton, John Vangelis and Rick Wakeman, along with a bunch of American football nuts pulled together by a bloke called Frank Barcelona. I went to Lawrie and asked for the summer off because Ossie had said he wanted me there and I would be back for pre-season anyway. Richard Dinnis was the manager, but I soon discovered that the team was a ragtag and bobtail outfit. They brought in Johnny Giles of Leeds United and Republic of Ireland fame to strengthen the team.

We lost, but the club gave me a 5,000 US dollar bonus. The story now becomes slightly complicated because I had a few drinks on the plane; my mates met me at Heathrow and took me to Salisbury races, where I imbibed a little more. We had a wonderful day and at some stage during the afternoon my mates decided to buy a horse called Ashera. I stumped up the money, so that the cheque for the $5,000 was gone. As a form of sobriety reappeared I began to wonder how I was going to get out of this mess, as Lesley was bound to mention the bonus. She was always clued up to anything I was due.

I decided I would just say I had lost the cheque, but when she didn't ask about it I assumed she had forgotten. Two months elapsed before she suddenly asked me about the money. I told her they hadn't sent it yet but that it would be on its way and not to worry. She accepted that, but then began to get slightly worked up about the delay and decided to phone someone she knew in the office at the club in Philadelphia. I knew she was being fobbed off, but then a man came on the line to tell her in the most precise terms that he had been delegated to inform her that I had taken the cheque home with me and it had been cashed within three days of issue. Confronted by this evidence, what could I say? My next excuse was that I had given away my jacket and that the cheque must have been in the pocket.

That yarn was not accepted either and eventually the story came out that we had bought this flipping horse and stabled him with trainer Frank Muggeridge near Salisbury. Peace soon broke out and I suggested that the whole family take a day out and go and look at it. There were horses in boxes all around the yard, mostly looking out at the scene, but one in particular was nervously 'weaving', which means his head was swaying from one side of the door to the other. It was our horse, Ashera. It was so useless it never saw a racetrack and eventually we gave it to a girl who promised it a good home to ride as her hack. I know it is hard to believe, but the mates I was with when we bought the horse were the types who would write on the back of a cheque, 'Sorry, done boots at races, please let this one through.'

It may not have been funny for Lesley, but everyone had to laugh at events surrounding my debut in Philadelphia. Anyone who knows me recognizes my seriousness about football, but this was hilarious.

I was to be introduced as the new captain, a World Cup winner, and a legend in international football as an England stalwart. As soon as I had my playing kit on they led me from the dressing room and up a ramp and sat me on top of an old Philadelphia fire engine. Eventually the fire engine was driven down the ramp with sirens howling and me ringing the big bell right into the heart of the Vets Stadium, where we played our home games. As we reached the pitch a helicopter hovered overhead and dropped the ball on a small parachute.

The referee ran under the ball and caught it. Peter Frampton's music was belting out as I threw away the long-nosed firefighter's helmet and we lined up for the kick-off with me feeling as though I was involved in some Las Vegas spectacular. I began to wonder what I was doing there.

It was football from a different planet. We had some fun. Peter Osgood was injured at one time and watched one of the matches in a private box with all the family. The Fury team had a cry of 'Get furious'. Peter was in the box and he said to our Jimmy, who was two at the time, 'Come on, Jimmy, get furious.' Jimmy said: 'I can't.'

In the brief period that I was in charge of things at the club we had to go on the road in Florida to play three teams, two of them being the very strong Tampa Bay Rowdies and Fort Lauderdale strikers. I announced the team before we set off. Peter was still injured but I called out the eleven names and said that Osgood would be on the bench as substitute. He was furious, asking how could

I possibly consider putting him on the bench with so many Muppets ahead of him. He told me never to even think of doing that again. He said I had insulted him.

I told him that if I hadn't included him on the trip I would have had no mates in Florida and he would have had to stay behind for treatment. Couldn't he see that I was giving him a week's break in the sun? He said he'd never looked at it that way.

While I was at Philadelphia, Frank Worthington joined us, as did a Yugoslav coach, Marco Valec, who had some weird and wonderful ideas of his own like staying for two hours after training trying to sleep in little bunk beds. He was not a bad coach by any means, but his methods were not for us; I was traded halfway through the season for my first taste of the Whitecaps and the magnificent, cultural city of Vancouver.

I went into a good team that included the compulsory two North Americans, Buzzy Parsons and Bobby Lenni-duci, along with our two centre backs from English football, Roger Kenyon and John Craven. We had the Scottish international winger Willie Johnstone, as well as Steve Kember, Carl Valentine and Ray Lewington, who is now the manager of Watford. Up front we had Kevin Hector, who had played under Brian Clough at Derby County and Trevor Whymark, previously with Ipswich. Bruce Grobbelaar was also at the club, but he was understudy to goalkeeper Phil Parkes.

The whole time there was an amazing adventure. Lesley and the kids were with me and we adored every moment of our time there. It was a pleasure to play in the stadium and we were such a good side that we saw off every team, with special pleasure coming from the defeat of New York Cosmos, Franz Beckenbauer and all, in a semi-final.

When I first landed, the Whitecaps put me in a hotel and provided me with a small car, a Honda Accord. On the first morning I awoke early, slightly jet-lagged, to set off for training at the stadium. They had given me the route, something about going along the coast road and you can't miss the stadium. Signs all the way, they said. I wasn't sure of the way so I put my foot down that day, and as I came around a corner I was confronted by a policeman aiming a huge speed gun at the car, which was blue and white and had 'Vancouver Whitecaps' plastered all along the side.

I was pulled over and became terribly polite and English as I apologized, explaining my newness to the country, my jet lag, the fact that I had just signed for the Whitecaps and was running late and that it would never happen again. He said: 'Buddy, I've been in this job a week and you are the quickest. That'll be a sixty-dollar ticket. Have a good career and enjoy your time here.'

We did. We won games, the stadium was packed with over 20,000 people most of the time and we had real quality time off. Lesley would go skiing on Grouse Mountain with the kids up the mountain in the morning, and in the afternoons we would often all be out on the lakes, either sunbathing or swimming, or else cruising around in a boat owned by a man who became a great friend, Fred Burns, who was football daft. Sometimes we would cruise to the islands for dinner. It was a gloriously idyllic life, and Vancouver became the one place where you truly felt you could happily spend the rest of your days.

Lesley's mother and father, Jack and Hilda, came over for their holiday of a lifetime. Sadly, when they returned home Jack went into hospital for an operation and never came out, having passed away under the anaesthetic. Lesley's grief was slightly tempered by the fact that they had enjoyed such a fantastic holiday.

Alan Hudson was playing for Seattle and after we had played them at home, beating them, of course, there was a reception. Afterwards Lesley said she would drive him back to the Rembrandt Hotel where I had stayed when I first arrived in Canada. We were driving in the area known as English Bay, which was a haven for prostitutes and druggies, and had a homosexual beach. It was not a place for hanging around. We had a young Canadian player, Paul Nelson, in the car, as well as Huddy, Lesley and me. We dropped Huddy off because the bar was closed and drove away in a back-street area and, quite honestly, I was dying for a leak. I saw a skip parked in the darkness and told Lesley to pull in so that I could spend my penny, so to speak, behind it. My aim wasn't very good, or perhaps it was breezy, but my trouser leg was suddenly damp so I rolled it up and returned to the car and we set off for where we lived, a route that took us downtown.

We seemed to hit every traffic light just as it turned red and had to get through an area called East Hastings, a name synonymous with drunkards, when we heard what we presumed to be police car sirens or ambulances. I remember Lesley remarking that somebody must be in trouble, and just as we approached another set of red lights, police cars and motor cycles approached from all directions and surrounded us. The young lad in the back was terrified and his language mirrored his predicament. I was in the front seat, slightly the worse for drink with my trouser leg rolled up. The doors of the 'paddy wagon' were opened and one particularly gruff officer ordered us out of the car. At first I refused until the lad in the back advised me, in no uncertain terms, that stubbornness would not be a wise option in the circumstances. I stepped out with my trousers rolled up like some unsteady, Masonic mimic but Lesley adopted a different approach. She pulled herself together and said in her most precise, authoritative manner that she did not wish to get out and when she was asked for some ID she conjured up one of the most marvellous sentences I have ever heard. She simply told the officer: 'My dear fellow, we are British visitors and as such we have arrived from a nation that has long been at pains to preserve the status of civil liberties.'

She still had to step outside and the three of us were lined up on the pavement as the police scoured the car, virtually ransacking it. The Canadian lad, who was shaking with fear, whispered that they were looking for drugs. We knew we were innocent on that score but we stood there, looking down, with our hands behind our backs like serious suspects and me with my trouser leg still rolled up, wondering what might happen next. Then around the corner came this Mountie with the biggest feet any of us had ever seen and we just set off with the giggles. The police were not amused. They found nothing and I asked what the problem had been as they concluded the search.

It transpired that they had seen us drop Alan Hudson at the hotel, get back in the car and then stop and disappear behind the skip. Their surveillance had created the impression that I had gone into the hotel with Hudson to collect drugs and gone behind the skip to use them, and then we had driven off. If only they had realized that I went into the Rembrandt to see if the bar was still open. The police insisted on taking the car away for further examination and said we could collect it the following day. I asked how we were to get home and would they have some transport for us. The officer just looked at me as though I was something on the bottom of his shoe and said: 'Yeah, we pay for drunks to get home.'

The young Canadian reckoned it was only the fact that we had English accents that kept us out of the Black Maria and a night in the cells. I went with Fred Burns to collect the car the next day and gave Lesley the fright of her life when I returned and told her the police wanted her to go back for questioning. She was so shocked that I thought she was going to faint, so I had to tell her sooner than I intended that I was joking.

The episode did not seem like fun at the time but looking back it was all part of the richness that made our time in Vancouver so memorable. On the pitch we were a very, very good team. In a play-off between the two groups, separated geographically, we had to play the famous Cosmos, who seemed to win the championship every year. They came to our place first, a small ground reminiscent of The Dell, with a bevel almost gently crowned like one of those north of England bowling greens. The stadium packed the people in to welcome a team that contained several international players with worldwide reputations, including Georgio Chinaglia, Carlos Alberto, Beckenbauer and Dennis Tueart. We beat them 3–1 and went off to New York for the most bizarre match I have ever been involved in. After an 8 p.m. kick-off we played the ninety minutes (0–0), then over time (0–0) and then a shoot-out, which they lost making it one game apiece. Typical of American football, or soccer as they always called it over there, we had to play a second match on the same night. By now it was 10.45 p.m. and it was decreed that we would play half an hour each way. That ended 1–1; there was no scoring in over time and now we were down to a shoot-out again. It was the best of five. In a shoot-out you start twenty-five yards out and have five seconds to beat the goalkeeper. It came down to Derek Possee, the former Millwall winger. If he scored we were into the final. His choice, which you had in this situation, was to either dribble the goalkeeper or chip him.

Derek took two strides and, showing amazing com-posure in such a pressurized situation, chipped with precision and we were through. The crowd, most of them New Yorkers or immigrant football fans from other countries, were stunned into silence as we went potty with our celebrations. It was midnight by the time we left the pitch, four hours after we had started.

A week later we beat Tampa Bay Rowdies, 2–1 in the final. It was 1979 and Rodney Marsh's last match. I flew my dad out for the final, after which each player received a gold watch. I gave it to him. He had a wonderful time. I had told Lesley to organize a flight for him, first class, something special because I wanted to treat him. After the final I came home with Lesley, missing the celebrations in Vancouver. Everyone told me the city was awash with joy, as I knew it would be.

Of course I was contracted to go back the next year, which I did, but my heart wasn't completely in it as I had signed to be Blackpool's player-manager and was anxious to get on with the job. Blackpool, so I thought, was the start of my new life.

I had visited Blackpool and Bloomfield Road – the starting point of my career – with them in the Third Division before leaving for the Canadian stint. I had Ted MacDougall with me and was greeted by Stan Ternent, who had just been sacked but knew I was taking over. I was overwhelmed by Stan's kindness, understanding and generosity as he stayed for three or four days, showing me the layout, handing over the keys and pointing me in every right direction. I found it hard to understand why he had been dismissed. He took me around and I met the office staff and spoke to the groundsmen at Squires Gate, the training ground and the pitch where I had been the teenage muck-spreader all those years ago.

Stan said to me on our brief tour that I should meet our chief scout, who had been kept on. He described him as a fabulous chap whom I would love to death and pointed to an office along the way. I knocked on the door and walked in ready to introduce myself as the new manager, but as soon as I saw who was there my jaw dropped and my prepared words evaporated. Sitting in front of me were two absolute legends of the game, Peter Doherty and Len Shackleton, two white-haired heroes of my father and his generation and many more besides. Peter was the chief scout and Len, the genius of his day with every trick in the book, had come to visit him. We just sat and chatted about football, and I told them how much my father had admired them and how often he had talked about them.

By the time the new season started we knew we had to make changes. Ted had been in charge but we had a few players who were at the wrong end of their careers. Bob Stokoe, a previous manager, had signed four of his ex-Sunderland players. They were old pros who had done it, seen it and were on big money. All four had played in the 1973 FA Cup Final, when they surprisingly defeated Leeds 1–0, but they were now out of date as far as I was concerned. They were a problem I wanted to sort out and they were soon gone, so that I started by drastically lowering the age of the Blackpool team by including youngsters. I told the directors that was my plan and that I was going to trawl the country looking for promising boys and free transfer players.

One of my first signings was Paul Stewart. I got him for nothing from Manchester City, and he went on to play for England when he was with Tottenham Hotspur. There was David Bardsley and the two sixteen year olds, Colin Greenall and Eamonn Collins, eventually made the club £1.5 million. We started off all fresh and new and had a fabulous early match at Sheffield United, where we lost 3–2, but we were both at the top of the table.

Everything was moving along nicely. Ted was playing and scoring goals on a regular basis as he always would, but then after the Sheffield United game he confessed that he was having trouble in his marriage. I lost him that night. My right-hand man was leaving. It was the first chink in my newfound happiness. Things started to go wrong. I had so much to cherish. My best player, a little winger called Colin Morris, was really turning it on. In the treatment room I had one of the finest physiotherapists in Alan Smith, who was recruited by the FA to be England's physio.

There were many positives, but after six weeks the chairman who had been instrumental in taking me back to Blackpool, Peter Lawson, had been voted off the board at the annual general meeting. I was soon to start some serious learning about the politics of running football clubs. Peter has always been a good friend and when he appointed me he knew I was raw. I was coming straight from the playing side after Southampton and America. I didn't know the rules of buying and selling and scouting, but I was always quick to absorb knowledge and use it.

I needed time but after Peter had gone I seemed to have a succession of know-alls, with board meetings every two weeks and one director in particular making himself a nuisance. And that is the correct description of Tom White, who was an ex-player and the brother of John White, the Tottenham and Scotland player who was killed while sheltering from lightning on a north London golf course. I rarely saw Tom White, but he was an ex-Blackpool player who seemed to want to be managing the club. He was constantly trying to pull all sorts of strings. Nothing I did could ever be right in his mind, as far as I could see. I could not wear a kid glove with all the politicking that was going on. I was my own man. I was straight and to the point, as forthright as you would expect from anyone who had been brought up the way I had been by my father.

He had told me all along about how to get on with directors but I wasn't getting there. I lost the boardroom, in effect, the way some managers lose the dressing room – and there were others apart from Tom White who made things difficult.

Another director, Cliff Sagar, whom I never saw until later in my term as manager, always made noises off-stage, as it were, like an absentee chairman. Then Allan Brown, who had been a crowd favourite as a player and had been manager for a spell, came into the picture with his

ABOVE LEFT: Beginnings . . . at St Peter's C. of E. School, Farnworth. I'm in the first row, far left. ABOVE RIGHT: Reading the first write-ups with Dad.

ABOVE LEFT: *Daily Dispatch* Shield winners, Farnworth Grammar School. Second left, bottom row with sports master Mr John Dickinson. ABOVE RIGHT: Scoring against Liverpool on my Mersey derby debut in 1967. BELOW: Me and Dad – 'My mentor'

Early days at Blackpool.

Happiest day of my life, when I married my childhood sweetheart, Lesley.

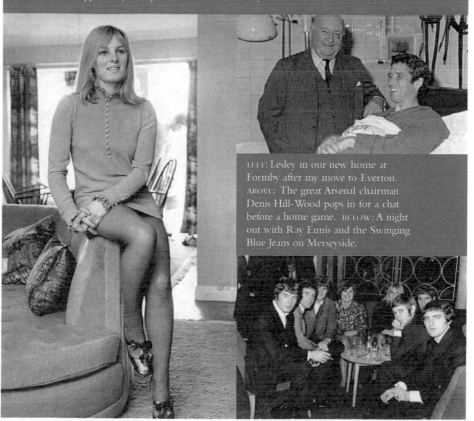

LEFT: Lesley in our new home at Formby after my move to Everton. ABOVE: The great Arsenal chairman Denis Hill-Wood pops in for a chat before a home game. BELOW: A night out with Ray Ennis and the Swinging Blue Jeans on Merseyside.

ABOVE: Champions at Everton. Skipper Brian Labone
was injured that day so I led the side and collected the trophy.
BELOW: A much appreciated telegram from Bobby and Tina Moore.

DE119 AP8 1550 LONDON T 28 GREETINGS
MR ALAN BALL C/O SOUTHAMPTON FOOTBALL CLUB WEMBLEY STADIUM WEMBLEY

GOOD LUCK FOR TODAY LITTLE FELLOW SHOW THEM ALL HOW YOU
CAN PLAY

    BOBBY TINA AND KIDS

ABOVE LEFT: 1966 post-match party. Lesley and me dancing.
ABOVE RIGHT: A night out at Danny La Rue's club with my old mates
from the squad of '66, Geoff Hurst, Nobby Stiles and John Connelly.

ABOVE: 'Flash, Bang, Wallop' . . . the launch of photographer Kent Gavin's
book with Malcolm Macdonald, Bobby Moore and boxer John Conteh.
BELOW: With two of my most enduring friends, Paul and Anne Phillips.

ABOVE: My favourite picture of a lovely woman, my Lesley.
BELOW LEFT: My Everton debut at Fulham brought World Cup pals together.
With Ray Wilson and George Cohen. BELOW RIGHT: Two of my best friends in
football from Arsenal days, Frank McLintock and George Graham.

ABOVE: In awe of my first child, Mandy.
BELOW LEFT: The happy face of a man who has just signed for Arsenal.
BELOW RIGHT: Two England captains on Brighton beach.
With Tony Greig (England cricket captain).

Happy sunshine days with little Mandy on holiday in Majorca.

thoughts and ideas, which hadn't seemed to work when he himself had been in the hot seat.

Results started to go against us and I began to feel very uncomfortable. I was on my own. Ted MacDougall would always have fought with me and for me but he had gone. I had the two Fred Davieses, one my reserve team coach, the other an older man, to help me with all the background stuff and to watch my back, but it was all too much for us.

Old Fred was one of Lawrie McMenemy's men who knew all the ropes and dodges. As things deteriorated and I lost the chairman who had taken me to Blackpool I decided I was getting out. I was becoming increasingly lonely and isolated. I was fighting everybody again which, I suppose, is part of my nature. Blackpool were halfway up the table but it was one of those turnaround seasons of transition and the league position was only to be expected. I told Lesley of my intentions and went to the board meeting, where I told them of my need to speak to them all collectively since the main man, Sagar, had not been seen and I wanted him there because of what I had to say.

I told them I believed I had 'gone' as a player and that I realized that as a player-manager, meaning that I was doing two jobs, I had become quite expensive for them. As I was on a two-year contract and felt unable to see it out on the playing side, perhaps we could come to an amicable financial arrangement for me to leave as I would be saving them a reasonable amount of money. As expected, Tom White said I should not take any money because I had not done the job. I told him those words were exactly what I had anticipated from him. I disagreed and said we should do things properly.

I realized I had made a mistake in taking the position at Blackpool. I was not yet ready for boardrooms and the machinations of football club directors. But I pointed out that I was leaving the club with some good young players. I said I would take half the value of my contract. It was a very long meeting, with no Cliff Sagar.

When I arrived home I told Lesley straightaway that I had quit. She had expected it and, as always, she was supportive. There were issues that might have been worrying. We had bought a lovely house in Lytham, the kids were settled in school and it was a delightful place to live with the sea and all that fresh air.

As if by second nature I rang Lawrie for some advice, knowing that whatever he said would be sound. I told him the boardroom side had driven me mad and was ruining my love of working with players. He listened to me and said he had always thought that I would find trouble with the directors, adding that only experience can get you through those situations. Lawrie had known a few awkward directors in his time. I told him I had helped Blackpool over the money due to me and he just said I would have to live with whatever I had decided for myself.

Then he said, out of the blue: 'How fit are you?'

I told him I was in great shape and that I had hardly missed a game. He said: 'Right, I am flying to Spain tomorrow. The Southampton lads are out there for a few days. If you fancy coming out, you are welcome, and we can have a look at you.'

It was in the spring of 1981. I was in Spain within twenty-four hours, trained with them, resigned on the Thursday when we got back and captained the team on the Saturday at The Dell, where we beat Manchester United 1–0. It was as if I had never been away, but here I was in my second spell at Southampton. I should never have taken the Blackpool job in the first place. I wasn't ready for it. I soon realized the magnitude of management in football. You have to be involved in everything – tours, travel, contracts, buying and selling – with everything being put in front of the chairman for his tick or his veto. All the time at Bloomfield Road I was doing this and training and playing as well.

With young Eamonn Collins there were other issues. When I first saw him at the age of fourteen he was tiny, but he could play. We had to get a child-size shirt for him and sew on a number because the club shirt was so big that it tucked down into his shorts, taking half the number with it. We had to get special permission to take him out of school in Ireland on the promise of a contract. I took him to Southampton, where he played in the First Division, as he did when I recruited him for Portsmouth. I took him everywhere with me. He never grew, but he had a shrewd footballing brain and was always great fun.

I had two years and some good matches when I returned to Southampton. It was one of the best moves I ever made, though I probably drove Lawrie mad. I knew that I would want another crack at management. I was prepared to go as low as possible in football to learn more. Lawrie was a terrific adviser. He listened, and when he spoke you knew he was weighing every word in that careful Geordie way of his. I had this thirst for knowledge. I was always popping in for our question and answer sessions.

He gave me so much to think about and there was even more to feel good about at Southampton. I found myself playing with Keegan again. Golac was there. He couldn't speak a word of English when he arrived from Yugoslavia and neither could his wife, but I like to think we looked after them well, especially with Lesley taking them to the butcher's shop and making mooing, flapping and grunting noises to help them identify the different meats.

Lawrie was big on lucrative foreign tours. He took us to Malaysia on one trip. Kevin, Mick Channon and myself were the attractions or, at least, we were the recognized names in far-flung parts of the world. Kevin was the main attraction and wherever we went he was the one in most demand by the fans and the promoters of these friendly, fund-raising games. We were due to play in Kuala Lumpur but at lunchtime on the day of the match Kevin complained of feeling unwell.

He grew worse in the afternoon and we left for the stadium without him. As we neared the ground, the crowds began to thicken. Soon they were jumping up at the sides of the bus chanting, 'Keegan, Keegan.' When we arrived there were so many people surrounding this rickety old bus that we were penned in; still they called for Kevin, the only man they apparently wanted to see. I turned to Lawrie and told him he had a problem. We could be lynched if they didn't get to see Kevin. Lawrie disappeared but later returned to the dressing room to say that the lad was lying in his bed back at the hotel doing a vivid impersonation of death itself. However, he was going to make the effort. We were looking on as he arrived on a motorbike policeman's pillion, wearing a crash helmet. It was one of the funniest sights imaginable but he did his best and saved the day, because I feel sure there would have been serious trouble had he not made it. That was typical of Kevin, who would not want to let anyone down.

That was the day I realized the enormous impact of television. Matches were being beamed all over the world and names that we thought were confined to Britain and the rest of Western Europe were registering and being idolized in the Far East. They had seen Kevin playing in England and Germany and in international football and had taken to him. The world was embracing him.

Kevin is one of the true gentlemen of the game. When I came back to Southampton for the second time we had nowhere to live at first. Kevin was the first one to consider that we might have a housing predicament. On one of the earliest days of training he invited us, Lesley, me and the kids, to stay at his place. We had sold the house that Lawrie gave us in lieu of a signing-on fee first time around when I moved to Blackpool. Kevin said there was plenty of room for us and we could stay as long as we liked until we got ourselves a home of our own. He was always very friendly, ever ready to do a good turn.

Lawrie took the team to play in a three-cornered tournament in New York in the summer of 1981 and naturally we went racing at the first opportunity. We were not having a good day so Kevin, Mick and I pooled our money and gave it to Channon and the money was down. The horse romped in with us screaming it home.

We couldn't wait to collect our winnings. No more going for an advance on our expenses. We were in for a fistful of dollars. Then we saw a downcast Channon lumbering towards us. He had put the money on the wrong horse. To say we gave him a verbal hammering would be a massive understatement.

We won our first game in the tournament, as did Celtic, which meant we had to play them in the final. Lawrie was very good on trips and this one was no exception. As is usual when on tour he said there were no curfews. He said we were professional people who knew how to look after ourselves and would not step out of line. He said he did not want to be on tenterhooks worrying about us and having to act as a babysitter for grown men. Throughout his time at Southampton his attitude remained the same and there was never any trouble.

On the morning of the match against Celtic, Lawrie called us together and stressed how much their manager was a stickler for discipline, especially when it came to how to dress when representing the club.

They were staying at the same hotel as us and Lawrie predicted that they would be immaculate in their green club blazers, white shirts and green club ties. He told us that we, too, would wear shirts and ties because we didn't want to be appearing scruffy in their smart presence. Fair enough, we concurred. I had gone for my rest after lunch and Channon had disappeared. He came in half an hour later, threw a packet at me and said, 'Here's your shirt and tie for tonight.' He had been out and bought shirts that had a tie and buttons painted on with a rose on the pocket. He had one for himself but I said we couldn't possibly wear them because Lawrie would go berserk.

Typically, Mick said we would be all right because he was going to make Keegan wear one as well. Fair play to Kevin, he had an infectious enthusiasm for anything humorous, so we wore these shirts with their round collars and came down in the lift together, the three senior players.

As the lift doors opened, sure enough the Celtic players were standing there as pristine as tailors' dummies alongside the manager. This was their Cup Final, if you like, Glasgow Celtic against an English League side. But right opposite as we emerged from the lift was Lawrie Mac. He closed his eyes as if in disbelief and Keegan just said: 'Well, you did say shirt and tie, boss.' He laughed and we just got on with it. That was the way he handled players. You could always have impish fun with him.

Around that time, 1982, I had become friendly with Charlie Watts, the Rolling Stones drummer. I had met him through Frank Muggeridge, with whom we had stabled the ill-fated Ashera. Frank was taking me to Cheltenham but said we would stop off on the way to see Charlie, who had had horses with him when he trained at Lewes, near Brighton.

While we were in New York the Stones were also in the city recording their album *Tattoo You*. As far as I was concerned it was just a coincidence. We were there to play football and they had the recording to get along with, so never the twain shall meet. We arrived back from training one day and there was a note in my pigeonhole from Charlie just saying he had heard I was in town, they were doing a recording, starting at midnight and would I like to come along and bring a pal.

I mentioned it to Kevin and he fancied the idea. We arrived at the studio around midnight and stayed all night until seven o'clock in the morning. It was an incredible experience, just the band and technicians along with Kevin and me and caterers popping in now and again with food. There was no liquor, not a drop of alcohol to be seen. We had some breakfast, had our photographs taken with them and walked into the hotel as Lawrie and the rest of them were having breakfast. 'Just got in, boss,' I said, before he could ask where we had been. He was as impressed as anyone when we told him we had been out all night watching the Rolling Stones doing a record- ing. I rather fancied it was something he wouldn't have minded experiencing himself.

Lawrie's easy-going reaction was typical of the man. He could deal with any situation in his own way and always made us laugh whenever we went racing at

Plumpton or somewhere else within striking distance. We, Channon, Keegan and myself, were the experts. We read the form and studied the ink off the racing papers. We spoke to trainers we knew. Lawrie, on the other hand, would go off and back something because he fancied the horse's name and then he would come back beaming, waving his winnings.

It was a big plus that he was such a good mixer in any company, especially at a football club where there were big stars, journeymen and juniors, some promising, some having to come to terms with careers outside the game. I found it hard in management to be as phlegmatic as he appeared to be. I was probably more hands-on at the business end but wanted to keep players at arm's length afterwards. I never had to deal with the Keegans of the football world when I was managing. Matt Le Tissier was the biggest name I had under me, but he was easy because he just needed an arm around him.

Lawrie's final favour to me, and there were many, came as I decided that I could no longer reach the standards I had set for myself as a player. I may have managed to get through another season as a Southampton player but I did not want to peter out with my speed of thought and deed on the slide. Lawrie talked about a testimonial match but I said that I didn't want South-ampton folk putting their hands in their pockets for me so I never had a benefit match.

I knew the time was right to move on and I asked Lawrie if he could manage to get me a three-month contract in Hong Kong to see me through the summer while I decided on where I wanted my career to take me next. In my final game for Southampton we defeated Everton 3–2 and I was on my way to the Far East. I had a great contract to play with Eastern Athletic. There was plenty of money for the short period I was there and one of the attractions of the trip was that I would be linking up with Bobby Moore again.

Sadly, that aspect of it became something of a nightmare because his marriage to Tina was in difficulties. Lesley and I and Bobby and Tina had become very close, often going out together as a foursome. Lesley had sensed something might be amiss between them but I hadn't an inkling that Stephanie, a long-haul air stewardess, was not only in the background but that Bobby had fallen in love with her.

I slowly began to suspect something before Lesley arrived. Bobby and I had fabulous suites in the Royal Garden Hotel on the island, but often when I asked him if he fancied a beer after training he would say something vague about having business on. I never pestered him or queried him but I missed his company and it became obvious later that whenever Stephanie's crew were in Hong Kong he was off seeing her. At the time I just thought that perhaps things were not going too well for him generally.

We had quite a decent team generally made up of five Europeans and six Chinese but the trouble was that as fast as we were scoring goals the Chinese defenders were letting them in at the other end. You never knew which way they were going to play or what mood they would be in. They were probably getting the equivalent of a bowl of rice for playing and we were pocketing big bucks. The only way they could make money was by betting on the games, which led to some unusual situations. I simply could not come to terms with this but I rapidly discovered that you couldn't criticize a Chinese player because he loses face. I was not popular, except when I was able to pass on racing tips.

The players were all demented gamblers and one lad took a particular shine to me. He was the most serious gambler and wanted to keep on the right side of me to pick up any tips. One morning the Europeans managed to get some bacon and eggs fried for breakfast, which completely baffled the Chinese, especially that one lad who was trying to eat a runny egg with chopsticks.

He came in one morning and when I asked after his well-being he said, in his pidgin English, that he was 'velly tired, no train today'. He kept repeating it, as I said tiredness was no excuse and he had better get his kit on, pronto, or there would be trouble.

When 'Mooro' came in I told him that the unthinkable was going on; a player reluctant to train because of some small fatigue. 'Mooro' softened and explained that he was a dustman and had been on the all-night shift moving tons of Hong Kong's refuse. A rest and a shower were all he needed. I had to admit that I would not have been anxious to train after that kind of a night.

The European contingent had some awesome nights out and wherever Tommy Hutchison went people wanted to touch him. His mazy, dribbling style had made him a great favourite in the colony. We had a Christmas Day lunch on a boat in a bay on the South China Sea. We swam and we drank, and by the time we arrived back on dry land we were providing a whole new definition of the term leglessness.

We ate in the best restaurants. One meal in particular unfortunately left a nasty taste, which leads me to putting the record straight regarding an allegation made in his book by the late singer Adam Faith, who said we shopped him over his affair with the tennis star Chris Evert.

He wrote that he was in the restaurant with Chris and that Bobby and Tina were there with Lesley and me. A few days later their liaison was reported in the paper and Faith concluded that we must have provided the evidence. I suppose he reckoned that because we were the only Britons in the place it must have been us. Nothing could have been more wrong. Perhaps it hadn't registered with him that there are so many journalists in Hong Kong that they have their own luxurious foreign correspondents club.

Then there was a sad meal when Bobby and Tina's differences surfaced. Until then all our nights out had been packed with fun and laughter. The four of us were in a big restaurant and a British Caledonian crew came in for dinner. I am not sure if Stephanie was with them but it threw Bobby completely. He became quite odd and it all went off. Bobby and Tina began exchanging insulting, sarcastic remarks. It was awful, and although Lesley and I tried to placate them, things became worse. Soon afterwards we took Bobby and Tina out on a junk but Tina, who could at times be unpredictable, disappeared from the table at a quayside restaurant.

When we found her she was sitting among a group of meditating religious people. It was all very strange. Bobby cried and said he had no idea what he should do. It was a grim end to the Hong Kong story. Lesley and I love Tina and we often reminisced about times gone by.

They eventually divorced; he married Stephanie, and after Bobby's untimely death at the age of fifty-one Steph has continued to work tirelessly for cancer charities.

8

TRAGEDY STRIKES

Tragedy invaded my life on 2 January 1982 and I knew that things would never be the same again. It was never anticipated. Life was wonderful. I was loving being back at Southampton. We bought a house back in Chandlers Ford after spending a few days living with the Keegans. Hampshire was a wonderful place to live. And when Mick Channon invited me to go clay-pigeon shooting with some of his mates, I leaped at the chance even though I told him that I had never picked up a gun in my life and wouldn't have a clue how to handle one. Guns may be lethal but unbeknown to me something just as damaging was happening far away in Cyprus as I joined the shoot. I went off with Mick and his brother Phil to a place somewhere the other side of Romsey. It was a cold, crisp winter's day. There was not a cloud in the sky but plenty of frost about. They sat me in a little area and my job was to launch the clays. I put them in the trap and when they shouted 'Pull!' I pulled for a couple of hours as they shot. They had given me half a bottle of brandy so I was quite content sitting there, and eventually we all trooped back to the pub, the Malthouse, on the Stockbridge road.

It was one of those days when everything just felt right. Southampton had won on New Year's Day, the pints were coming in foaming and the fire in the hearth was cheerfulness itself. There was a lot of laughter and the whole day seemed aglow. I had my back to the door and was talking to Mick, who suddenly seemed to be looking over my shoulder and was no longer listening. He was mouthing 'What?' Instinctively I sensed something was wrong and knew that whatever was happening involved me. I turned around and there was the huge Geordie figure of Lawrie McMenemy framed in the doorway. As I walked towards him I knew something dreadful had happened. It wasn't the kind of visit you get when a transfer is involved. His face was serious and as I went towards him I was asking myself who, what, where?

He almost buried me in his arms as he said quietly: 'Your dad's died in a car crash.' I was unable to say anything. I didn't say goodbye to the boys I had spent the morning with. All I could do was mumble to Lawrie to get me home. He was wonderful as he always would be in such situations. All I could do was mutter and mumble as Lawrie did his best to comfort us. My own life with my father rose through my numbness, the times we had together, the knowledge that I had him to thank for my life in football, his humour, his caring, and his George Formby songs.

It was late that night before we heard how he had met his death. I knew he was flying to Cyprus to be interviewed for a coaching position. The first Lawrie knew about it was when he took a call from the Foreign Office, who told him that Alan Ball had been killed in Cyprus. At first Lawrie stressed that it would have been impossible because he had been with me the night before. He thought it must have been my father, but he phoned the house and Lesley answered the phone. He asked her where I was and she told him I was out clay-pigeon shooting. He then asked: 'Where's Alan's dad?'

Lesley replied that he was in Cyprus and Lawrie just said: 'Oh, my God. He's been killed in a car crash.' She told him exactly where I was and he said he would go and find me and tell me.

The facts began to unfold slowly and I will be eternally grateful for a lovely Lancashire lad called Mike Ferguson who was coaching out there and got involved sorting the logistics as soon as he heard what had happened. He rang and told us that he would sort everything out with regard to any inquest and getting Dad transferred back to Britain, and that there was no point in us flying out there. It wasn't as easy as that because there was lots of paperwork to be done involving the Foreign Office and the Greek government before they would release him.

Apparently this is what happened. My dad landed at Larnaca and was met at the airport to be driven to Limassol by an official of the Eyagoras club, who were interested in taking him on. He was out of football in the UK at the time. It transpired that the driver had overtaken a car about 300 yards from a bridge over a dried-up riverbed. He was unable to straighten the car and they finished down the bank. Dad was thrown clear but he was dead. Subsequently, Lesley went to Cyprus with my sister, Carolyn, for the court hearing. Peter Cormack, the former Liverpool player who was managing out there, was a great help. The driver of the car was given a year's ban and Mum was awarded £25,000. It was scant consolation.

On hearing the news of the crash I left home straight-away to drive to Bolton to see my mother. I knew her emotions would be wrecked by the news. All the way north I could not think straight and every half hour my father's death was on the radio news. It was an awful drive. I was still stunned. I could not cry or grieve properly, and yet I wanted to. I do remember, though, being told about the first time my mam and dad met. He would be direct, of course, and asked her name, and when she said 'Violet Duckworth' he said, apparently, 'What sort of a name is Violet Duckworth?'

He said: 'You'll never be a Violet to me. You will always be a Val-er-ie.' He called her Val all his life.

When I arrived at the house I was clearly not myself. The curtains were closed and several people were there, the way families and friends gather when this type of thing happens. I was uncharacteristically short with them, said I wanted them out of the way and asked where my mother was.

They said she had locked herself in the bedroom and I thought no wonder, with that lot moping around. I knocked on the bedroom door and I could hear her wailing inside. She let me in. I knew my main job was to comfort her. He had been her strength, her provider, her confidant and her unshakeably loyal husband.

She was never the same from that day. She became jumpy and suffered with a mental illness afterwards. It was as though whatever had been lying dormant had been brought forward. They had been an utterly devoted couple. She doted on him, smoothed his path. She was a wonderful mother, too, making sacrifices for my first pair of boots, taking jobs to give us a better quality of life.

That afternoon following my father's death, I tried my best to placate her, to tell her that there was nothing we could do and that we had to try to get on with our lives as normally as possible until we could get him back. I told her that Mike Ferguson, who had been a friend of my dad's, was out there linking with the British Consul and making sure the autopsy and everything was being done correctly. It did not calm her down and there was the added distress of not knowing precisely what had happened on that road between Larnaca and Limassol. Lesley spent a lot of time talking to the Foreign Office, who were not particularly helpful, and there were a lot of expenses to pay including those for bringing him back. Throughout, though, Ferguson was just fantastic with his time, help and understanding, and to this day I cannot thank him enough. Dad's brother, my uncle Trevor, was also a great support.

In effect we had three episodes of mourning: when he died, when he came back and when we had the funeral. He was cremated but had always said that when he died he wanted to go looking smart, wearing his best suit with a tenner in his top pocket just in case there was anything going on 'up there'.

Not long before his accident he had remarked on a story in the *Bolton Evening News* about scams going on at crematoriums with items disappearing from bodies. He told us to forget about the tenner because he didn't want to be robbed in his coffin, but we put it in his pocket anyway.

The night before the funeral Southampton were playing Everton at Goodison Park and Lawrie told me that obviously he did not expect me to play. I just said: 'Lawrie, if I didn't play because I am burying my dad tomorrow, he would go berserk "up there". I am playing.'

Joe Mercer, one of the most lovable legends of football as a player with Everton and Arsenal and manager of Arsenal and Manchester City, came to the game that night and put his arm around me, saying: 'You go and play for him tonight.' We drew 1–1 and the funeral was the following day.

The main man had gone. Now I was on my own but even to this day his guidance is there. I have always said that he is not dead while I am alive and I honestly believe that. I know the way he would have handled situations and sometimes I follow that pattern to the point of stubbornness. His funeral stamped his continuing presence within my heart and soul. It was a wonderfully moving service with an absolute sea of familiar faces, football faces.

Tommy Docherty came up to me as I walked out and

said something that will also stay with me. He said: 'Good luck, son. We didn't always get on, your dad and I. In fact we rowed like cat and dog, but I am here because he was a proper football man.'

Those words rang very special to a son who had just lost the father he revered. I reflected, and still do, that life and football should be like that. The 'Doc' is like me in that he is not everybody's cup of tea but he is high on my list. Still, the great man, my father, had gone and as I drove back to Southampton and many a night after that, right until this day, I recalled the lengths to which he had gone to help me pursue a career in the greatest game of all.

He was there whenever I was rejected at Bolton, at Wolves and when I first went to the England Under-23 set-up. He encouraged me when I was down and nailed my feet to the ground if ever I showed signs of becoming uppity. When I became the first player to wear a pair of white sponsored boots all those years ago, he simply said: 'You'd better be good to be wearing those.'

I always thought he was indestructible because of the way he went about his life, but he did have a couple of heart attacks that slowed him down for a time – although not for long. The first time was when he was in Sweden in 1980 managing a team and Mike Ferguson was involved again. This time Mike rang my mother to tell her Dad had had a heart attack and was in hospital. No one knew anything about it. We didn't know which hospital he was in, so Lesley started ringing round and eventually located him. He had a scar on his heart and was told to take it easy. He did until he was back in Preston playing in a charity match. He said he had a tingling down his side. They took him to hospital again and said he'd had a heart attack. He was not long past fifty and this time it really shook him.

I was so convinced of his invincibility that when he had the heart attacks I just thought something like, oh, he'll get over it. When I did show some concern he just told me not to worry and go out and play my football because, as he always said, he could look after himself.

I saw him truly hurt just once and I was hurt for him. I was playing for Everton and he was manager of Preston North End at the time. I had just finished training when he rang me to ask if I was driving home to Worsley that day. I told him I was and he said: 'Can you come via Preston because they've sacked me and, you won't believe it, but they've taken the car off me and I have to get home to Bolton on the train.' I pulled up outside Deepdale, North End's famous old ground; he was stood there, trying to look proud, with a black bin-liner containing all the personal belongings from his desk.

He was not one for tears but I could tell he was devastated. It is probably fair to say that he had not been that upset since his father died. He doted on his dad. It must be a trait that runs through the family where, incidentally, every male member has James in his name. He was Alan James Ball, as indeed I am, and our son is Jimmy.

We had some fun times to look back on. When Vancouver reached the final in New York the club

invited Lesley over and paid for her ticket, but I wanted
Dad to be there so we bought an airline ticket for him.
I had a friend at British Airways who was useful for the
upgrades so as Lesley and Dad boarded the plane she was
saying to him, 'Turn left, turn left.' He saw the luxury of
first class and was clearly impressed. The stewardess
offered him the usual complimentary buck's fizz of champagne and orange juice and he, of course, said: 'How
much do I owe you, love?'

Lesley told me what happened next. He became mischievous, which was normal, and began to talk in a
louder voice than usual, saying to Lesley: 'Where would
you like to go when we get to New York, darling? I'll
get them to radio forward to get the jet waiting. It's very
inconvenient when you have a private jet and you have
to fly commercial.' The stewardesses soon cottoned on to
his game and played along with it until the aircraft ran
into the edge of hurricane David. The turbulence quiet-
ened him down somewhat, but they eventually landed at
JFK International Airport to hear an announcement
directing first-class passengers to their own designated
carousel.

Some of the world's most expensive luggage, Louis
Vuitton, Gucci and so on, was coming off and then
Lesley, who had checked in separately, spotted this old,
battered suitcase with a few torn stickers and held together
by a belt.

She said to him: 'If you pick that up I'll kill you.' She
made him wait until everyone else had collected their

baggage and gone. He thought it was hilarious. They checked in at the hotel and Dad, as was typical, decided he would explore Manhattan.

When he reported back he said he'd had a wonderful time. He'd been for a walk in Central Park and he had been in a bar and met a very friendly Swedish woman who wanted to talk, so he had bought her a bottle of champagne. He never guessed that she was a hostess whose job it was to get the punters to buy bubbly. The night before we were due to fly home was the final. There was a reception and there he met a lot of old footballing mates, including Noel Cantwell. He was in his element with them and had such a roaring good time until 5 a.m. that he missed his flight. No problem – he feigned illness and jumped the queue of those in front of him.

Eight years after his death my mother passed away. She lived with us for a few years and then with my sister Carolyn, who had a pub at Cark-in-Cartmel, a village in the south of the Lake District. One day in January 2000, my sister phoned me to say that Mother had fallen and had been taken to hospital. That night I woke up at 3.30 a.m. and something told me I had to see her. It was an intuitive thing. Our Jimmy was with me as we drove the 400 miles to Furness General Hospital in Barrow-in-Furness. As I walked into the room a doctor appeared to be attending to her. I told him who I was and that I had come to see my mother. He looked at me and said: 'She has just this minute passed away.'

It was as though she had been waiting for me. All the memories came flooding back as they did with my dad. I could not have wanted for better parents.

On the long drive home from Barrow Mam and Dad were always on my mind. There was a question I would have liked to have asked Dad but never got around to it: how do you end your playing career? Many an old player advised me to keep going out there as long as I physically could, and after the renaissance at Southampton as well as Vancouver and Hong Kong, I sensed it was probably time to roll up the curtain and keep the boots as souvenirs. I was twiddling my thumbs, wondering what to do, when I took a call from Bobby Gould who was managing Bristol Rovers.

He said he had a chance of promotion and had a collection of young players who might respond to having my kind of experience in their midst. I told him I wasn't fit but he persuaded me to give it a go for a month or two on a match-to-match payment basis. It was true they had some talent; it included Keith Curle, who went on to play for England, and Ian Holloway, who had a good career and went on to manage QPR. I knew my legs had 'gone' and when we received a good hiding at Walsall I knew that the time to say goodbye to the playing side had arrived. Management was calling again, though I didn't realize it at the time and I no longer had my father to turn to for advice.

I think I know what he would have said when I took a call from Portsmouth early in 1984. I was sitting at home wondering where my next move might take me when I was asked if I would like to meet the chairman, John Deacon, with a view to taking charge of the youth team job at Fratton Park. Bobby Campbell was the manager. I knew him as a good coach, a sound manager and a Liverpudlian with a sense of humour. I saw the challenge of galvanizing the youth team and developing the skills of young players as only part of the immediate future. I accepted that Blackpool had been something of a nightmare, but this offer represented a chance to learn much more about football club management. I saw the job as my apprenticeship before having another go at coaching and managing.

It was the beginning of five amazing, roller-coaster years on the south coast. My first weeks in the job were not auspicious. The previous manager, Ian St John, who had to work under serious financial constraints, had scrapped the reserve team, and Bobby Campbell, who had just eighteen professionals, was trying to rebuild things. Pompey were in the Second Division and I found myself working with just five young lads. They were the start of the youth set-up.

I began to work with a man called Derek Healey, who turned out to be the best spotter of talent, the best judge of a player I have ever known. He came with me when we went to watch players. His influence and knowledge were invaluable. We looked everywhere, starting off in the local leagues just hoping to spot that special touch and intelligent thinking that separates the very good from the simply good. Our Jimmy was still at primary school but he was playing on Sundays so I would watch his team, as any father would, sometimes casting an eye over the other games that were going on around.

The grapevine was working overtime and soon it became common knowledge that Alan Ball, youth coach at Portsmouth, was watching these games. As a result, youngsters became anxious to join in, so we had no problem attracting recruits. Slowly but surely we began to get a decent youth squad together with the likes of Lee Sandford, Robbie Taylor, Mario Walsh and Brendan O'Connell. The thirteen and fourteen year olds we were getting into the schools of excellence were all full of promise. Among them was Darren Anderton, who eventually went on to play for Tottenham and England. This was all happening during my managerial apprentice-ship, as I called it, and I imagined I would be working with the youths for ages. I never gave a thought to the possibility that I could be made manager of the club and that I would be in complete control, appointing my own people.

Then, before the last game of the 1983–4 season, on 12 May, Bobby Campbell decided he'd had enough. If results had gone against us we could have gone down to the Third Division. The chairman asked me if I would take charge for the last match of the season while he decided during the summer who would be in charge for the 1984–5 campaign. I enjoyed the one-match experi-ence, especially as we won 5–0, with Alan Biley scoring a hat-trick and Mark Hateley reaching his twenty-five goals for the season on that day. Also in the team was Neil Webb, another man who made a great career for himself with Nottingham Forest and Manchester United before a bad Achilles tendon injury affected his pace and led to him leaving the game probably earlier than he should. When I last heard of Neil he was working happily as a postman in Reading. The club had done well to sign Webb and Hateley for a tidy sum, estimated at £200,000 apiece, Webb from Reading and Hateley from Coventry.

As the summer seemed to be hurtling along and there was no sign of an appointment to the manager's job I was on tenterhooks. I was enjoying my work with the young players, but I'd had a taste of the first team with that match against Swansea, and there was also the concern that they might give the position to someone whose ideas might not be compatible with mine.

Eventually I got the call to go and see the chairman, and soon the ball was rolling and bouncing in a way that was spectacularly unpredictable . . .

9

POMPEY TIMES

There have been numerous twists and turns to my life in football and many of them seem to have been encapsulated in my time at Fratton Park. List all the emotions you can think of and I've experienced them, but even when the club was stricken by poverty we were usually rich in humour, often ironic, as I found when I sat down for the first time as manager with the chairman, John Deacon.

Obviously he asked me how I saw the future of Portsmouth FC. My idea, I told him, was that we could eventually go forward with a team based on a youth policy. There was talent in the area, there were lads dying to pull on the blue and white, but it would take patience. We would need to be honest with the supporters and tell them what we were planning. It was not necessarily a case of buying time, but of being sensible and making sure that everyone both inside and outside knew what we were planning.

He listened, or at least I thought he was taking it all in, but then he switched tack and said that I had players already on the books whose sale would generate money. There had been inquiries from other clubs, he said.

This was not the initial meeting I had envisaged. Already I was beginning to sense that some kind of mind games were being played, and when he said that Mark Hateley was the player he had thought of when it came to selling I was dumbfounded. I told him of the implications. Here I was, newly in the job, and he was telling me to unload my best player. What was I going to tell the supporters? The announcement would give me the worst possible start to my new career. Hateley was a crowd favourite, he scored goals on a regular basis and if we were to get anywhere we needed him in the side. He had scored a goal for England in the Maracana Stadium in Rio de Janeiro on his second of thirty-two international appearances in June 1984, only a few weeks earlier.

No doubt Mark had been attracting the attention of the bigger clubs. The pound signs were almost visibly dazzling the chairman's eyes as he said selling was the way to bring in the cash. I could see he had set his eyes on a big transfer so I asked him how much of the transfer fee I might receive to spend on the team. I told him that we could probably get £1 million for Mark but I knew I had to do something to keep faith with the Portsmouth public. The last thing I wanted them to believe was that I was the man doing the selling. I was grateful to a local journalist, Mike Neasom, for helping to get the right story, with just a hint of the right spin in the local press.

Portsmouth newspapers were fed the line that, having

finished fourth bottom of the Second Division, I knew the supporters wanted change; that there was a revolution in the air and that I had been assured by the chairman that I would be given a huge lump of money to rebuild the team. This seemed acceptable to most of the fans, although I was as reluctant as the Hateley fans when we decided to contact AC Milan, who had been the most persistent with their inquiries. A meeting to discuss the probable transfer was arranged for London. I went with the chairman to meet two representatives of the Italian club. It was convenient because we had to be in London to appear before a transfer tribunal, who were to fix a fee for Billy Gilbert, a central defender I was trying to take from Crystal Palace. It was good that we could announce that day to the supporters that we had managed to secure his transfer.

We stayed the night in London so that we were on hand to meet the Milanese. We went to an Italian restaurant. It probably made them feel at home. I sat downstairs and left the negotiating to the chairman, but as he left me I kept insisting that he must make sure that the price was £1 million and not a penny less should be considered. I told him I would eat downstairs but he knew where I was should he need me. Twenty minutes later he came shuffling down to me. It was the first of a series of low-grade shuttle runs from him. They had offered him £750,000 and I simply said absolutely, positively not. He returned and was soon back again – so try £850,000. The look on my face told him that was not a goer, either, so off he went. Hardly a minute had elapsed when down the stairs came a Milan official in the most crumpled suit I had ever seen, accompanied by an interpreter.

Crumpled Suit, I cannot remember his name, sat down beside the interpreter, who told me that they could not understand why the chairman kept leaving the table to go downstairs to consult me. I chose my words carefully, saying: 'Yes, I'm his new manager. I have had the job for no more than a week and I am losing my best player.'

In the back of my mind was the knowledge that they had taken Luther Blissett from Watford earlier and it had turned out to be a mistake. He had been poor and had cost them plenty of money. I knew they had been as disappointed as Luther that it hadn't worked out, so I almost challenged them: 'Ask me about Hateley.' I had in mind a lesson from my dad when I asked the question. Tell them the truth, he always said, because you might want to do deals with them again. Tell them the strengths and the weaknesses and they will recognize the honesty.

I told them: 'In my opinion he is streets better than Blissett who, I know, has not been successful with you. If you are looking for a lad who is quick, likes balls delivered over the top, is brave and has a great left foot but an ordinary right foot, scores goals, is terrific in the air competing for balls and meeting crosses, then he's your man. If you are looking for a lad to play with his back to goal, to link up with everyone else, then forget him.'

I could tell Crumpled Suit was impressed with this forthright approach. The interpreter said something about looking for a player who was quick on the left side and could get on the end of things and then they were gone, back up the stairs.

As I sat contemplating the state of play the chairman was back again within minutes. He said we were nearly there. They were talking £950,000 so I suggested he went back, and nudged them up the extra £50,000, then we could be all done and I could get some rest because I had work to do and other players to talk to next morning including, of course, Hateley. He was clearly excited by the prospect of playing in Italy, which was to become a fulfilling place for British players. Everything would surely be sealed without a hitch, but Mark had a problem. He needed an extra £50,000 to buy his Midland home outright and wanted the money to be put on top of his transfer or he would not sign.

AC Milan, with the player just about secure, quibbled no further and the deal went through. As an introduction to management it was in the league of further and higher education and we had still to kick a ball in the new season that was about to start. All the paperwork was done and the Portsmouth supporters accepted the situation. I suspect there was an air of inevitability about the transfer in that it would have been a struggle to hang on to such a blossoming talent.

Although we were losing a striker, a proven goal scorer, my first priority was a centre half. I sat down with Derek Healey and we went through all the pros and cons of his reports and those that had come in from others.

We plumped for Noel Blake from Birmingham and landed him for £150,000, which was roughly the amount it took to obtain Billy Gilbert. Before that I had signed Mickey Baxter from Preston on a free transfer with the original plan to play him alongside Gilbert. I also brought in Mick Kennedy from Middlesbrough for £90,000, so that Gilbert, Baxter and Kennedy were in before Blake.

The need to go for Blake became apparent as we prepared for the opening pre-season friendly at Salisbury. Throughout the training Baxter had done well. He was six feet two inches, had a decent touch on the ball and looked immaculately fit. I could not understand, and nor could he, why he was so desperately tired after every training session. He was the perfect professional with a delightful wife and two lovely children. He was from a footballing family and did all the right things. He trained as hard as he could but it was obvious that he was in trouble so a day or two before the Salisbury game I suggested he get himself checked out by the doctor.

Within half an hour of being in the surgery the doctor was on to me telling me that Mickey's condition was potentially serious and that he needed to take some tests. He had them straightaway and it was not long before we heard the dreadful news. He had cancer. I told his mate, Kennedy, first and then had all the players in a room. Kennedy was still in a state of shock as I told the rest of the squad. They stood there in silence. Their thoughts, their hearts, went out to the big man who stood for all that was decent in the game. I told them, look, we've got a game to play so let's go and win it for Mickey. We won 2–1 but the match was a non-event as far as we were concerned.

After telling the players I went to see the chairman. He had his critics over the years but he handled this situation perfectly and said that Baxter was one of us and the club would do whatever possible to help him. We realized that in all probability he would never play football for us again and that the insurance was nothing compared to a life. Deacon paid him all the way through his contract but he never kicked a ball for us again. Mickey eventually went back to Preston North End and did some marvellous work with their youth and football in the community schemes.

Without the clearly stricken Baxter, the chairman released the funds to bring in Blake and he and Gilbert became my central defenders. Their behavioural records caught me cold. I knew I was getting two hardened, experienced pros, but my own novice status as a manager jumped up to bite me when I realized they were both suspended for the start of the season. They had both been rascals on and off the field too with their previous clubs.

I felt I had pulled a decent squad together for the 1984–5 season, with Alan Knight in goal, and then there was Gary Stanley, Paul Hardyman, Neil Webb, Mickey Tait (who went on to manage Darlington), Scott Mc-Garvey from Manchester United and Blake and Gilbert. We needed to get off to a good start and it happened. There were 13,000 inside Fratton Park for the first match. We won 1–0 with a goal from Alan Biley. I was on my way. A run developed as we drew one-apiece at Oxford, drew 0–0 at home to Barnsley, went to Leeds and Birmingham and won both matches 1–0. We beat Shrewsbury 3–0 at home, drew 2–2 at Charlton, beat Sheffield United at home 2–1, won 2–1 away to Cardiff, beat Grimsby 3–2 at Fratton and then lost 3–2 at Wimbledon. It had been a ten-match unbeaten start. I could hardly have asked for more in my first stint as a manager.

We were top of the Second Division after the Grimsby match and were still there at the beginning of December. Everybody was happy. The Pompey Chimes were ringing out and it seemed we were going places. Confidence had been in short supply in the boardroom but our success was making things happen. I bought Vince Hilaire from Luton and David Bamber from Walsall. Kevin O'Callaghan came in from Ipswich and we were able to reject a £250,000 bid for Webb from Queens Park Rangers. Thankfully, Webby didn't fancy the move anyway. We signed Paul Sugrue on a free transfer and Ivan Golac came from Southampton in January. I had made any number of changes but everything was working and towards the end of March we were lying second and a hot tip for promotion to the top flight.

We were lying third when Manchester City came to visit us on 27 April, right at the end of the season with the top three to be promoted. It was then that I made one of the biggest mistakes of my managerial career, leading to the 2–1 defeat that prevented us from going up. At 1–1, I had ordered everyone forward, going for the win when we should have consolidated. If it had stayed like that we would have been celebrating not long after, because although we won our three remaining matches so did Manchester City, and we were beaten to the third promotion spot by City on goal difference. After winning 2–0 at Huddersfield on the final day, City won 5–1 at home to Charlton, who fielded an inexperienced youngster in goal. We sold Neil Webb to Forest for £250,000 at the end of the season and he went on to win twenty-six England caps before injury took its toll.

Losing out on promotion was a huge disappointment, of course, and in a sense I blamed myself, but once I had calmed down and looked at things objectively I was prepared to tell myself that overall it had been a good first season. We had given the crowd plenty to shout about, the situation was looking healthy and I had the summer to plan the strategy that would take us just that one, vital step further.

There had been a lot of changes made, I had sold our best player, Hateley, but everything around the place shone with promise. To that we added a burnished smile when Mick Channon, my old Southampton sparring partner, race-goer and scorer came to join us at the start of the 1985–6 season.

He knew he was joining a great set of lads. When I say the likes of Kennedy, Gilbert, Blake and many more of them were mongrels, I do so in a complimentary way. Nobody liked playing against them and they had reputations that suggested they would be difficult to manage, but I put into practice all I had learned from Lawrie McMenemy, who knew just how to handle the truculent, the mean, the mischievous, the skivers (not that I had any) and those who inhabit every dressing room and seem unable to do right for doing wrong.

I had an enthusiastic mixture of people and outlooks. Alan Knight, the goalkeeper who is still at the club and was on the bench at Aston Villa as substitute in January 2004 at the age of forty-two, was a model professional. Kenny Swain had played under Brian Clough at Nottingham Forest, which meant he was a creature of good habits. Paul Hardyman, who had been at the club as a kid, went on to play for the England Under-23 side.

Kevin Dillon was the original one-man awkward squad. We had a love-hate relationship, but there was always a lot of respect for each other. He was an oddball. I would remark that he was looking happy and he would reply: 'Yeah, I'm always happy when I'm sad.'

I remember talking to him after a cup tie at Blackburn during which he had scored a goal that would have made David Beckham proud. It was, indeed, reminiscent of the goal Beckham scored against Crystal Palace at Selhurst Park when he beat Neil Sullivan from fifty yards. Dillon's wasn't lobbing. It was a half-volley from the halfway line that was still rising as it entered the net to win us the tie. Afterwards I congratulated him on a fantastic goal and asked him what he was thinking when he went for the shot.

He said: 'I saw your face on the ball and hit it as hard as I could.'

Whether it was despite our peculiar relationship or because of it I have no idea, but I must say he played some tremendous football for me. We were getting even stronger as a team.

Nobody fancied playing against Gilbert and Blake, whose mere presence on the team sheet was intimidating enough and when we went forward we had width with Vince Hilaire, who had won Under-21 and England B caps with Crystal Palace, on the right, and Kevin O'Callaghan, a Republic of Ireland international, on the left. Vince loved the Portsmouth area so much that he still lives there. He seemed to light up the game every week. Through the middle I had Mick Channon and Nicky Morgan, who came from West Ham. Young lads such as Lee Sandford and Paul Wood, who had been at the club as youths, began to push for regular places in the side.

It was looking like another fantastic season and I had the feeling that we would make it this time. Everything about the place, on the pitch and in the financial ledgers, was looking healthy. I was being given time to do the job properly and that is the secret of management in a football club. You have to be given time. I knew I had the basis but I was forever looking round, wondering how I could change things for the better. Even though we were playing good, entertaining football the search for improvement was never ending. I had to accept that Morgan and Channon were not getting the goals that our approach play warranted. In twenty-eight appearances Morgan had scored fifteen but my old mate Mick managed just six goals in thirty-four matches and neither of us needed to say anything. We knew he was coming to the end of his career so I went for a big buy; someone who I reckoned could increase our scoring output.

I had been watching a lad called Mick Quinn play for Oldham and he had usually impressed me. He was a boisterous player with an eye for the goal. I signed him from Joe Royle for £150,000 and he made his debut against Barnsley on 8 March, perfect for the run-in. He got me six goals in eleven games but the season, though successful by most people's standards, was to end in disappointment. We were in second place until 19 April and looked to be going strong. Losing at Stoke was a blow and though we drew at Sheffield United and beat Bradford City 4–0, we somehow managed to drop to fourth. We lost it at Stoke really. For all that my planning was on course because the accepted philosophy of a manager taking over a club is that the first year is for sorting everything out, the second year is to make your moves and the third year is the one for achieving your aim.

Quinn's arrival came after I rejected the offer of a £25,000 bung for another player. This lad had been playing for us on loan and had done quite well. Mr Deacon called me into the old boardroom with its roaring fire and said he had agreed a £75,000 fee with the player's agent. I just said: 'Mr Chairman, I don't wish to take him.'

The agent suggested we have a talk outside. He said my chairman was happy, he was happy, the player was happy and there was £25,000 for me. It was the first time I had encountered agents. I turned it down. My heart was set on Quinny.

The summer of 1986 was a time for contemplation and looking forward but there was a frightening family crisis that took my mind off things. It was a Monday night in July 1986. Usually Mondays in summer meant an evening at Windsor races, but for some reason I decided to stay at home and was signing some cards for the club shop. Missing my Monday racing was out of character. It had nothing to do with the fact that Mandy, who was eighteen, had been unwell, and that Lesley had taken her to the doctor that morning. She was worried that, as Mandy had become a vegetarian, she might not be getting enough nutrition.

The doctor concluded that she had a virus and suggested that if we gave her some aspirin and put her to bed she would be all right. We did all that but she was sick and in view of what happened subsequently it was as well that her stomach rejected the supposed remedy. Her illness became progressively worse and when her friend came round to see her she was unable to get out of bed. This was not like Mandy, who had also gone desperately pale. She managed to come downstairs to say goodbye to her friend, and as she was going back to bed, Lesley promised to come upstairs and see her in a couple of minutes.

She had hardly disappeared when we heard a bang. We knew instantly that something was wrong. Lesley dashed upstairs and shouted for me to follow. Mandy was in a collapsed state, half on and half off the lavatory. She was bleeding down below. She wasn't breathing, and her pupils had gone right back into her head. We knew we had to give her mouth-to-mouth resuscitation. I could not get her mouth open. Her teeth were clenched. In our panic we didn't realize that we could have done it through her nose. I managed to force her mouth open and she bit all my fingers but that didn't matter because we got her breathing again. Lesley had telephoned for the ambulance.

We tried to get her into the bedroom but the bleeding was profuse. We managed to move her to the landing and suddenly she went rigid. Once again we gave her the kiss of life and she started breathing. By this time the ambulance had arrived but Max, our Alsatian, would initially not allow the medics in. It was a horrible, frightening and worrying experience.

Eventually we moved Max out of the way and the ambulance men wrapped Mandy in red blankets and carried her out. There was blood everywhere. We travelled behind the ambulance in the car and more drama was waiting at the hospital. Only junior doctors were there and they could do little other than tell us that she had lost half the blood in her body. Lesley was screaming for action. I was arguing and shouting at everyone within earshot. We signed all sorts of forms. We were convinced there was no blood in her legs. That may have been in our imaginations. It was clear, though, that the people on duty hadn't a clue what to do.

Eventually one of the nurses got through to me, telling

me to calm down. They had phoned for the duty surgeon and he was on his way. It turned out that he was the top man in this particularly mysterious field. Nobody could be sure of the problem at first other than the fact that she needed a blood transfusion, having lost so much blood. In her anaemic state they could not find an artery in her arm. They were forced to go in through her jugular and give her the blood that way.

She was stabilized in the operating theatre and then the problem was revealed under the scrutiny of the radiologist. It transpired that her umbilical cord (this has no blood supply and normally withers and dies after birth) had for some inexplicable reason attached itself to the wall of her bowel and filled up over the years with a corrosive fluid. Eventually it had to give way or burst and suddenly the blood vessels had broken under the pressure. She was operated on and, thankfully, has had no problems in that area since.

At times like this, and bearing in mind Mandy's other fight with breast cancer and Lesley's ongoing battle with her own illness, football seems a triviality.

It was soon back to business, though, and after a summer of even more careful planning it was time to try again. I had agreed with Mick Channon retiring and brought in Paul Mariner, another England international, on a free transfer. He formed an instant understanding with Quinn and things looked good once again. Now we had to get up there, among the Manchester Uniteds, the Arsenals and the Liverpools. Both strikers benefited from the service supplied from the flanks by Hilaire and

O'Callaghan. We went top on 11 October with a 2–0 win over Birmingham City, with Quinn getting both of them.

We won a succession of matches to hold top position and I began to get the certain feeling that this time it was for real. We stayed on top of the Second Division right until close to the end of the season, when we had a couple of hiccups in an otherwise flawless run and finished second to send Pompey into the First Division. Mick Quinn had been absolutely superb. Not only was he a character in the dressing room, full of the almost adolescent humour that the environment provokes, but also he was a leader in every sense of the word, providing twenty-eight goals in thirty-nine games. We were very much a one-for-all, all-for-one team, and had played enough good football to deserve our place. The irony for Joe Royle, the man who sold me Quinn, was that Oldham finished three points behind us in third place.

We were such a together bunch. The players called themselves the Gremlins because I had plucked them from all over the place, put my faith in them. They appreciated that, I believe, because most of them came with the baggage of disciplinary records and bad reputations. We happened to be the right people in the right place at the right time. Portsmouth can be a tough town. They expect you to fancy a scrap. No room in Pompey for your fancy Dans. It was a proper man's club. I told them all what I expected of them and the chairman allowed me to get on with it. I was able to sell Neil Webb as well as Hateley to fund my recruitment drive.

They both went expressing how much they had enjoyed their time working with me, which was good to hear.

All the time Derek Healey was unearthing gems. He was marvellous at spotting talent, and then there was another fellow, Kevin Leahy, who to this day I call Tonto. His range did not stretch much beyond Basingstoke, but he was in a class of his own, bringing kids to the club's School of Excellence and coaching them himself. Wherever I have been Tonto has been by my side. I brought in Peter Osgood to join the coaching staff. He loved the game with a passion and had a charisma about him that everybody appreciated. Graham Paddon came back to be by my side. We all made sure we put plenty of time in at the School of Excellence, myself, Ossie, Graham and Kevin, because we all saw youth as the foundation of the future. We worked our socks off imparting our knowledge to kids who were hungry to hear. Their thirst for learning was the rewarding element that drove us on with them, although no youngster was ever pushed too hard.

The first teamers were all fighters and the marriage we had was understandable. Most of them had been let go in their twenties and felt they had something left to prove. I was as desperate as them to prove myself on the managerial side. It was a combustible arrangement to say the least. There were many fiery incidents and several that tickled me. They bonded well and socialized together, but nothing was ever predictable.

When I went into the office on a Monday morning I never knew who was going to come through the door. It could be a policeman, an irate husband, a tax inspector or a bookie's representative looking for unpaid bets. Much of our fun in training was at a place called Money Fields, which we leased. It wasn't the best of training facilities, but I had the groundsman cut a special square of grass, like a cricket square. I called it Wembley and it was there, on Thursdays, that we used to play our short-passing, one-touch football. Those whose feet weren't the best hated it, but it provided valuable practice in the basic skills as well as creating its share of humour.

I'll never forget the day I came in and gave the order, Money Fields one to six please. There was a communal groan. One to six meant run a pitch length, and then walk one. Then run two pitch lengths and walk one and then run 300 yards up to 600 yards. They were still moaning when they started and as they ran I was puzzled why this group of twenty players happened to be running so close together. They had done about three runs and as I looked closer I could see a pair of feet dangling, not touching the ground as the pack ran on. I quickly realized it was Billy Gilbert who had come in so pissed that they were carrying him. Just as they thought they had finished, having got away with it, I ordered them to do the reverse, six down to one, which was most unusual.

I walked away and just kept glancing at them. They were still carrying him. It was simply unbelievable but it left me with a kind of admiration for the team spirit that was being shown. When they had finished I just said: 'Right, six stretches, please, and a stretcher for you, Billy Gilbert, and thank your lucky stars that you have got some good pals here.' I knew I was on the right lines with them if they were prepared to carry a teammate to that extent.

We had some fascinating escapades. Quinn, for instance. We lost him to three weeks in prison for driving when disqualified. He was only half a mile from home, he told me, and his wife, who was heavily pregnant, was not feeling well so he said he would drive the rest of the way. He swore somebody must have shopped him and called the police, who were soon pulling him over. It must have been a long three weeks for him in Winchester jail but when he came out we had a fabulous party. It may not have been the politically correct thing to do, but we loved the big fellow and all his daftness.

There was an unforgettable day when we had just started training and two police cars arrived. The police said they were taking Clive Whitehead, who had joined us from West Brom. They bundled him into one of the cars and took him to the station. As he pleaded his innocence they said it had been reported that he had driven to training. He was a Quinn lookalike, but as soon as it was pointed out that the real Quinn was doing his porridge they realized their mistake and brought him back to training. It did not end there. The lads, being incorrigible rascals, had a photograph of Quinny copied and made into masks so that they were all driving around Portsmouth as Quinn's doubles. The police were not amused, but it tickled the players and me no end.

I was always devising ways of winding up the players; tricks to get them at it. A league cup tie at Wrexham springs to mind. We went two up and were playing well when suddenly we became unusually sloppy. I barked at them but it didn't seem to make a lot of difference, so I left the dug-out and started walking down the track so that they could see me go. I was saying that we would concede a goal, making it harder for ourselves in the return leg.

As I walked down the tunnel with time just about up I heard a roar. Sure enough, Wrexham had scored with a penalty. As our lads entered the dressing room I blew my top. I was ballistic. I ranted: 'You cannot be pros, can you? I could see it all coming, getting sloppy, foot off the pedal, jack the lads, two–nil away from home against a team from two divisions lower. You are not learning enough. I am fed up. How many more times?' A voice piped up saying they had won 2–1 and would murder Wrexham back at our place.

I told them it should have been 2–0. They could have no excuses and there would be a surprise for them the following day. We stayed the night in Wrexham and as we set off in the morning I told the coach driver to go straight to Fratton Park, dropping nobody off no matter where they had left their cars when we picked them up on the way to north Wales. I was stewing inside. I'd decided I would nip any complacency, the maker of sloppiness, in the bud.

Mariner was the first who expected to be dropped off but I told the driver to keep going and informed Mariner and everyone else that we were all going back to our own ground whether they liked it or not, so sit down.

I got them all in the dressing room when we arrived and told them we were going to have a chat about their unprofessional attitude. I told them how unhappy I was and then I switched and said: 'There's a board meeting going on down there. I am not getting anywhere with you, and things aren't improving. I am going in there and then I am off. I am resigning.' I honestly thought I had taken them as far as I could.

With that I picked up my overnight bag, walked out and slammed the door. As I was halfway down the corridor I suddenly realized it wasn't my bag. Now I had to return without losing face to collect my own. I opened the door knowing exactly where my bag was, about five yards inside, but I hardly had a foot inside the room when they all gave a collective roar of laughter.

I just stood there and could not help laughing. I gave them another burst about how they were frustrating me. I said: 'You do my head in, you lot. I am sorry, but you know what I mean.' They said they did and I told them to forget about the resignation and the board meeting but that we had to work together to get it right.

It was indicative of the kind of relationship I had with them. We pulled together because we were moulded from the same metal. There was a togetherness that was always going to hold out under pressure even if they could be seen as a bunch of rogues and vagabonds.

They fought for me. They went in where it hurt and won matches. They were lads who had come together with like minds and a sense of fun. They could be frustrating at times but I grew to love them all with all their idiosyncrasies.

In an effort to root out occasional pockets of bad behaviour among the crowds, the police began to put plain-clothes officers at the bottom end of Fratton Park. A good idea. We had no objection because it could only be good news if it rooted out the occasional racist or foul chant that had become too prevalent in modern football. We never realized that an element of guilt would be laid at our own dressing-room door. We came in after a win and there was a knock on the dressing-room door.

I went to answer it and there was a uniformed officer saying he would like to interview Quinn and Wood as there had been allegations of foul language on the pitch. I asked Quinny if he had been using what is euphemistically called industrial language and he gave me the answer I expected: 'Doesn't everybody?'

Well, the police officer took them down to the interview room and I decided to go with them to keep a paternal eye on things. The copper seemed a decent chap and he said to Quinny: 'Before we start, Mr Quinn, have you got a police record?'

The reply had me in creases. He answered in that rich Scouse accent: 'Yes. Walking on the Moon,' which of course had been a hit for the band Police. The policeman smiled and they were let off with a caution. It was just another episode with a terrific bunch of lads.

Although I had learned much from observing Lawrie McMenemy and Bobby Campbell and the way they confronted problems or handled difficult situations I had my own set of rules. I had been disappointed in myself during that brief spell at Blackpool, the job that had come too soon for me.

I adopted the third person to deliver my mantra as I told the players my rules, which I wanted them to know from the outset rather than have them find out for themselves. I was firm, precise and unwavering as I told every group of players who were in my charge: 'If you want to stay in an Alan Ball squad of players and if you want to stay in an Alan Ball team, Alan Ball likes people who give everything they've possibly got for the cause. Alan Ball likes people who work hard at their training, work hard at their football and work hard on the pitch. Alan Ball can accept poor performances from a trier; Alan Ball will accept things going wrong because he has been there himself. Alan Ball can accept defeats. Alan Ball has been beaten but Alan Ball, when he played, never gave less than 100 per cent.

'To me, that is an easy way to stay in an Alan Ball team. I won't accept anything less than that. I have been a person who has been first to the bar and last to leave the bar – at the right time. I have been caught speeding in cars and can understand that. What I can't accept is people not being 100 per cent honest in everything they do. They can fail trying. They can be wrong but honest. If they adhere to those rules they will get on fine with Alan Ball.'

There was a little of Lawrie McMenemy in that but basically it was my own mission statement. I hadn't been an angel during my playing career. I had been on the odd bender with the lads and I had been on the wrong end of many a curfew. I told them there wasn't another trick left in the book that I hadn't worked. Been there, done it and seen it, I told them, so there would never be any point in trying to pull the wool over my eyes. I told them that if they followed my rules everything would be fine.

Cross me, I warned, and you will find you have big problems. I had given them fair measure of my tolerance levels and I also made it clear that I would not keep unhappy players at the club. I had been sold when I didn't want to go and sold when I was anxious to get away so I was experienced in that area as well.

They were the ground rules I had laid down from the very beginning, but it was not a speech that I had delivered at Blackpool. It was after that unfortunate episode that I sat back and had a whole rethink about how I would handle management if I was given another opportunity. I grew up very quickly as Portsmouth's boss and I have to say that the players grew impressively and loyally, too.

The first two seasons were an emotional roller-coaster ride. We were knocking at the promotion door all the time, only to find it firmly shut in our faces. The third time they let us in. All the time I was learning, gaining experience, though initially it all happened very quickly. I had to learn the nuances and intricacies of buying and selling, handling the press, making sure that the supporters were informed about what was happening at the club. I tried to become a fully rounded, complete manager, and to arrive at that situation you have to have lived through the highs and the lows that are the weekly diet of any professional football team.

Nobody let me down. If we lost, we went down fighting. I had players sent off and they would probably agree to this day that, by and large, they were a collection of lovable rascals. I handled them the way I thought was best. They knew I was on their side. It was important that I was the last person to see Quinn before he went down, and equally important that I was the first person to greet him on his release. Lesley made a point of visiting when he was inside as if to emphasize the family spirit that existed.

When there were sacrifices to be made it was imperative that the manager be part of the perceived hardship. That was something I learned from my dad, as well as another of his nuggets of wisdom that said a manager's best friends were his chairman and his secretary. He also stressed the importance of a good physiotherapist, arguing that you would not expect men to go into battle without good back-up. I insisted that we had the best available physio so that any player putting his foot in and getting hurt would know that the man running on to treat him would not be a clown.

I recruited John Dickens and he was superb. Injuries decreased and players got back to full fitness with excellent recovery times.

I was fortunate in that, apart from the knowledge I had gained from Lawrie and my dad, I also had some good friends outside the game whose sheer common-sense approach to everything helped me make decisions that applied to the game.

Barry Taylor and his wife Wendy lived at Marwell Manor. I met him when I first played for Portsmouth, and he was managing director of Olympus Cameras at that time. While the chairman was very good and ticked most things in my first three years, Barry would help me if I had a problem that needed solving. He also helped calm me down. I remember going to him one day, saying how I badly needed new players.

I was saying Pompey couldn't play and I needed new players in just about every position. He asked me who I wanted as my goalkeeper and I said Shilton and Banks and people of that calibre. Barry gently pointed out that they were either not available or too old and that I had Alan Knight anyway. He went through the Pompey team, listing each player, and by the time he had finished I had grasped his logic and was no longer talking at wild tangents. He was the sensible, wise old head that I needed and I turned to him quite a lot.

I was not good at handling setbacks. If we lost, Saturday night was a write-off. Perhaps I should never have gone home on those occasions, as I usually inflicted my misery on Lesley. On the other hand, winning points would have me euphoric and eager for a wild night out with Lesley and our friends. My head was usually clear of those celebrated twin impostors, misery and despair, by Monday morning. Either state was between the final whistle on a Saturday and training two days later. I was totally possessed by the state of the team, the rate of progress and the performances of individuals to the point where the family came about tenth in my order of priorities rather than second. Football had become the all–consuming number one and I know now that this was wrong. I also knew at the time that success was all the family wanted from me.

That came with promotion, but it was a nail–biting end to the 1986–7 season when Joe Royle took his Oldham Athletic team to Shrewsbury Town needing the win that would have pipped us on goal difference. They would have been promoted with Derby County, who were already crowned champions. We should have clinched it earlier ourselves with a draw at Crystal Palace in our last away match of the season, which would have put our points totally out of Oldham's reach.

It would have clinched Pompey's return to the top flight twenty-eight years after being relegated with the lowest points total in the club's rich history. The fans were beginning to celebrate at 1–1, but they should have known better after the near-misses of the previous two seasons. As the match entered the last five minutes I had an awful fear of foreboding and sure enough, Palace's seventeen-year-old substitute John Salako knocked the ball across the six-yard line and there was Ian Wright to sweep in the winner. To add to the agony of waiting for the final matches of the season to unfold, Paul Mariner had what appeared to be a perfectly good goal disallowed.

Our destiny was still in our own hands with Sheffield United due at Fratton Park. Twenty-four hours after the Palace defeat Oldham had that trip to Shrewsbury.

That was going to be a key game. John Deacon went to see the show *Les Miserables*, and I went to Kempton Park's evening race meeting while the Shrewsbury–Oldham match was being played out so many miles to the north on that quaint old ground by the River Severn, Gay Meadow. There was absolutely no way that I was going to stay in the house that night. At the races, my friend Neil Wilkins had champagne on the bar but I vowed not to touch a drop and asked someone, anyone, to please try and get the score from Shrewsbury.

A man next to me was trying to pick my brains about the favourite in the next race but my mind was elsewhere. Neil came back and said the words, 'Shrewsbury 2, Oldham 0', and went for the champagne. 'No, no,' I said, 'it's only half-time.' The race meeting was coming to an end and eventually I set off for home knowing that the second half was being played. The radio was not giving out results and there were no mobile phones in those days, so I was driving down the M3 just wishing and hoping and occasionally thinking that perhaps we had flunked it again.

I turned off the motorway and made my way home, and then I saw the happy, smiling faces. The kids and the neighbours were jumping about under a banner that said BALLS UP!

We had an outrageous party. I rang the chairman and he said: 'Young man, I am the happiest person in the world. Come round to the house now.' We did, Lesley and I, arriving around midnight. He had just arrived home from the show and was smiling in a way

I had never seen before as he opened a bottle of champagne.

He said he would like to give me a present for all that had been achieved. He went on about how much I deserved to be rewarded and said that I should spend up to £25,000 on whatever alterations we needed to make to the house and to send the bill to his building company. I thanked him and then he asked Lesley what make of car she was driving and she said it was a Metro. Did she like it? Yes, of course she did, so he told her a new one would be hers and he would foot the bill. He asked us where we were going on holiday and when we said we were going to a friend's apartment in Florida he said he would pay for the flight tickets for the five of us, Lesley, me, Keely, Mandy and Jimmy.

The fare came to around £1,100 and that was the only thing he did pay for in real terms. Yes, Lesley was provided with a new car that was in the club's name. She had not had it very long when she received a phone call from the club saying that they were coming to collect the car because they needed it for a basketball player who was with the club the chairman had just bought. When Lesley protested his secretary told her: 'Mr Deacon says it's our car and we are coming to get it.' As for the house renovations, nothing.

It may have been that the purchase of the basketball club was the beginning of the financial problems that eventually became too much for Deacon. To be fair, he had tried to do his best for the club and me as manager. He gave me a three-year contract and allowed me to bring in John Kerr, a talented American boy. I took Ian Stewart and Mick Fillery from QPR on free transfers. The chairman sanctioned the buying of Terry Connor from Brighton for £200,000, Ian Baird from Leeds for £250,000 and Barry Horne for £60,000. He went on to be sold for £3.4 million.

I had changed the face of the team with seven new signings over a short period for around £600,000, but I also brought money in by selling Kevin O'Callaghan to Millwall, where he had started his career, for £100,000, while Mick Tait went to Rotherham for £30,000. Sadly a bad pre-season injury to Noel Blake meant that I had to bring in Malcolm Shotton from Oxford United for £70,000.

We got off to a poor start the next season and everything started to go downhill very quickly. I had a friend, Jim Sloan, who kept me informed of everything that went on in the boardroom. We were third from bottom in early January when the chairman put his question, or rather a statement that had a questionable ring, to me.

In hindsight it was a funny scene because he just said, with no preamble: 'I'm going to need £645,000 pdq.'

I had to ask what pdq meant and his son, David, piped up 'pretty damned quickly'. At this point everything turned against the future of Portsmouth FC as I asked for a reason. They hit me with a thunderball. They had received a winding-up order from the Inland Revenue and that amount of money was required almost instantly. They said I would have to sell some players. I was upset because I knew that the basketball team was draining what meagre resources the club possessed while I was within my budget.

I must be fair here and say that whatever faults people may have found with John Deacon his heart was with Portsmouth FC because he was always putting his hand in his pocket, loaning the club money. Instead of consolidating the football side, however, making sure it was on a level financial footing, he mistakenly decided that the city deserved a top basketball team.

He imported several American players on inflated salaries, all of which put a drain on the football side, and it all came to a head that January. I had to sell Kennedy to Bradford City for £250,000. Now Deacon was looking for another £400,000. I sold Baird back to Leeds for a cut price £185,000 so I lost two key players. As the club's history of that season said in summary: 'Collective belief in the club's ambition was shattered.'

We were struggling. You can always look back over a season and nominate the 'what ifs'. What if Kevin Dillon hadn't missed two crucial penalties? What if . . .? and so it went on as we were relegated after just one season among the elite. We went down third bottom of the First Division amid rumours of an imminent buy-out of the club. The strain of it all had finally taken its toll on Deacon. He was getting on in years and had handed much of his property business over to his son.

The rumours would not go away and as much as Deacon denied it, the constant theme was that Jim Gregory, who was a London garage owner and regarded as something of a hard man, was looking to take over. He had owned Queens Park Rangers but a heart attack had compelled him to sell the club. He was clearly well enough to be considering buying a new club. I still had time to reflect on the season that had just passed as I prepared to go on holiday.

There had been some highs, like remaining unbeaten against Southampton, which gave the fans bragging rights that they enjoyed to the full. Against such moments there was the frustrating business of having to work with my hands tied by financial constraints.

We received our good hidings, losing by six goals at Highbury, but there was always effort and team spirit until the possible effects of the winding-up order began to invade the players' minds. Negative thoughts crept in no matter how we tried to protect the players. I looked at that stupid basketball team's existence with little more than contempt. I had no quarrel with the players and their right to be there, but Deacon might just as well have opened his windows and thrown the money out into the street.

At least a little might have blown back. I felt as much for the supporters as anyone and that includes myself. They had been down to the Fourth Division with Portsmouth but they had battled back up. We should have been consolidating during our year in the First Division. Young players like Anderton were maturing to the point where you knew they would go on to have great careers.

I knew we were building for a brighter future until

211

the Yankee slam-dunkers came along and I was powerless to do anything about it. It was bad chairmanship on Deacon's part but I must stress that I thought the world of him. He allowed me to manage in my own way without interference; he was happy to go along with the kind of football I wanted the team to play and never questioned any of my motives. A lot of people disliked him because he came from Southampton, our big rivals, and some people didn't take to him perhaps out of misguided envy because he was ploughing huge amounts of money into Fratton Park – until, of course, his huge mistake with the funding of the basketball team. Few people could see any sense in that, especially as the football side began to suffer because we could not afford to bring in new players and had to sell established crowd pleasers.

After we had been relegated Deacon came to see me and asked me why I was looking sorry for myself. I told him: 'Chairman, you have made it hard for me since Christmas. I've just not been able to do it the way I wanted.' He listened sympathetically, but what could he do?

I went away on holiday and heard that Deacon had sold the club. His quote in the local paper that summer's day in 1988 was relayed to me. He had said something to the effect that if some of the supporters did not like him, 'just wait until you get the new guy'. Jim Gregory was on his way.

The fun days were clearly almost over. I say fun because there was never a dull moment when the director

Jim Sloan, the cheerful ex-matelot who kept me informed of boardroom matters, was around. He was a real supporter in every sense, an ex-navy man who lived his life to the full and no one was ever going to change that. When he travelled with the team he drank on the way to the game, on the way back and during the game. He was a phenomenal figure and could truly hold his drink. It only enhanced his capacity for mischief.

When we lost 6–0 at Arsenal it was my duty to go to the boardroom to exchange the usual pleasantries with those extremely proper people, the Hill-Woods and so on. They were directors of formality and etiquette. As an ex-Arsenal player I knew I had to face whatever was coming my way in the wake of such a heavy defeat. As I walked through the door I could see that Jim was well refreshed as he put his hand up and waved me over, calling out so everyone could hear: 'Here's my manager. Bally, come in son, I've won in here.'

The Arsenal directors loved it, although Ken Bates, the Chelsea chairman, was not so sure about Jim one day at Chelsea. As they walked into the boardroom, Jim said to the waiter so that Bates could not fail to hear: 'One wink for small, two winks for large.' He duly received a hefty looking whisky mac, downed it in one and turned the glass upside down, asking Bates where it had been made. It was his way of letting Bates know the glass was empty.

Jim knew all the old navy songs and kept the lads amused on long away trips by singing to them. One night in the Midlands, where we were staying overnight, the

213

players had gone to bed and Jim and I were just sitting there talking. Well, I was listening and he was doing the talking, spinning all these old navy stories. I was always fascinated with his yarns. No football talk, just fond reminiscences.

All of a sudden, just after midnight, a group of weirdly dressed young men came in and Jim, typically, asked them if they would like a drink. It turned out that they were the rock group Whitesnake. They had just finished a gig. I told Jim that I was off to bed as the lads would be up fairly early in the morning for a light run. Jim said not to worry; he fancied having a bit of fun with these lads and their roadies.

When I came down the next morning there were bodies lying all over the floor and chairs of the hotel foyer. Jim had wiped out Whitesnake and as I went in to breakfast he was sitting there, bright-eyed, saying: 'Morning, Mr Manager. Breakfast? Same again?'

On another occasion we stopped at Frimley Green for lunch on the way to a match in London when suddenly the police were in the hotel saying there had been an accident; they said the road was blocked and we should get under way, with an escort, as soon as possible. The police walkie-talkies were going off and everybody was present and ready to leave except Jim.

We had people scouring the bars but there was no sign of him. Then, poking through the trees, I spotted a marquee, which suggested there might be a wedding going on. I raced across and there was Jim shuffling to the front of the welcoming sherry queue. I shouted at him to get a move on as we were leaving. He grabbed one dry sherry and one sweet sherry and said he wasn't sure if he was with the bride or the groom.

The happy days were soon to end.

10

THE WOODEN CIGGY

Headlines everywhere told the world that Jim Gregory was taking over at Fratton Park in 1988. From the very beginning a second sense told me it was not a welcome appointment. He came in and was on the supporters' side straightaway when he started smartening up the ground. It was a cosmetic exercise, and as I went to see him for a first meeting at his business office at the top of the A3 I spotted something else that wasn't all it was supposed to be. I was shown upstairs and was sitting waiting when he came in. He thanked me for being there and said we'd have a chat about things, but there was no warmth. He was gruff and deadpan. He was smoking a cigarette, or so I thought until I looked a little closer. It was wooden with a glowing, red end to make it look real. It reminded me of those sweetie cigarettes you could buy as a kid, making imaginary puffs before you ate it. Here he was pretending to smoke. Perhaps he was trying to kick the habit and this thing was his crutch.

He went straight to the point. Bluntness, even rudeness, was his speciality. He announced that he was changing my job. I was no longer to be known as the manager but as chief coach. At that point I saw no advantage to be gained from arguing. I still had two years left on my contract. Then he said I had to change my staff. Graham Paddon was my right-hand man, Peter Osgood my youth team coach, Dave Hurst the youth development officer and Derek Healey chief scout. He told me to get rid of Ossie.

When I asked why, he said: 'I don't like him. You'll need to replace him. You need to drop Paddon to youth team coach and your new right-hand man will be John Gregory.'

He was no relation to the chairman but had played for him at Queens Park Rangers, and was a former Aston Villa midfielder who had played six times for England. He was thirty-four, had just finished playing and was totally inexperienced on the management side. I was having him foisted upon me.

I listened to my new chairman and told him I could not do as he asked. He puffed on his wooden ciggy and just said: 'It's up to you, son.'

I thought for a moment and said: 'Basically, what you are trying to say to me is that you are going to put your own man in next to me, who is eventually going to take my place, and you are asking me to sack one of my people because you don't like him. You know that I, being a loyal person, cannot accept that. You are hoping to get rid of all my lot and me very easily. You want me to walk away.'

He just said: 'Have it whichever way you want, son.'

I left that office boiling inside. I had wanted to talk to

him about the squad, where it needed strengthening, where we could cull players and what was needed to improve the situation, but it seemed like it was all about him bringing in his own people. I drove back in turmoil. I really was fuming that he could behave in such a cold, brutal way when people's careers were at stake.

I rang Ossie and Graham and told them I needed to speak to them. They knew I had been to see the chairman. Both suggested I had bad news to pass on. I told them, no, it's not bad news, its shocking news. We arranged to meet because I needed their input at this turn of events. I told them exactly what Gregory had said, Ossie out, Paddon demoted, John Gregory in. In my opinion, I said, there were two ways of tackling the situation. I could go back to him to try to negotiate settlements on our two-year contracts and we could all quit together, or Ossie could be sacrificed while Graham and I stayed to scrap it out to try to improve the situation.

Ossie stood tall that day. He said that Gregory would have disliked him because of the old Chelsea–QPR West London rivalry and that he would leave, but that Graham and I should fight on. I said we should be prepared to go en bloc, but Peter was positive and said he would go and just hoped that I would be prepared to negotiate a decent pay-off on his contract. I wanted to stay because I wanted to fight Gregory from day one. I had taken a dislike to him and for the first time in my life I despised someone from the very first meeting. I made some inquiries about him, and those who had worked beneath him could not come up with a kind word. Jim Smith, the 'Bald Eagle' who had been around the block a few times, just said, 'Good luck.'

Clearly, I was going to need it, but the fight that has always been part of my spirit took over. I rang Gregory back, put on my confident voice and said: 'I'm not going and neither is Paddon. Osgood will go but I want to make sure he gets his proper tax-free entitlement.' Gregory said there would be no problem with Ossie's money, but they made him wait month after month until the matter reached the steps of the courts before he was paid up.

There was misery all around, but I told the chairman that I wanted to get on with things even though Ossie had gone and Paddon had gone down to work with the kids. John Gregory made his appearance. It did not take a lot of working out to see what was going on.

The chairman was pushing me, making life uncomfortable, as if he was wanting me to crack so that he could put his man into the manager's job. I did not yield. I was learning more lessons. He used to say in that cynical manner of his: 'You've got to play games, son.' But he was playing his games with people's lives and careers.

I was given money to spend and signed the Sheffield Wednesday winger Mark Chamberlain for £200,000 and then, typically, Gregory did a deal without even consulting me when he told me he had bought a fullback, Warren Neill, from QPR. I told him I neither needed nor wanted a fullback either to play or to sit on the bench. It was typical of a man with a bulldozer mentality.

Then I bought Graham Hogg, a big centre half, from

219

Manchester United for £150,000. I was always aware of the need to balance the books and allowed Vince Hilaire to join Noel Blake at Leeds for £200,000. The buying and selling had been clean and businesslike, but I still fancied taking striker Warren Aspinall from Aston Villa. Jim Gregory was on his yacht in the south of France at the time. The new season had yet to start. The fee of £350,000 was a club record at the time.

I rang Gregory and told him what I had in mind. I listed Aspinall's plus points. He was a good young player, a regular goal scorer just creeping into the England set-up, and was a lad with a bright future. He sanctioned the deal, and told me to get on with it. I rang Graham Taylor, the Aston Villa manager, and we agreed to shake hands over the phone on the transfer. Straightaway I called Gregory on his boat to tell him the business was almost complete, and he just said there would be no deal and I was to cancel it.

I said: 'What do you mean, cancel it? I have just given my word over the phone after you had said it was OK to go ahead. Don't you dare. Don't even think about making me do that.'

He just said 'Cancel it' and put the phone down. I sat there with Lesley, perplexed. I did not know what to do. My word is my bond and now I was faced with calling Taylor and backing out of our agreement. I said to Lesley I just hoped that Graham would understand and realize that I was dealing with a chairman who was madly unpredictable. I was trying to compose the right things to say when the phone rang. It was Gregory again. He said: 'Hello, son, do the deal.'

I asked him what he was up to and he said: 'Playing games, son. You've got to learn to play games.' I told him I didn't fancy his games.

Aspinall was suspended for the first three games but we started like a train. We took ten points from the first twelve, beating Leeds 4–0 at home with Hilaire and Blake coming back, and we went to the top of the league. I went up to the boardroom and into Gregory's inner sanctum, where women were not allowed. It had been pleasantly refurbished and was a sort of boardroom within a boardroom. Everything was pukka. The champagne was always open on match days. The best of everything was available although I knew my relationship with the chairman was not right. It was deteriorating. That day I walked in and the Leeds chairman, Leslie Silver, came up to me and offered his congratulations, saying: 'Well done, young man. That's the way football should be played. It was a fantastic exhibition of how the game should be played even though we have been beaten 4–0.'

I nodded towards where Gregory was sitting and said something like 'You wouldn't think so looking at him.' He looked as if he was grinding his teeth, and here we were top of the league. His problem was that he wanted John Gregory to be running the show and it would be difficult to make that happen while we were at the top, although I was aware that with this particular chairman I should never be surprised at any turn of events. I still had the overwhelming belief that as soon as anything went wrong I would be out of the club.

John Gregory arrived, was given his own office and reported to the chairman every day. He appeared at training in his baseball cap and walked around the ground, watching everything I did from beginning to end, and I would see him writing things down. It was an unpleasant environment. He watched the youths, the reserves and the first team, but did nothing himself. He just watched. That, presumably, was his brief from above. I used to openly call him 'the vulture' in front of the players. I would say: 'The vulture is here. He's your next manager.' He just took it on board. He was hard faced, never batted an eye when I came out with such a thing. He did not want to take a session, nor did I want him among the players. He knew he just needed to bide his time and Jim Gregory would have him working in my place.

I gave him a torrid time and I made a point of telling Jim Gregory that I knew exactly what was going on. I knew I was making things hard for myself but I was honest with the players. I told them that if they wanted me as manager they had to win games because the two Gregorys were working to get me out.

Jim Gregory challenged me to a walking race outside the ground after one night match. He remarked that I was quite a fast walker and I agreed. He immediately said he was faster than me and we should race. Silly man didn't have a chance.

Around that time – and I don't think the events were connected – he brought in Ron Jones, a former international sprinter, as a public relations man. He was a lovely, decent individual, quite the opposite of the chairman. I was late getting up to the boardroom one particular night after probably spending too much time with the press. The main room was still busy but the only people in the inner sanctum were the chairman and Ron. I accepted a glass of champagne and the chairman barked: 'Jones, get your guitar.'

Ron produced the instrument and started strumming, and the chairman bizarrely told him to play something for me. He had just started to play when Gregory ordered him to sing. Jones, playing gently, started to sing softly, but Gregory jumped up, walked over and gave him a mighty slap across the face, shouting that didn't Jones know he did not like the song. Jones went down on one knee.

It was a flashpoint for me. I jumped up, pinned Gregory against the wall and told him: 'You are at it again. I want to smash you all around this place.' As I went at him I thought that he was trying to get me to strike him. If I did that I knew I would truly be gone.

I was fuming. I was shaking. I told Ron Jones that he should never accept such treatment and then I walked out. His chauffeur whispered to me: 'He's a bastard, that man.' As I made my way through the main boardroom Gregory's wife looked at me in a way that suggested she sympathized with the tough time I was having with this horrible person. I could tell from her face.

Still, the lads were doing well. I bought Martin Kuhl from Watford for £125,000 and we went on a run, taking seventeen points out of twenty-one to be top of the table after a 3−0 win over Barnsley on 19 November. We beat Brighton 2−0 to make it twenty points out of twenty-four, and promotion looked on the cards again. All the time, John Gregory was in the background ticking away at the politics, but my team were doing it for me. They were winning games for me.

By this time I had given Gregory the reserves to look after. He was having to use his own knowledge and it just wasn't happening. I drew no pleasure from the fact that they were losing almost every match. They were just not playing for him. But around the Christmas period events surrounding the first team took a downward turn.

We lost an FA Cup third-round tie against Swindon in a replay and with that result some of our confidence went. We had injuries, which meant I had to play Kit Symons, who was just seventeen, on his debut alongside another of Jim Gregory's signings, Gavin McGuire, whom he bought from QPR for £225,000. He was another I didn't necessarily want pushed on to me. We lost 2−1 at Leicester and deep down I realized that my time was up. We had lost three in a row and I knew Gregory would pounce on anything to get rid of me. We had been lying third on Boxing Day but that defeat at Leicester was the killer. Right after that match, when I felt as low as I had done in years, I received a telephone call to say that Mickey Baxter, who had been battling cancer, had died at Preston. His death put a lot of things in perspective.

I had brought in Paul Moran from Tottenham in an

attempt to shore things up, but I was on my way out of Portsmouth with the team lying ninth in the Second Division. It was a weekend of contemplation and heart-ache, although I was still the manager. Everyone knew the pressure was on but nothing was said. Then on Monday night, after I had gone to bed early, Lesley took a phone call from Florrie Gregory, the chairman's wife. It was unusually formal, no first name terms as was normal. It was hello, Mrs Ball, and is Mr Ball there? Lesley told her I was asleep so she just said that I was to see the chairman in his office at Alton House at 10 a.m. the following day. This put Lesley in a quandary. She didn't know whether to wake me, as that would have been to tell me that in all probability I was due for the sack the following morning. She waited until the morning and as I stirred, she just said that Jim wanted to see me. I had to drop her off somewhere on the way and as I did she told me that if anything dramatic happened I was to phone her immediately, because she did not want outsiders, reporters and so on ringing her up to say I'd got the sack.

No worries, I said half-heartedly. There was no way he could sack me, I thought, because we were lying ninth, and once I got all the players back from injury we would be off and running again. Lesley did not share my confidence.

I went up to his office and he made me wait again before he came in and just said: 'It's time to call it a day, son.'

My response was direct. I can remember exactly what I said. I went: 'OK, but I would just like to tell you something about yourself. What I have had to do and the way I have had to manage with all your messing about, and what you did to Peter Osgood at the start, is despicable. If you can live with yourself as a person after all the things you've done to me, there is something seriously wrong. I stayed here purposely to fight you, even though I knew you were just waiting. You have given the job to a fellow who hasn't got a clue, by the way, but if he is prepared to do your bidding as you want him to, then you deserve each other.

'Just make sure my money is correct. There are only eighteen months to go on the contract and I want the proper money and not in the way you messed Peter Osgood around. You've more money than anyone and you play games, as you put it. I don't want any games played with me, please.'

He just ground his teeth and played with his ridiculous wooden cigarette. 'All right, son,' he said, as if I might just have got through to him. I was livid. I was just holding my temper. I left the office and went back to the ground. By now it had filtered through that he had sacked me. Before I left to see Jim Gregory I phoned John Gregory and said that as I had to see the chairman, would he take the players for a run until I returned. He said he would but the lads told me he was in his suit in his office at 10.30 giving a press conference about his new status as manager. He had known all along. I was out of work and he was the new boss.

The family were devastated. Of course I told Lesley and she phoned the school and arranged to collect the kids at lunchtime. They knew, of course, that something serious was afoot, but when I told them their dad had been sacked, Jimmy just said: 'Thank heavens for that. I thought my nana had died.' That made us all cry. For all the family, Pompey was our club.

I had been there six years, five as manager, and we had enjoyed some great times.

Looking back I recalled the first day I went down to see the kids at Portsmouth after John Deacon and Bobby Campbell had brought me in to see if we could get some kind of a youth policy going. I had just three players when I spotted a young black kid looking through the railings on his bike.

I said he looked like Cyrille Regis and asked him his name and he said it was Darryl. I asked him about his boots but he said he had none, so I told him to go home and come back with his trainers and he would make up a little two-a-side kickabout. He was Darryl Powell who went on to play Premier League football with Derby County, and international and World Cup football for Jamaica as their captain.

Lots of kids came through – Anderton, Mark Kelly, Kit Symons, Andy Awford and one very special signing that I set up just before Jim Gregory got rid of me. That was when I bought Guy Whittingham out of the army. Somebody had told me about this lad who was scoring regularly for the forces' teams and for Yeovil Town, who were part-timers in the Conference league. We heard there was an important match being played at Aldershot, the army versus Combined Services.

I took my star spotter, Derek Healey, with me and we were a bit late because the match had already kicked off and it was a long walk from the car park. As we walked from the car to the pitch we heard two particularly loud roars of the kind you immediately identify as the accompaniment to a goal. As soon as we were in we asked the score and were told that the army were two up and that Whittingham had scored both goals. We sat down and watched this big, strong lad playing up front. We had just decided that we would leave before the end of the game when the main man, the officer in charge, approached me and asked if I would present the trophy after the match. I agreed and by half-time the player had convinced me. He looked a natural goal scorer. At half-time as I was talking to the officer I let him know that we were quite interested in Whittingham; we felt he could have a good future as a professional footballer. I asked about the possibility of signing him.

He said it would take £450 to buy him out of the army, but added that if we were really serious and were ready to offer a contract, he would tell Whittingham that if the move didn't work out, his job in the army would stay open for two years. I spoke to Whittingham after the match and the deal was done, although I never saw him play for Portsmouth. I was gone soon after and John Gregory took him over.

There I was, out of work and, not for the first time, wondering what would happen next in my life. I was wounded by the Portsmouth experience, but not mortally because I knew I had given the club six hard-working years. There had been a lot of fun for the fans and the players. We had been close to promotion, then we made it and the awful shame was that we were just not allowed to consolidate. It provokes a quirky, catchy quiz question: which English football club was relegated by a bastketball team? The answer is Portsmouth and that was without the man with the wooden cigarette.

Not surprisingly there was an offer to resume work almost as soon as I left Portsmouth and it was with one of the game's true characters, Jock Wallace, the manager of Colchester United. One of the problems, however, especially in dealing with Gregory, was that until you were paid your money you could not take on another job.

Although I was anxious to get back in the game as soon as possible there was around £110,000 due to be paid to me as severance by Portsmouth. Why couldn't they just sign the cheque, make a clean breast of it and let everyone start again? People had said to me that if I thought it was difficult working for Jim Gregory, just wait until I tried to get my money off him. It was very obviously wrong that I was kept waiting, and as he haggled I said I just wanted to get away from him and settled for £30,000.

A commitment to visit Doha, Qatar, for British week, where UK products are promoted at a fair, had already been agreed when Jock phoned. He had been a good pal of my father's. I had only met him once before at a charity golf tournament near Leicester, when the boys of 1966 got together. I enjoyed his company although I did not know him well. He was clearly a huge enthusiast, one of those people who had never lost his sense of purpose, his sense of humour and his sense of wonderment.

When he rang and reintroduced himself he said he needed some help at Colchester United and asked if I fancied going there as his assistant. I told him that I had to visit Qatar and that when I came back I would get back to him, but that his offer was very appealing. I didn't know where Colchester were in the league, probably because I had been totally consumed by the Pompey affair. When I looked in the paper, trailing my finger down the two lower division tables, I stopped at the last place. There they were, Colchester United, bottom of the Fourth Division by eleven points with eleven matches remaining. It was 10 April and I rang him to say I would be over to see him. It was the beginning of long weeks of absolute fun. I have never laughed so much in all my life because Jock Wallace had an enthusiasm for life and football that was incredibly rich. He was everything you wanted in a football man. He was Bill Shankly, he was Harry Catterick, he was my dad and he was Sir Alf Ramsey all rolled into one. He was serious and funny at the same time. We drew four of our last ten matches and won six to stay in the league.

He just loved being with football folk. He could laugh at himself and his players could laugh at him. They loved him like a father but there was always a fearful respect for him. Winning, not that Colchester had much experience of it, was a deadly serious matter.

The laughter came afterwards. I was not impressed with the team in our first away match. I think it was at Darlington and I remember going home and wondering aloud just what I had got myself into. Smiles galore were just around the corner.

The next match was against Exeter on a Tuesday night. There had been no time for any real input on the training pitch and the league position hadn't changed. The situation was still dire but I had not yet seen Jock in full flow in the dressing room before a match. As the lads filed in, Jock, with his rich, rasping Scottish accent, announced the team and told them to get ready. 'We are going to war,' he said, like a Rob Roy commander in some Highland battle. 'This is war.'

When they were stripped, I did my spiel. It was obvious stuff and Jock just sat on the side silently as I launched into my tactical plan in coach speak. We were going to play tight and push up as a unit. It was mainly simple, uncomplicated stuff. I made them aware of when and where not to play off-sides and all the usual stuff – keeping it simple, getting the crowd behind us with some confident play early so we could start the run that would get us off the bottom.

I was doing my rousing best and Jock was saying nothing. Good, I thought, he is letting me get on with it. Just as I finished he stood up and the no-frills, no-nonsense Scottish voice announced: 'Right, twenty past seven, kick off at half past. You, Tony English, my skipper, stand in the middle of the dressing room and sing. By the way, I dinnae like the name, son.'

Tony stepped forward looking slightly embarrassed and heard another strident order to sing. 'Sing what?' he said, desperately puzzled.

'Nae surrender,' commanded Jock. The lad started quietly murmuring 'No surrender' and Jock exploded. 'It's nae surrender,' he shouted to Tony. 'Louder,' roars Jock, and gets the rest of the team in a huddle all singing 'Nae surrender.' I could not contain myself and escaped to the physio's room to peep through a little cubbyhole. Jock was in the middle of them with his 'Nae surrender' and then he hit his captain a full blow in the stomach, elbowed somebody else, gave another a crack and the buzzer went for them to get out on to the pitch. They ran out and walloped Exeter 4–0 and I cried laughing.

They started to win and escaped from the dreaded bottom zone. Jock was a one-off, a sensational man. I did all the work, all the training, and he left me to get on with it as he stood and watched. I did a little bit of coaching but don't take credit for them staying up. Maybe a little, but Jock was the mad motivator. He had an antipathy to anything green and white because he had been a Glasgow Rangers man through and through and anything green was associated with the dreaded Celtic. The lads used to wind him up all the time over this and were forever leaving green items around the place. When he found them he would rage and go hunting down the culprit.

Every match we played had me wondering in advance what he might get up to. We had two mascots, delightful blond twins dressed in Colchester blue with little boots

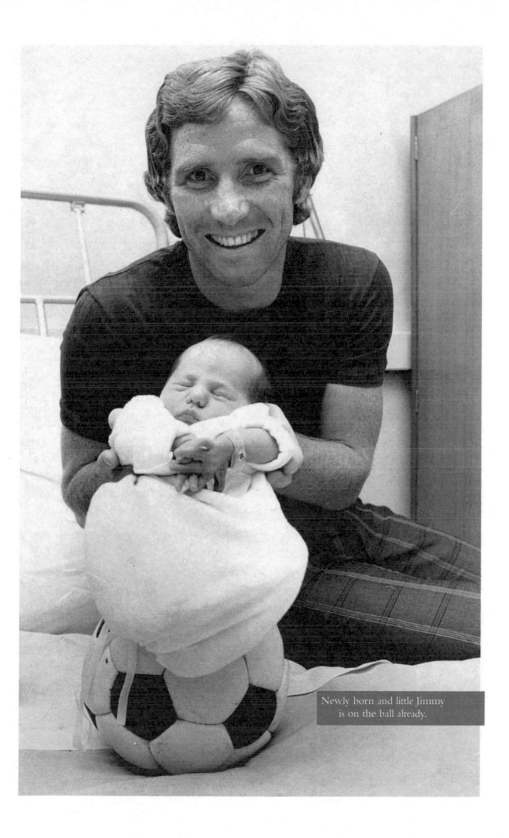

Newly born and little Jimmy is on the ball already.

ABOVE: Having a laugh with Willie Johnstone (Vancouver Whitecaps) before the Soccer Bowl final in New York, 1979. BELOW: On a break in Las Vegas with Lesley, and Willie Johnstone and his wife.

ABOVE: The big No. 9 is Georgio Chinaglia, the New York Cosmos captain.
BELOW LEFT: First exciting job in management at Portsmouth.
BELOW RIGHT: Me and Jimmy celebrate winning promotion with Portsmouth.

ABOVE: Smile, please . . . Lesley, Keely, Jimmy and Max, the German shepherd dog.
BELOW: The wonderful Jock Wallace greets me at Colchester.

ABOVE: My favourite lovely Cornishman, Stuart Dawe, who took me to Exeter City.
BELOW: All aboard. The lads of '66 on a Mediterranean cruise a couple of years ago.

ABOVE LEFT: Two princesses, Keely and Mandy.
ABOVE RIGHT: Mandy and Jimmy at the finish line of the 2003 London marathon.
BELOW: All the family with the MBE
(from left: Dave, Mandy, Lesley, Alan, Keely and Jimmy).

With two of our old Blackpool friends, Ian and Anita Smith.

ABOVE LEFT: Jimmy (Keely's son). ABOVE RIGHT: Louis kissing Lacey.
BELOW LEFT: William Harrison-Allan (on the right) co-owner with me of a good horse called Pick Up Sticks. BELOW RIGHT: The two Louies in my life, grandson and Labrador.

Mandy and Dave's wedding day, 3 July 1999.

on their feet. They were a picture of pure innocence. One day after I read out the team, Jock walked across the tiny dressing room and picked up one of these three-year-olds and nutted him. I'm not quite sure what was in his mind, but he did, and naturally the kid started to scream and the other one kicked Jock on his shins. He thrust the one he was carrying at me and was hopping round the place trying to get the one who had kicked him when the twins' father comes in, and sees the children crying and all the players trying to hide their faces. Now Jock would not have harmed a child for the entire world. He was just trying to give him a little tap, like an interpretation of the Glasgow kiss. Inwardly the players just cracked up, and the fuss took away the pressure and we went out and won another game.

Jock was a marvellously funny man. I took a small flat in Colchester, with the family back in Chandlers Ford. Jock and I used to go out for dinner. Seven o'clock on the dot, he always insisted. He was never late, never early, and he always ate every scrap of food because, as he said, he had been in the jungle in the army doing his National Service. He kept me enthralled for hours with his stories of the hardships of fighting in jungle warfare.

I found him the most captivating company. He was truly an amazing man who had been through so much, but here he was also telling me that the manager's road was as hard as it comes. He was wonderful and incredibly funny. I remember going away with him and the team for one match, wondering where the green and white might appear because the lads would certainly be up to some mischief. They fixed him. He went to the flip chart to write down the team and without looking started to write. The lads had substituted the pen so that he was writing in green on a white background. As he turned around shouting 'You bastards,' the lads just went: 'Gotcha.' They had done him again. It was a hilarious moment, again before an important match.

He asked if I wanted to stay around the following season and that if I did I would probably inherit the job. I'd had a marvellous time and we had saved the team from going down. Jock and Colchester had rekindled my love for the game. The bad taste left by Jim Gregory had gone. I was on only a modest £300 a week at Colchester but job satisfaction in working with the great man Wallace, an understanding chairman in Jonathan Crisp and players who wanted to learn were rewards in themselves.

I assured Jock that I wanted to stay. I knew he was coming to the end of his managerial career and I wanted him to go out on a high. Eventually I sat with the chairman in London and said that if he could give me a year's deal at £600 a week I would be more than happy to continue the good work alongside Jock, who had told me he would be gone in a year anyway. It was decided that I would stay, and Jock used his contacts in Ireland to bring in two good young players, Mark Kinsella, who eventually went into the Premier League with Aston Villa, and Martin Grainger, who went to Birmingham.

For pre-season, Jock decided that we would go north and use the facilities at Stirling University. He must have had a contact there as well. Before we started at the university we trained in the park, and we took them to the barracks to let the army have a go at getting them fit. It was a good move because it brought variety, but then we left for Scotland. On the way to Stirling, Jock had us stop off at Ibrox to see the home of Glasgow Rangers, which was a shrine to him. We toured the impressive trophy room and had a thoroughly good mooch around before moving on towards our destination. We were in students' quarters. Basic would be the right word. There was a narrow bunk on the floor, a washbasin and that was it.

Once we had settled in I decided to give them what I called a thought session. It was a quick-fire affair designed to sharpen their thinking on the pitch, trying to take them to a mental state where their thinking would be yards ahead of the opposition, where they would always be looking for alternatives. I was just attempting to put things in their heads. Jock sat and listened. He had said to me before we set off: 'You take them. They are all yours.'

The session was nothing strenuous and afterwards we had our tea and Jock said he had been impressed with the things I had been saying. I said I wasn't sure the players were bright enough to take it on board. Ever the optimist, he said there was no doubt they would pick it up and benefit from it. Then he took me over to Terry Butcher's pub, where we had a very pleasant evening yarning away about the game. None of our players was about because they were confined to the university.

When we returned to the room I felt that warm,

gentle tiredness that comes at the end of a long, pre-season's day, when you seem to have been on your feet all the time, your mind has been buzzing and you get back after a few beers just yearning for your bed. Not that mine carried any slumberland guarantee. I was just relaxing, about to fade into sleep, when there was a tap on the door and Jock came in carrying a bottle of Glenmorangie malt whisky and two glasses and suggested we might have a 'wee dram'. I tried to protest that I was tired but he was having none of that. He sat on the stool, I was on the bed and he allowed me to put a drop of water into the whisky he had poured. It was about 11.30 and he left his stool and opened the curtains. As I added the water I drew the curtains again and he went on talking about how much he had enjoyed the thought session and how we should have some more of the same.

I told him that I could vary it. Next time I would put on an options session where you've got options on the ball and what to do and what options the other players give you by their movements. I also told him that a couple of days later I could put on a movement session and he said: 'Aye, I'd like that, son.' We carried on talking about football and about my dad and just chewing the fat, but he opened the curtains of my room every time I closed them.

Finally I asked him why he kept opening my curtains and he said: 'You wee English bastard. You know, don't you?' The more I protested that I didn't know why he kept opening the curtains, the more he insisted that I did. In the end he told me to open the curtains, which I did, and there lit up was a huge statue of the legendary Scottish hero William Wallace. He thought I'd kept shutting the curtains because I didn't want to see the statue. I said I hadn't known it was there.

He pinned me to the bed and said: 'That's William Wallace, son. He chopped the heads off all you English-men and you did nae want to look at him, did you, son? I put you in this bedroom on purpose so that you would have to look at him every day.'

What could I say? I couldn't move. I was a victim of his passion and humour. I didn't realize that a few days later I would be immensely saddened by an incident relat-ing to Jock Wallace, whom I had come to love and admire in equal measure. We were still in Scotland playing a Highland league team. We knew it would be tough. Jock knew that they would be trying to put one over on the team from the south of England but we prepared them well. What happened in the match soon became incidental because as the players ran onto the pitch I was following Jock and he seemed to be waddling as he walked.

There wasn't the usual coordination. I didn't think much of it but I overheard one spectator, who was leaning on the fence, say in a loud voice: 'Wallace is pissed.' I suspect Jock heard it, too, but he kept walking and sat down in the box. I sat next to him and asked if he was all right. There was a tear running down his cheek. He just brushed it away and we got on with watching the game. It ended one apiece and when we got back to the students' hostel he was still quiet and said he was having an early night, which I intended anyway.

I went to my room and had a smile as I looked out at the William Wallace monument before drawing the curtains. There was a knock on the door and Jock came in with what was left of the Glenmorangie. He looked serious and I could tell there was something on his mind. He poured a drink and said: 'I hope you don't mind if I share a secret with you. I was hurt today when that fellow said he thought I was pissed. I think I ought to tell you I've got Parkinson's disease. You know we didn't have a drink last night but I lose my balance sometimes. That is why I have only one season left in this fabulous football world. You have to know this secret of mine, son, because you are going to have to protect me at times.'

It spoiled the whole trip for me, but then I saw him battle that illness, never losing his humour, his sense of fun and his desire to make footballers play their best. When I put on my sessions he sat the players down and told them how fortunate they were to be having so much good coaching. He built me up all the time.

Halfway through the season we were doing quite well, comfortably in mid-table, and the youngsters Jock had brought in were showing plenty of promise, when he called me over. He said he had taken a call from Mick Mills, the manager at Stoke City, asking for permission to speak to me with a view to becoming Mick's assistant. I looked at Stoke's situation. They were in the bottom three; they had played twelve matches of this 1989–90 season and hadn't won a game.

I was torn. I was enjoying life with Jock and he again assured me that the Colchester job would me mine at the end of the season. Yet he was very good and understanding, as I would have expected, and pointed out that I would be going up two divisions and that Stoke, potentially, were a big club rich in traditions.

I knew that. My dad had coached there. Some great days under Tony Waddington, who made a speciality out of signing very experienced players and coaxing one last good tune out of them, had reignited passions at Stoke, where Sir Stanley Matthews began and ended his career.

With Jock's blessing I went to speak to Mick Mills, knowing deep down that I would take the job and accept the challenge of trying to keep Stoke in the Second Division. It meant leaving Jock. I was very sorry to go but that sadness deepened beyond description when I heard that Jock had died at the age of sixty in July 1996. I had just strapped myself into my seat for a flight to China with Manchester City's pre-season tour when I read of his death in the newspaper. I was devastated and unable to get in touch with his family. He was one of the true football men.

11

STOKING IT

First impressions have always been important in any decision making I might have to take. There was something odd about the mood at the old Victoria ground where my dad had worked and become friendly with that unique managerial maestro Tony Waddington, who had sadly died far too young.

Mick Mills had called me, but when I arrived in 1989 I found Sammy Chung there working alongside him and assumed he would be going to make way for me to form an understanding with Mick. I had always admired Mick Mills during his days with Ipswich Town, when he won forty-two England caps between 1973 and 1982 as a quick-thinking left back. Reliability was one of his strengths, but I soon discovered that he was in trouble as a manager.

The history of Stoke City and the knowledge that my dad had trodden the same turf appealed to me as part of the challenge. In truth, I was walking into a shocking mess. They lost 6−0 at Swindon. There was rot everywhere from the rafters of the stands to the hearts and minds of the players. The fans were jeering, the pressure was intense and nobody was feeling it more than Mills. I was trying to work with him but our views were often going off at tangents, and in his despair Mick told me to take the players for training to see if I could somehow find the key to unlock the misery that was enveloping everyone.

I could see the awfulness of it all around that Swindon match. Some supporters were doing a mickey-taking conga around the ground. In effect they were laughing at the manager. Some of the players seemed to have given up. After that match I took it on myself to lock them in the dressing room and nail them with some vital invective that was seriously strong but constructive.

There were moments when I had doubts about the move. By now, though, I wasn't moving the entire family around the country. Mandy had her own place in Portsmouth and was engrossed in her creative work as a hairdresser while Keely, who would have been a star footballer had she been born a boy, was enjoying life as a dancer on the cruise ships that sailed out of Southampton. We found a nice house outside Stoke, which Lesley quickly organized, and Jimmy found yet another new school.

Mick Mills had tried several changes to the team, which involved the sidelining of men whom I had previously regarded as reliable professionals. They were probably approaching the back ends of their careers, but I still felt that people like goalkeeper Peter Fox, centre half George Berry and winger Peter Beagrie, who had all been victims of the purge, had experience to offer and should be brought back.

It was clear that Mick, who is one of the most genuine people you could ever meet, was under intolerable strain, as the vociferous protests from the stands had left him puzzling over a solution to the club's plight. His decision to ask me to take the team cannot have been an easy one, especially as rumours about his future were beginning to circulate.

After I had recalled Fox, Berry and Beagrie I sat everyone down in the dressing room and asked for their support. I told them I realized how badly their pride had been dented at being left out but the time had arrived for them to bury their disappointments and fight for the cause, which was to lift Stoke City.

Perhaps I should have taken more notice of the problems that existed before I agreed to take the job, but when Mick and Sammy Chung departed 'by mutual consent' I was left on my own. Those words, 'by mutual consent', seemed to be the only polite expression to be found anywhere near the place. The chairman, Peter Coates, asked me to stay in charge until the end of the season. I pleaded with the old pros to show their professionalism. I brought in Noel Blake, Mickey Kennedy and Lee Sandford, players who had worked their socks off for me at Portsmouth, to try to bolster the side. Tony Ellis from Preston came in as well.

We all worked hard together but we could not stem the tide. Sometimes you can turn things around, but not at this club. It was a tough place to manage because so much was wrong in the background. I could handle all the internal difficulties, but the players seemed to be affected by the strife in the boardroom and the inadequacies of some of the backroom staff, although I had great support from Bernard Painton, chief scout, and Tony Lacey, who was with the youth team. Winnie the kit lady and Ron the kit man were two of the most cheerful people around the place.

Potteries people, I discovered, are insular folk, and some of the changes did not go down well. They were angry when I sold Beagrie, a crowd favourite. He went because I had to raise money in the same way that I had sold Mark Hateley and Neil Webb to generate funds at Portsmouth. The shouting went on because it didn't work and we were relegated from the Second Division.

Everyone was hurt by that and I quickly realized that I had a chairman, Peter Coates, who appeared to be more concerned with his personal business interests than throwing everything into attempting to preserve the club's survival in the Second Division. There was an unhealthy, uneasy feeling, and I was soon to learn about the cause when I went to a meeting of the directors in the boardroom. Of course events on the pitch added to the turmoil, I did not have a contract and a strange kind of bleakness was everywhere. There were some decent men about. Maurice Nield was a director who was a lovely man with the red and white of Stoke City running through his veins. Mike Loftus and Ed Weetman were others with whom it was easy to get along. The only thing the boardroom lacked was stability.

As I wandered in one day Weetman was there, just back from his holidays. He was a big, bluff haulage contractor who did not waste words on anything or anyone. I can see him now, as I entered the room. He was almost lying back in his chair, dangling his shoes on the ends of his feet as if he was about to drop them off. I asked him if he had enjoyed his holiday and he said: 'Aye, lad, until I came back to this.' I wasn't sure if he meant the state of the team or some other issue that was bugging him. The chairman came in along with the others and Weetman launched his tirade almost before any opening pleasantries.

'Before we start,' he said, 'why has my name been taken off the licensed premises board at this club while I have been away and Lindley Catering, your company, been put on top?'

He was talking to Peter Coates and there began the biggest row that I had heard in a boardroom for a long, long time. It culminated in Weetman storming out with Nield and Loftus following, which left a dumbfounded fourth director, Keith Humphreys, looking at empty chairs. He said there was little point in carrying on with the meeting. The situation, he said, had left him with plenty to think about. I went out of the room leaving Humphreys and Coates to themselves. There was enough on my plate for me not to become too worked up about boardroom friction.

In the middle of all the issues of trying to get the team on a winning streak, with injuries and form losses, there was another damning example of the way the club was being run.

We were battling away against all the odds when one

of my stronger players, Chris Kamara, came to see me. Chris is currently a Sky TV pundit and tabloid columnist. He was a reliable player, no trouble, until that fateful morning after training when he asked to have a word.

He told me he had a problem involving money. The situation was serious. He said he urgently needed a loan to pay off a debt and escape the trouble he was facing. Failing a loan he said he would have to be sold in order to be able to claim a signing-on fee and clear whatever he owed.

I told him that selling him was a non-starter. I would have been lynched, I said, and I sensed I was heading down a very difficult cul-de-sac. I was also very unhappy with him. I said I could not understand him coming to me with such demands when we were all battling against relegation. Talk about needing a hole in the head! He continued to pester me about the loan. I knew there was little chance of the club helping him but I rang the chairman anyway. By this time Peter Coates was in the chair. His reply was instant. No.

Kamara's response was to tell me that with this debt hanging over him, he was in no state to play for the club. He said he was far from happy and needed to leave. If he was miserable I was doubly concerned. What was I going to tell the supporters? I realized he had to go but told him that when someone asked him, in the fullness of time, why he had left Stoke, he would tell the truth about how I had tried to do him an enormous favour. I knew I would be the one to suffer in the immediate aftermath of his transfer.

I rang the chairman and told him that Kamara wanted to go, did not want to play for us and that as the club was not prepared to provide him with a loan we should sell him. I told Coates that Bruce Rioch, the manager at Middlesbrough, had made several inquiries about Kamara, and that I believed we could get £150,000 for him. He was coming to the end of his career and we would get no more than that. The chairman told me to go ahead and organize the transfer if Rioch was still interested.

I rang Bruce and told him the goalposts had been moved. Kamara was now available because he needed the money that would go with a signing-on fee, and that it was up to Rioch to sort out that aspect of the deal. Bruce was keen, the fee was right and we agreed on a handshake over the phone which, as far as I am concerned, means the deal has been done. I knew that would be Rioch's bond as well.

I said I would see Kamara, hand him all his medical records and he would be in Middlesbrough the following morning. Bruce replied: 'No, send him up tonight. We've got a match, I can see him afterwards and we will put him up in a nice hotel so that we can get cracking on the financial straightaway.'

As soon as the phone was down I called Kamara and told him what was happening. He came in, collected the records and even his boots, and set off for Middlesbrough after shaking hands with me. I told him never, ever to get into financial trouble again and to thank me whenever he had the chance because when the news was released next day I would be the one in serious trouble with the tens of thousands who cared for Stoke City.

On the way home that night and as I lay in my bed, I began to wonder how I would handle the inevitable criticism that would come hurtling my way. As soon as I arrived in the office the next morning I rang Bruce just to inquire how things had gone. His reply left me shocked and stunned.

'What do you mean, is everything OK?' he asked rhetorically. 'He's signed for Leeds.'

Not surprisingly Rioch was displeased. He even resorted to understandable sarcasm, 'Thanks a lot, that's no way to do business.'

Trying to explain myself was not easy because I was completely in the dark over any Leeds business. I assured Rioch that I was absolutely sincere in my belief that he was on his way to Middlesbrough with all his papers and a firm desire for the transfer to go through as quickly as possible, so that some essential funds could be released. I said he must have been highjacked along the way and that I would speak to the chairman to see what was going on. I promised to call Bruce back as soon as I could.

As soon as I rang Coates his voice dropped. He told me that Bill Fotherby, the Leeds managing director, had called to ask him about Kamara to be advised that he was on his way to Middlesbrough and that the fee was £150,000. Fotherby had suggested Kamara might want to stop off at Elland Road on his way north.

Leeds pinned him down there and then. I told the

chairman of my disappointment. If I'd known, I could have told Bruce Rioch of the sudden development and given him Kamara's phone number so that, at the very least, he could have got in touch with the player on his way to Leeds. I told Coates in no uncertain terms that I felt as though I had broken the code of conduct that exists among managers. I was embarrassed by the lack of communication and now I had to ring Bruce Rioch to tell him what had happened.

All I could do was apologize as I detailed Coates's explanation. I was blazing and the anger did not subside readily. It festered. Things were never the same again. I was slaughtered in the media but Kamara's financial problems remained a secret between us. His transfer cleared whatever debt existed and as far as Stoke City were concerned, business resumed as normal.

Not long after the Kamara affair there was a re-enactment of the England–Germany World Cup game at Leeds in aid of the Bradford Fire Disaster Fund. Fifty-six people had been burned to death on the last match of the 1984–5 season between Bradford City and Lincoln City when the main stand caught fire.

England won again, and afterwards there was a splendid banquet for both teams and other guests in an impressive room in the new stand on the far side of the pitch, opposite the tunnel. The place was beautiful, the food was good and I was complimenting one of the commissioners on the grandeur of the set-up when he told me that the club had recently hired new caterers, Lindley Catering from Stoke. Even during my time at

Manchester City, later in my career, Francis Lee was telling me about the rent people paid for various outlets. Lindley ran the catering and bars in the Umbro Stand, and when I asked him if any deals had been done during the period when the franchise was being released, he said that two players had indeed gone from City to Stoke.

Lindley Catering has stuck in my craw ever since, but the other haunting aspect of my time at Stoke is that we were relegated. Few people knew of the turmoil that was going on in the boardroom. It was hard for me to handle and I turned to my old companion and coach, Graham Paddon, to come in to help. The spectators were making plenty of noise and everyone expected us to return to the Second Division straightaway.

We were going well, lying second on New Year's Day 1991, but things started to go wrong in January and February. We had injuries, we lost form and then the supporters turned into some kind of unspeakable hate mob. Not all of them, of course, but there was an element who were ugly, foul-mouthed and unable to accept that you cannot win all the time. They quickly made up their minds that I had to go.

My last game was at Wigan, when we lost 4–0. Stoke's yob element did their infamous conga again. They turned vicious. They spat, threw things and bawled the vilest abuse. That day at Wigan I went out to look at the pitch and a Stoke fan, a young lad of about nine or ten years of age, spat at me. As he ran away I chased him and a policeman intervened before I could give the lad a clip around the ear. The policeman escorted me back to the tunnel with some stern words, warning me against taking the law into my own hands.

I showed him the spittle that was all over me and in the end I just sighed: 'What is going on in this world?'

Then the team went out and played some of the most pathetic football I have ever seen. Their hearts were not in it. Whatever confidence had existed had long evaporated. The Wigan supporters kept up their malevolent chanting and there was nothing I could do about it. As soon as the referee blew his whistle I was on my way to the boardroom when normally I would have been among the players.

I was angry. I was raging inside over the sarcasm and vitriol of the so-called Stoke supporters. I could neither fathom nor stomach their verbal violence. We were in mid-table but they were showing their disapproval because it seemed as though we were not going to bounce straight back into the Second Division. I was not under contract, I was working on a monthly basis and I had just about had enough. Being spat at by a child was the incident that probably made up my mind that I should go.

As I climbed the stairs to the Wigan boardroom, Coates was on his way down. I pulled him and said: 'I'm out of here. Forget it. I'm gone.' He said he was on his way down to see me 'about that'.

'Forget it,' I repeated. 'I'll come and see you on Monday when it's all died down. Accept my resignation now. I'm finished.' I returned downstairs and told Paddon what I had done. I urged him to hang on as long as he could, but not to say a word to anyone on the coach back to Stoke. I said that when I got off the bus he would not see me again.

My anger was such that I told people I was absolutely finished with football. I didn't like the area. I didn't like the people and the way they turned on me. They had been just as vicious with Mick Mills and Sammy Chung and I had seen, first hand, just how it had affected these two decent men. I was determined that I would never be in the same shaky mental state as those two. I just wanted to get away as soon as I could.

Lesley had been at the Wigan match listening to everything and reminded me of the week before at a home match. The fans had been outside hurling their abuse. The women, wives of the directors and so on, had their own room on the first floor looking out over the mob. They all moved out, frightened that something might come through the glass, but Lesley was so furious and defiant that she went and stood in front of the window as they threw their stones.

Away from the club we had a lovely house and some great friends, particularly David Pedley, a local business-man, and his wife. After I had made my decision to leave we went to see them. They sympathized. Although David was an avid Stoke supporter he said he had been disgusted by the behaviour and I feel certain that he never went back to the club again.

We lived in his brother Robert Pedley's house, a beautiful little farmhouse in a pretty village, but I had to cleanse myself of the Stoke City business. I could have happily driven away that night. As we eventually set off down the A500 a few days later, past the industrial buildings, I thought to myself that if I never had to drive that road again it would not bother me. I could not get away from Stoke fast enough. On reflection, I had been angered by the mob. Maybe I had given them some false hope at the beginning of the season, when I had predicted that we would be promoted. Sometimes you should be sparing with your predictions. I was trying to build confidence about the place but there was neither willingness nor patience from the Stoke public once things began to dip.

Before that memorable drive away from Stoke I looked in at the club on Monday morning. There was no real money involved, no contract to be paid up. I was probably owed about £5,000, which was handed over. I shook hands with the chairman and said I thought that Paddon was a good young coach and that was me out of the door, out of a home and apparently out of football.

I had quit in such a hurry that there appeared to be no place for us to go until a friend asked me about taking a pub near Ascot with a view to turning it into a pub-restaurant. It was something neither of us had ever contemplated, but our determination to rid ourselves of all things Stoke made up our minds. We renamed it Winnigans, transforming it into a sporting bar with a racing theme. I went in with two pals, Mick Walsh and Barry Lewington, as a partnership and we really threw ourselves into it, with Lesley especially industrious.

We slept on the floor upstairs. There was a hole in the

ceiling. It was very basic and spartan at first. Jimmy, the only child left with us as the girls were now pursuing their own careers, thought it was fun. Lesley and I looked at each other and wondered what we had let ourselves in for. We completely revamped the place from top to bottom, applied for the licence on a Thursday and opened on the Saturday with lots of friends around. It was a different life and we busied ourselves as we began taking good money. I must admit, I was not very good at the till.

I could not add up, never could. I would pull the pints and pour the drinks and half the time charge the customers what I thought was to the nearest pound. I would chat football at the bar with the customers and we all enjoyed it. Up to a point.

Slowly but surely, for all the fun we were having, it dawned on me that I was simply a football man, and although I had vowed never to get involved in the game again I knew I could not escape it. I was a World Cup winner who had been steeped in football from the womb.

Some people used to say that as a player I was tireless and that I had the lungs and the energy to run all day. That may be true but there was a weariness that often came over me, making me long for my bed, at the end of a long day running the pub. You always had customers who were reluctant to leave at closing time. One particular night when I was tired and they didn't seem like going I put on my George Formby records in the sound belief that his ukulele and Lancashire voice would clear the place. Not so. They started singing along, especially the older ones, who knew snatches of the verses and were really getting into it.

One night at about 11.45 p.m. when it was past closing time I said to one chap: 'Let's be having you. I'm tired now. I'm going to bed.'

He looked at me cynically and said: 'What do you mean, you are going now? Don't you know you are just a drunk's waiter now?' I was livid, turfed them out and went upstairs and said to Lesley: 'That's it. I can't be doing with this any more.'

I meant it, but not really, because the reality was that we had nowhere to go. The remark had hurt me, though. I was able to look inside myself and wonder. After my successful playing career, culminating in so many trophies and awards, was this what I had come to be, a waiter for some disrespectful drunk? What was I going to do?

A few days later on a Sunday morning, the telephone rang and a rich, fruity Cornish voice introduced itself: 'Right, me old beauty. You don't know me but I have been watching you for years. My name's Stuart Dawe and I am a director here at Exeter Football Club, and we are in a mess. I want you to come down here and be our manager. It's pre-season so you've got a bit of time to sort things out. Tell me you'll come down here and be our manager.'

I told him I thought he was having a laugh. I told him I'd had enough of football. The game had driven me mad. He gave me his telephone number and suggested I have a think about it.

Now I was in a quandary. I repeated the conversation

to Lesley and as usual her common-sense approach to the subject worked. She knew that, deep down, my heart was still with the game that had been my life despite my protestations as I drove away from the bad Stoke memories. We decided to drive down by car in time for a pre-season friendly Exeter were playing on the Friday night. I watched the first half in the directors' box. The quality of play was poor and I sensed a familiar restlessness among the supporters.

At half-time I went to the boardroom and suddenly there was a dreadful banging and raised voices. The disgruntled supporters were trying to barge their way into the boardroom and the police were fighting to keep them back. I knew then exactly what Stuart Dawe had meant when he said the club was in a mess. I met him as all this nonsense was going on and here was this lovely man pleading with his moist eyes for me to take the job as the din went on in the background. We shook hands. I said I would take it and drove home along the M5 having promised to return on the Monday, when they had another friendly fixture, to complete all the paperwork. I was smuggled out of the ground after making my promise and told them to announce in the papers that I would be taking the job.

My contract was a pittance. It was for three years but there was barely enough to live on. They paid for accommodation and provided a car and I set about doing the job. I had a wonderful time there and referred to it as my three years of convalescence. I loved those little windy roads and villages we saw as we sought somewhere to live. Eventually we found a place to rent in the village of Shobrooke. It was a converted barn. We loved the place and the area, and had the most fulfilling time of our marriage there. We loved the pace of things; those little roads where you sometimes struggled to get above fifteen miles an hour, and the scenery with both Dartmoor and the sea within easy driving distance.

We had some laughs. I invited Dave Hill, a smashing lad who had been the steward on the players' entrance at Southampton, to come and stay with us. Dave must have weighed twenty-five stone. Lesley and I were in bed one night when we were woken by this loud thudding noise. I just said that will be Dave falling out of bed. There was no point in going to help because I would not have been able to lift him. Next morning we discovered that Dave had slept like a baby and that the noise had been part of the barn collapsing.

I started to build a useful little team. My appetite for the game had returned. We survived in the Third Division for two years, 1991 to 1993, and had tremendous cup victories at Birmingham and Bolton. We made £75,000 profit in the second season and old Stuart threw a huge party after the annual general meeting but I had to sell players. I sold Scott Hiley to Birmingham for £350,000 and goalkeeper Kevin Miller to the same club for £250,000 after a very interesting incident.

There was real interest in Miller. There was an offer of £200,000 for him. I stuck out and said it had to be £250,000 or there would be no sale. On the Sunday night we received a sinister phone call. Lesley answered and a mysterious voice said: 'If Mr Ball will sell the lad for £200,000 there will be an envelope on your doorstep in the morning.'

We just laughed it off and insisted through the right channels that the fee was £250,000 and not a penny less. Birmingham paid up in full and later sold the lad for huge money.

One of the joys of working in deepest Devon was that I was alongside a board of directors who had a great love for the game. They were simply nice people. I could say that they didn't have much of an idea about the way things should be run but they were also without any grandness. Inevitably, though, there was some politicking, mainly emanating from the all-powerful president, Clifford Hill, who liked to put people in their place, including the chairman, Gerald Vallance. Hill owned most of the shares but he had a generosity of spirit and no one could deny that.

With my love of the game restored I looked forward to going to the Cat and Fiddle training ground every morning to work the players in a setting that many much bigger clubs would have envied. The training facility was owned by the president and he rented it to the club at peppercorn rates. After the rigours and traumas of Stoke it was the kind of therapy I needed and I was able to do things my way with a good youth-development man, Mike Radford. We hit it off straightaway and shared the realization that the best way forward for the club was to produce our own players, as I had done at Portsmouth.

While we worked along these lines I brought in Steve

Williams, a midfielder whom I had known as a young player at Southampton, from Arsenal to be player-coach. I saw that as a good coup. He was a leader and would be my voice on the pitch, but he later let me down after being courted by a director, Alan Trump, to take my place.

I bought Ronnie Jepson from Port Vale for £15,000, which was a lot of money, but Ronnie turned out to be one of the best buys of my career. Others who came in included John Hodge, Russell Coughlin, Steve Moran, Stuart Storey, Scotty Daniels, Peter Wiston, Andy Cook, Danny Bailey, Andy Harris and so on. We paid peanuts for them all. Miller was there in goal so that, with Stuart Dawe's blessing, I brought in an almost entirely new first team while Mike Radford carried on scouring the area for youngsters who could be developed. We knew a youth policy was the best way to build a club despite all the signings.

That first season was a scrap. We were fighting relegation all the way and although we lost 5–0 in the last match of the season we just managed to stay up. We survived the following year as well and were going well in my third year, when we should have gone to Wembley to contest the final of the Auto-glass Trophy. As titles go, it may not have been the mightiest trophy in football, but to the people of Devon it meant a great deal. To say we were robbed in the second leg of the semi-final is a massive understatement. We lost 2–1 at Port Vale and when the second leg came to our ground, Steve Moran scored the goals that made it 2–2 on aggregate and we went into extra time. If it had stayed like that we would have won on the away goals rule. A minute and a half into injury time and Exeter City were on an all-time high. We were not only glimpsing the famous twin towers, we could have been booking the hotel. All we were waiting for was the referee's whistle to end the game.

He blew all right, but it was for the worst penalty decision I have ever seen and Port Vale scored from it. I was incensed, so angry that three months later I was up before the FA disciplinary panel to be judged on the actions of that night down in Devon.

I ran onto the pitch along with the enraged crowd. The three officials were knocked to the ground. Not by me, I rush to add, because I was further away. But I have never seen anger like it and the lad who was adjudged to have hit the referee had never previously had as much as a traffic offence against his name. It was all so unlike the Devon crowd to show such anger. They were and probably still are the most placid supporters in football. I was called to London to be dealt with because they interpreted my actions of going on to the pitch as leading the general revolt. I was heavily fined but there was no suspension because I believe they realized that I had every reason to be angry at the penalty decision.

In my third season at Exeter, 1993–4, we began to look a decent side. The young players were beginning to push for first team chances. Then, not for the first time in football, there was a problem within the boardroom. The wrangling was apparently due to a bid to restore a former director, Ivor Doble, to the board. This was causing divisions because he'd had problems with the Football Trust and more or less been compelled to vote his shares back to the president.

The club was in strife, with its future becoming uncertain, as the arguing went on. Then Freddie Starr, the comedian I had known as a pal from my Everton days, came down and said he wanted to buy the club. I had been telling him about the problems and the politics and he said he might be interested in buying Exeter City. I told him to come down to the town with a view to purchasing the club 'to frighten the life out of them, have a bit of fun and see what is going on'.

I never imagined that we would see him but, sure enough, he appeared on the Friday and came to the training. The players hardly believed it as he joined them. He was chipping, juggling and executing all manner of tricks with the ball. He was telling jokes, moving around with his funny walks and then when he knocked the ball into the net he went down like Elvis Presley, calling 'Yo' as he lay there. The lads were in creases with laughter and he got up to tell them that if anybody scored in the following day's league match the manager and players all had to go down giving it the Elvis 'Yo'.

Next morning, before the first team match against Wrexham in the afternoon, the youth team that included my son Jimmy had a match and Freddie went into the dressing room. Again he was larking about, juggling with the ball and cracking gags. They won well, with every goal accompanied by the Elvis call. I had signed Jimmy under the government's youth training scheme. Most clubs had YTS boys on their books at that time. He was living in digs in Exeter because he didn't think it was right to stay with the boss!

After a light lunch following the youth match we beat Wrexham 5–0, the most goals in a match they had ever scored in my time there up to that point. It was a hilarious afternoon. Freddie turned up in his Hitler outfit and went onto the popular bank, the open end. There were several others wearing Hitler uniforms in the ground because there had been a lot of publicity about his interest in buying the club and his likely attendance. The whole afternoon took on a Freddie Starr theme and after ten minutes Ronnie Jepson scored.

All the players and I were jumping out of the touchline box shouting 'Yo' and by the time the second goal went in the whole crowd had picked it up and were giving it the big 'Yo'.

We had made our point. We'd had some fun on one of those days when everything turns out right, but then things turned a shade nasty when it became obvious that Freddie was not going to buy. I told him he could slip away, no problem, but some people acted as though they had been used when, in fact, Freddie had given us a lift. By this time Ivor Doble was back on board and became chairman. I sensed it would be my last season, but one person with whom I stood together was Stuart Dawe, the man who had taken me to Exeter in the first place.

We were a good pair. I enjoyed his loyalty, his honesty and his innocence. He was a lovely old Cornish boy who made you laugh just by being himself.

I brought in more players, Jason Minett, Micky Ross, Alan Tong, David Cooper, Gavin Warboys, Simon Davies, Ronnie Robinson, Eamonn Dolan (who became manager), Eamonn Collins, Steve Wigley, Vince Hilaire . . . they all helped Exeter City.

George Kent, youth team assistant manager, and Mick Chapman, my physio, were both ex-Marines. The training ground suffered a break-in one night, with the thieves making off with some valuable training equipment. We replaced all the locks and tried to carry on as normal.

I came into training a touch early one morning and as I looked up I saw these two people coming from the woods with their faces painted and wearing camouflage gear. It was George Kent and one of his pals, who had spent three nights in there sleeping in bivouac tents without any of us knowing, hoping to catch the criminals if they came back for more.

George stood to attention and said in military speak: 'Gaffer! Kent here, reporting no sightings for the last three nights.' He then disappeared into the woods again.

January 1994 came and although we had slipped a bit from being tenth in November to sixteenth at the turn of the year there was no need for anyone to be worried. Then one day Ivor Doble came to me to say he'd taken a call from Southampton Football Club. They had sacked Ian Branfoot and they wanted Exeter's permission to talk to me about becoming manager with Lawrie McMenemy as my aide. Ivor said he could not deny me the opportunity and we talked about the possibility of getting some compensation for Exeter.

My last match in charge was the FA Cup tie against Aston Villa, big Ron Atkinson and all. We lost on a last-minute penalty after dominating the match and Ron said at the very least we deserved to go back to Villa Park for a big-earning replay.

I knew I had to listen to Southampton no matter how content I felt at Exeter although the rumblings left by the Freddie Starr affair had caused some disquiet. I appreciated Doble's understanding of the situation and his awareness that Southampton was a cause very much close to my heart. Then Lawrie Mac rang me at ten o'clock that night and suggested I drive over the following day to meet his chairman, Guy Askham.

It was clear I would be leaving Devon but I was going sure in the knowledge that I had left the happy little club in a healthier state than when I arrived. It has often been said and written that I took Exeter down. I did not. They were never relegated with me. Stoke, yes, Manchester City, yes. Exeter did go down the year I left but that happened five months after I had gone.

12

SAINTS AGAIN

Until that call from Southampton, inviting me back to work at the club that had been my spiritual home, I had just about decided that Devon was the place to be. And of all the ironies, the day we drove to The Dell coincided with the very date on which we were completing the sale on the house at Chandlers Ford, where the family had lived during my earlier days at Southampton and Portsmouth. Sod's law or something sprang to mind because we had loved that house and the people around the area but it was too late. We may have been going back to Hampshire but not to our old address. Even so, we had warmed to Devon. We had been given time to reflect on events at Stoke, on Jim Gregory's bizarre nature and on life in the pub (which we bought ourselves out of the partnership). We usually managed to laugh about those times and became so settled in our West Country situation that we took another pub in Tiverton with a good man called Reg Payne. We were settled, feet under the table and all that.

But driving over to Southampton, Lesley and I were like two kids again. We left Jimmy behind to pursue his footballing ambitions while Keely and Mandy were living their own lives, though keeping in constant touch, probably forever wondering where we were going next.

My old ambitions resurfaced. Southampton were in trouble, second bottom of the league and in need of a rescue act. I could not wait to get started. I knew it would be difficult but the consequence of failure never entered my head and whatever the wages I was up for the challenge. The personnel had hardly changed, but that did not matter. I went to see Askham in his office while Lesley waited outside in the car. He offered me a three-year contract with a £10,000 bonus if I kept them in the Premier League. He said that as both Lawrie and I would be working together he would pay us accordingly and I reckoned that he was splitting Branfoot's wages between the pair of us. I hardly gave the wages and the bonus a second thought. I would have signed anything just to be back at The Dell to manage this great club at this particular time of my life. It was January 1994 and I had just turned forty-nine. I felt I had unfinished business and that was to get them out of the mess they were in. I was going to build a team and I was going to be as good a manager as they'd had in a long, long time. That was the rampaging state of my mind at that time.

I told Lesley I wasn't bothered about the money, which was £60,000 a year with the ten grand bonus, even though I knew the average wage in the Premier League at that time was £225,000. It meant that I was bottom of the pile in the wages league as well as inheriting a club that was staring at the bleak face of relegation. I hardly slept thinking about training the next day and how I was going to change the world yet again.

We had the statutory press conference and everything was fine. I reiterated the massive job that was waiting to be done and that I was restless for the kick-off at Newcastle on the Saturday and my first home game against Liverpool on Sky TV.

Kevin Keegan was in charge at Newcastle and they were flying high and Liverpool were, as ever, a team as formidable as any. I had seen Southampton from a distance, watched them occasionally, but as the training session approached I realized that I did not know them properly. Lawrie went over to the players, who were standing in a group that first morning at The Dell, while I lingered about thirty yards away. He called me over and introduced me to the players. Once the niceties were over it was time for me to deliver my expectations. I told them I had been appointed to help get them out of the mess they were in but without their own commitment there would be no chance. Then I delivered my usual 'Alan Ball believes . . . Alan Ball demands . . . Alan Ball expects . . .' routine.

I told them there was no time for me to try to find out about them because by the time I did that the club would probably have been relegated and we'd all be gone. Instead I said I was going to tell them about me. I told them how I like people to play: 110 per cent and no trying to kid me. Then I said: 'We have got a fantastic player here. Will you stand up, please, Matt Le Tissier. Come and stand by me. Whether you like it or not he is the best player at this club by a million miles. His record of making goals and scoring goals will keep us up. For him to do that he can't run and tackle because he's useless at that, aren't you? I don't want him running and tackling.

'I don't want him to defend. I don't want him to get behind the ball, but he plays and he plays in every single game and he plays in this area, not on the right wing where the other manager played him, but right between the penalty box and the halfway line. He'll work hard in that area because you've got to work hard to get the ball to him. Now I am going to pick someone who is going to be able to pass the ball to him in those areas and the rest of you will have to fight like hell to retrieve the ball when we haven't got it. And those who scrap and fight and dig and run and head it will be picked, but the main man will be you, Matt. Can you do that?'

He nodded his head and said 'Yes.' I told him he had the hardest job because when we got the ball to him his job was to score or create a goal for someone else, and I urged Iain Dowie, the Northern Ireland centre forward, to put himself about up front as robustly as possible.

I was asking for nothing else and if he could win us six to ten free kicks in every match we would win most of the time and he would be a fixture in the side because Matt Le Tissier would score with free kicks from those areas around the penalty area.

Is there anything simpler than that, I asked them? Now it was up to me to pick the right team and up to them to impress me in the short time we had for training before the trip to Newcastle. It is always a long coach ride and I detected quite a bit of mumbling among the older players gathered at the back of the bus. I quietly hoped everything would go right because I had not hesitated over my words during the team talk at the first morning's training session. If the master plan failed completely I might not look as clever as I had sounded. We could not have had a better start. Early in the game Le Tissier delivered a perfect cross from a corner kick, Neil Maddison met it perfectly and put us in front. Andy Cole equalized and now our backs were truly against the wall. We made a break out of the pressure and won a free kick just where we wanted it outside the penalty area.

As Le Tissier was stepping forward, hopefully to register the coup de grâce, I turned to my assistant, Lew Chatterley, and said something along the lines that if Matt scored then everything I had said on the Friday would go up tenfold because he had done everything else that I had asked of him. And if he goes and wins the match he will fully believe in what I think is right to get us out of trouble. I was watching the Newcastle goalkeeper, Mike Hooper, prancing about, but Lew just said I had better start thinking about the eight minutes remaining because there was nothing more certain than a Le Tissier free kick finding the back of the net from this range. Lew predicted the top corner and it was 1–2. I just told them to keep the ball, to get behind it.

They did and we won. Keegan was spitting mad, beaten at home by the bottom team. That long ride home was one of the happiest I have experienced in football. We had lovely food and a wine waiter, and I just did not want the journey to end. It was usually an awful drag. I did not want to appear smug and with old Ted Bates on the bus there was little chance of that being allowed to happen. Ted, who sadly died in 2003 deep in his eighties, was Mr Southampton, having served them in every capacity from cleaning the boots to managing the team to becoming a director. Everybody loved him.

He had a rare, sage wisdom and on the way home he beckoned me to go and sit beside him. He said in that quiet way of his: 'That was fantastic. You keep him right, Le Tissier, and you will be all right and so will the team. Do you mind if I have a word with you after every game? It might be a minute. It might be ten minutes, but if you don't mind whatever I say . . .'

I told him of my profound respect for him and that he could talk to me anytime, anywhere. I was aware of his vast knowledge gathered in all his years in football. He kept his word, always had a little chat with me and was absolutely brilliant. It was always just a nice word or two, usually after games. He would pull me to one side and whisper something and I would be left amazed at the man's astuteness as he gently pointed out something I should have seen for myself.

On that first trip I did something that did not meet with the approval of the chairman, the directors and Lawrie McMenemy who, although he was working with me in an advisory capacity, was also a member of the board. My 'crime' was to join the players in their card school. I knew it was not usual for the manager to play cards with the lads but this was something I deliberately chose to do and when Lawrie chose to give me his views, as I knew he would, I had an answer for him. He said nothing at the time as I played cards, had a few laughs and a couple of drinks, and shared some sharp one-liners. I said my goodnights and went to the hotel where I was staying over the weekend until we found a house. We did some light training on the Sunday ahead of the Liverpool match on Monday, and it was at the training that Lawrie pulled me up. He asked me if it was wise for me to be playing cards with the players and was I sure that I was doing the right thing.

I told him I had anticipated him wanting a word on the matter. I told him I could stop playing cards at any time but it was essential that I got to know the players and their characters very quickly because before we knew it the season would be over before I had assessed them all. He said, fair play, lad, but I am just telling you that it is frowned on. I repeated that there was a very good reason for what I was doing.

The Liverpool match was a cruncher. I told them that the same instruction as at Newcastle had to be applied and I didn't want to see any showboating just because the television cameras were at the match. It was starting to snow. I told them it would be beautiful and crisp out there and that they should get stuck in. If they did we would win and lift ourselves out of the relegation zone, where the club had been for far too long. Again we had a dream start.

The match seemed to be only seconds old when the ball was knocked inside to Le Tissier and the next thing

I saw was the ball in the net with the snow that had attached itself to the rigging cascading down into the back of the goal like a secondary snowfall. It took a second or two for the crowd to realize what had happened. It had all been so swift and was such a blitz of a goal. It was the perfect start to a marvellous evening as we won 4–2. Matt scored twice more, both times from the penalty spot, and we were on our way out of danger.

I honestly believe that a combination of the simplicity of the team talk at the very beginning and the unmistakable genius of the boy turned the team around in that season.

All the time I was there Matt Le Tissier produced his essays of talent every single week. His consistency ridiculed those who said he was lazy. Some of his critics said there was no real position for him and that you couldn't put him into a system or you had to sacrifice the team ethic for him. Plenty of people echoed those things but I just laughed at them because he proved me right in every match and we began to climb the table until we were out of trouble. He scored twenty-five of Southampton's forty-nine goals that season.

When the final day of the season arrived we were not completely out of trouble but felt reasonably safe, because while we needed to go to West Ham and not lose, it was essential for Sheffield United to win at Chelsea if they were to stay in the Premier League. There were one or two other permutations that might have affected our status, but that was the gist of it. After about fifteen minutes at West Ham, Le Tissier found himself in possession and, as ever, a surge of anticipation filled my heart. He wriggled and advanced at an angle, and fired one into the corner and we were one up. Then he scored another and I could only stand there and marvel at his ability. From nothing he had the knack of fooling defenders and either finding the net or feeding the ball to another player in a scoring position. There were times when he seemed to be winning games for us single-handedly. I adored the lad. As the game progressed we were 3–2 up with two minutes to go when the West Ham supporters, those behind the goal to the left of the main stand, came over the wall and invaded the pitch. I couldn't fathom the motivation for this rush to get onto the pitch because West Ham were in a comfortable mid-table position.

The referee had little alternative but to bring the players off the pitch. I told our lads to go to the dressing room and I had a word with the referee, wondering if he intended to bring them back out for the final two minutes and he said he would.

As I was standing around waiting for the pitch to be cleared, a spectator shouted to me that Sheffield United had lost at Chelsea and that we were completely safe. At that point I didn't care whether our match resumed or not. I smiled to myself and looked around the stands, telling myself that this Premier League was my kind of world. The players came out and they had been told as well. I just told them to finish the game and then we could go and party. West Ham scored straight away on the resumption to make it 3–3. Imagine how I would have felt had I not known the Chelsea result. It was all so incredibly sloppy.

It was a stupid goal, so unnecessary that I could not get it out of my system when we should have been celebrating in the dressing room. I had a go at them. I was banging on about their carelessness and I remember one of the lads piping up and saying: 'Gaffer, leave it alone will you.' I tried, but I was still hopping mad for a while until we stopped off at the London branch of the supporters' club on the way home.

They provided us with a terrific reception and I soon forgot my complaints about that last West Ham goal and began to enjoy the moment. The more the evening wore on, the more elated I felt about what we had achieved. We had averted the big drop whereas it hadn't happened at other places. Saving Southampton from the drop was probably as big a challenge as I had faced. The situation at Colchester had been serious, but this was the Premier League and relegation would have meant the loss of the revenue from Sky Television, which was worth around £15 million.

That we did not go down was due to a set of lads who scrapped with unyielding comradeship, and a genius, as I called Matt Le Tissier. Our methods had been simple but they had worked, and that was the joy at the time. The £10,000 bonus was paid in full although I hadn't given it much thought. Already my mind was looking towards the following season, when I knew I had to consolidate. We had done well but there were still more markers to be reached. I was beginning to think that an extra year on my contract would be offered because that is the way things were done to preserve continuity when everything seemed to be working well. We had laid the foundations. I had good assistants in Lew Chatterley and Dave Merrington, while Lawrie was always at my shoulder with any advice he thought might be necessary. I imagined that all of us, myself and the staff, would be given an extra year. I did not want to push it too much so I decided that I would wait until they invited me in as I expected they would. When the time came I received something of a shock. The meeting with Askham and McMenemy did not produce what I had in mind but at the outset I had expected something cosy, especially as they had asked me to take Lesley along as well.

They were sitting at a table looking businesslike and I thought the signs were good until Askham said they were concerned about my friends, implying that they disliked the company I was keeping. I was amazed as well as being stung by someone questioning my friends. I asked for an explanation and Askham said that he had noticed two particular friends of mine who were in the boardroom on my private tickets. Then, with what I detected to be outright snobbery, he said that one of them was an ex-steward of the club and that it wasn't right for him to be there, and that the other was in the pub trade, as if that made him the lowest of the low. He was referring to my long-time friends Dave Hill and Terry Hussey, the latter of whom had become general manager of the prestigious Meon Valley Golf and Country Club.

I was dumbfounded. I insisted I could not see the problem of these personal friends being there. He said they were always the last to leave, again making the implication that they were shovelling the booze. I rebuffed that and said they were usually the last because they were waiting for me after I had done all the end-of-match duties, such as checking for injuries, getting changed and attending television and radio interviews and press conferences. I was bound to be late.

Lesley was so upset about the references to Dave Hill, the lad who had been the steward on the players' entrance when I had been on the playing staff, that she cried at the ridiculousness of it all. Dave had become a genuine friend who took Lesley to and from the matches. He always wore a jacket and tie in the directors' box and loved his new status as a friend of mine. Lesley told the chairman it was all a ludicrous class thing and I was upset, too, on behalf of my friends, particularly when he said it wasn't right that Dave, as a former steward, should have a seat among the directors.

They, Askham and Lawrie, said they felt the need to tell me. I could not believe their attitude at a time when the football was so massive and important. All of us on the playing, managing and training side had been working our butts off to try to get the club right and they brought up the subject of my friends in the boardroom. Surely that should have been the last thing on their minds, which now looked small indeed, in my opinion.

There was no mention of a new contract so I didn't speak up about one at that meeting because they had taken my breath away with their attitudes towards Dave and Terry. I decided not to bother then about the contract and we went on to have an excellent season when we started up again.

I just thought to myself that I had my bonus tucked away and I had my £60,000 a year so I carried on with all the old enthusiasm and we went on a pre-season tour. I kept the same players, more or less, and did not add any because they had done so well for us in retaining Premier League status. But I did have our Jimmy on board. He had been released by Exeter and I thought he deserved another chance. I used him as a non-contract player, which meant he had a few reserves games and scored a goal against Norwich City Reserves at The Dell.

He was not quite up to the highest standard but I always thought he could have made a playing career for himself in the lower leagues. He was showing an increasing interest in the coaching side and I allowed him to work with the youngsters to gain experience in that area.

For the first team squad's pre-season preparation I had found a perfect training camp in Holland. It had everything a club required and confirmation of the place's quality came with the arrival of the magnificent Barcelona team. If it was good enough for them, led by their legendary coach, Johan Cruyff, it was good enough for anyone. The team had arrived without him and he was to join them later. Over the years Johan had become a good friend of mine, so I was disappointed that he was not with the team. We went off to play a game and when we returned I sat down for a meal with Chatterley and

Merrington and the kit man. The players were at a table of their own and we, the staff along with the kit man, were at another. We were talking away about the match we had just played and whatever the topic of the day happened to be.

Suddenly the door opened and in walked the great man himself. The Southampton players reacted as if Nelson Mandela or the Queen had entered the room. They reacted with that overwhelming sense of being in the presence of greatness, for they had been brought up with the legend of Cruyff as a member of the great Dutch team of the Seventies. Cruyff took over the mantle of Pelé as the world's greatest player as Ajax won the European Cup three years in succession from 1971, and he was voted European Footballer of the Year on three occasions.

This very special person, followed by so many pairs of eyes, came to our table and asked if he could join us. He inquired after Lesley and the children and sat down with an ice cream. There was little talk of the football that night, but as we were settling into a conversation about families, life and travel, Matt Le Tissier came over with a piece of paper to ask for Cruyff's autograph. It was a spontaneous response to seeing a man he had admired for as long as he could remember. Le Tissier, who in my mind was starting to touch greatness himself, was in awe of Cruyff's presence.

After Matt had returned to the players' table I told Johan that he possessed a special talent. I told him about Matt's goals and the role he had played in keeping us in

277

the Premier League, and I was not surprised to learn that Cruyff already knew all about him. Le Tissier's presence meant that eventually we turned to talking about football until he said he had to go to bed as Barcelona were playing the following day and he was tired from travelling. He asked me if I was looking for players, if I needed anyone to strengthen the team, and I told him I was looking for a good, left-sided midfield passer.

He said: 'OK, Alan. I give you a present in the morning. You take him as a present from me. You can have him for weeks, months. You let me know if you want him. You don't have to buy him. If you don't like him, just send him back to me.' He gave me the business card of someone in Barcelona who would handle this temporary, possibly permanent transfer.

Next morning as Barcelona left on their coach to play a match, this lonely lad came walking over to us in his Barcelona tracksuit, his kit in a Barcelona bag. I felt sorry for him. His mates had gone, he was all alone and he was being sent in among strangers. He had come into a pre-season training camp with Barcelona and now he was being shunted off to us. He came with us to training after hasty introductions all around and I put him straight into action.

Within minutes I was marvelling at his skill, vision and control. It was Ronnie Eklund. The lad appeared to have everything. I was beside myself with admiration of his talent. He was way better than I had ever expected. He was comfortable with either foot, read the angles and moved with the easy grace that accompanies class. I

278

couldn't wait to call Lawrie to tell him of our apparent windfall, urging him to travel and to bring whatever paperwork was necessary to get him on to our books before we lost him to someone else.

Amazingly, that was how we came to sign Eklund, as a present from Johan Cruyff. With the pre-season tour over he was straight into our team for the Premier League campaign. His play was always top class, the crowd came to love him and I was constantly pinching myself over landing him on the basis of a friendship with one of the best players the world has ever seen. Proving that nothing lasts for ever, Ronnie injured his back and declined to have surgery and never fully recovered.

With such restrictions his career declined, but it was great fun while we had him. He was on the same wavelength as Le Tissier and the understanding they forged was enlightening and entertaining and certainly something the spectators and the rest of the team thoroughly enjoyed.

I have always believed in incentives for success and my philosophy with Southampton never wavered. They were all on respectable money with massive bonuses linked to playing success and attendance figures. Obviously the better they played, the more prolific the results and the greater the appreciation from the crowd. There was always a danger at any club that if you pay enormous wages, the players might be tempted to sit back in the comfort zone. I was a manager at Premier League level fulfilling a dream and loving every minute of working with a team that was doing terrific things. I was not interested in money. The kudos of winning and being recognized by my peers as someone who was doing a good job – that was my drug.

I did my best to take care of my staff. These days there is every likelihood that a new manager will want to bring in his own assistant and trainers, but I was content to inherit the people who were already in place. I have always been able to get along with anybody, and apart from the opening introductions when I said I hoped no one would let me down, we were quickly alongside each other. People often use military metaphors in football. In those terms we were alongside each other in the trenches. I knew my two assistants well, anyway.

Dave Merrington was one of those down-to-earth, solid, honest men who stood for loyalty. He was not a party animal, nor was he a drinker. He was just a regular bloke who knew the game inside out and had been raised as a footballer at Burnley, a club who had been pioneering in their nurturing and development of young players.

Lew Chatterley had been around Southampton a while and was so used to the job he probably could have worked wearing a blindfold. Don Taylor was the experienced and well-qualified physiotherapist and in Ray Graydon I could not have had a better reserve team coach, while Stuart Henderson was completely sound and reliable. They had all been there for some time so there was little I could tell them, apart from one or two of my own preferences in certain situations. My assessment that never wavered was that they were outstanding and dedicated professionals. None of them was a 'yes man'. We had some fascinating arguments where we begged to differ, but that was all part of the fun we had in being together. Whatever little debates we had made no difference to our relationships. They were totally supportive. My chief scout, John Mortimore, was the epitome of efficiency and trustworthiness.

Strangely, the one man I had problems with was Lawrie McMenemy, the person who had done so much good for me in my career. When it was first mooted that we could work together, with Lawrie more or less in the background, keeping me straight, it seemed a good idea and I looked forward to what I believed would be a perfect relationship. We have never actually fallen out and he is a great mate and confidant to this day, but we had our moments.

It struck me after a while that he probably had too much time on his hands. He wanted to be involved more and began talking to the staff, asking them questions. Why has Bally done this and why has Bally done that? He had brought most of the staff to the club and anyone who knows him will realize that Lawrie would want to be involved in everything. I kept him informed of everything that was going on but I did not want him questioning my staff. I was not beginning to feel undermined or challenged, but his presence, which was huge in more ways than one – after all, he was Mr Southampton and his six-foot-four-inch figure was well suited to his National Service in the Coldstream Guards – was becoming slightly unwelcome.

The air needed to be cleared before an unhealthy

atmosphere developed so I suggested we had a meeting. We did and we had a major row, but it was necessary and both of us benefited in the end.

I told him I did not want him questioning my staff about what I was doing, why I was playing this player and ignoring this one, why is so and so not training, why is so and so having treatment. I told him he was making life uncomfortable for them and that was wrong.

I said: 'These lads are working under me. They are my staff but you are looking at the old picture. They are close to me and they are beholden to me. You are making them uncomfortable because you are asking them questions about someone they want to be loyal to. You, in my position, would say exactly the same thing as I am telling you now.'

We had a big to-do and I know he wasn't happy about it because I let him have it in front of these people. To be absolutely fair to Lawrie, he took it on board whether he liked it or not. I am sure, when he thought about it, that he understood my position and the situation changed for the better. Harmony was restored and I bought a young striker, Neil Shipperley, along with Gordon Watson. I also brought in Bruce Grobbelaar, the goalkeeper well known for his eccentric antics, but an absolute star and crowd favourite during his time at Liverpool, when he played around 500 first-team games.

No one could have envisaged the problems that were about to surround him. I picked up the papers one morning in 1994 and there was the huge splash story all over the front of the *Sun* accusing Bruce of match fixing by throwing games. A Liverpool match against Newcastle and our fixture with Coventry featured heavily as the newspaper announced that it was handing over videos and interviews to the police. They had pictures of Bruce talking to reporters at Gatwick Airport as he was on his way out to play for Zimbabwe, his country of origin.

As soon as I saw the story I went off quickly to the training ground. I knew he had digs in Lymington and I thought he might have gone home after being interviewed by the police, who did not arrest him until March 1995 although he had already been charged by the FA on misconduct grounds. When I arrived at the training ground at Marchwood in the New Forest, it was crawling with cameramen and reporters and I was surprised to see Bruce there so early. It transpired he had arrived in the boot of a pal's car, an ex-policeman who used to drive him around. The scene was weird. There were people up trees, behind fences, inside the complex. The place was crowded and Bruce was sitting in the corner of the dressing room. With all the media attention going on and cars parked all over the place, the police arrived.

I told the officer in charge that we wanted to train, that this was private land and could he and his men do something about clearing the place. As they were doing that I sat down beside Bruce because I wanted the truth. I had played with him at Vancouver Whitecaps and knew him well. I simply asked him what on earth was going on.

He said: 'Boss, I would never, ever throw a game.' I believed him and said that Lawrie was on his way and he would be looking for an explanation, too. He gave Lawrie the same, firm answer and we told him to get warmed up and have a go at training. I watched that lad train for ten days. I can read the body language of footballers and judge the body language of men. Had there been the slightest sign of guilt or remorse, I would have spotted it. He was happy, he was flamboyant, he was open and he was the original jack-in-the-box in training. Even on that first morning when the flak was flying, his concentration was normal. Nobody could score against him. There was nothing about him to suggest that he had not told me the truth.

The press conference that followed training was always going to be interesting, but I had one firm line which I stuck by. I said I was going to stand by him because he had been proven guilty of nothing. I played him against Arsenal and we won. He had a fantastic game despite the immense pressure that was on him.

The charges were enormous, with all their career-threatening implications. The fans sang their songs and threw monopoly money about the place. Bruce borrowed a steward's cap and held it out for the Arsenal fans to throw money into it.

All the way through Bruce continued to plead his innocence, and does to this day, although the case probably brought about his financial ruin.

Bruce first went to court at Winchester in 1997 along with ex-Wimbledon players Hans Segers and John Fashanu, as well as a Malaysian businessman, Richard Lim. They were charged with conspiracy to corrupt and match fixing, but the jury failed to reach a verdict and a retrial was ordered. Later that year, at a second trial, all four were cleared when the jury again failed to reach a verdict. Two years later he was awarded £85,000 when he took the *Sun* to court for libel. The *Sun* appealed and the case went to the Court of Appeal in 2001. The judges reversed his successful libel action and ordered him to pay costs in the region of £1 million, as well as paying back the £85,000 he had received from the *Sun* in the first place.

Bruce felt he had to go to the House of Lords and there it all went wrong. Although Lord Justice Simon Brown said there was no evidence at the High Court that Bruce had ever let goals in deliberately, Bruce was awarded damages of £1, with the costs of £1 million being awarded against him.

What transpired, and this is my belief, too, was that Bruce was tipping teams he thought might win or lose. He was passing on information and when the gamblers' bets came up there would be a few quid for Bruce to slip into his back pocket. In a way, then, he was a tipster, though it was not as serious as a jockey whispering information to a punter. We had a match at Coventry that figured in the case and I had a bit of a to-do in the witness box with the famous barrister, the late George Carman, over the goal which he was trying to suggest was suspicious.

I tried to explain to him exactly what had happened. A long ball was played through the middle and our central defender, Kenny Monkou, tried to get in front of their striker, Dion Dublin. Everyone knew that Dublin was a strong player and he held Kenny off and half turned him so that the ball went over the top of both of them, but as Dublin had the advantage of his turn he was first onto the ball as Bruce began to come from his goal, as he had done many times, to meet the challenge. Suddenly the ball sat up with Dublin three or four paces from it. Bruce stopped and started back-pedalling, with Dublin trying to lob him. Bruce got a hand to it and tried to palm it over the bar, but only succeeded in pushing it into his own net.

Using a football expression I told the barrister that Monkou had gone in too tight and that Dublin had spun him. Carman reacted in a way that queried the expression 'spun him' and I could not resist suggesting that with him not being a football man he wouldn't have a clue. I tried to explain that spinning a defender is when he comes in too tight and misjudges the ball, which gives the striker the advantage over the defender who has tried to pinch the ball in front and has misread the flight of the ball. Trying to get the barrister to understand how that passage of play had unfolded took ages as I went through the play again, concluding that Monkou had made the mistake and that Bruce was trying to rectify it though being caught slightly out of position.

I also thought it was ludicrous that anyone would throw in a goal with the game just three minutes old. Trying to convince the barrister of my true view of things was one of the most difficult things I have ever had to do. He made me feel as though I was a criminal. I had to explain the expression 'palm it' because I suspected he might play on it as meaning a back-hander or something similar. As it happens we won the match 3–1. Some fix!

No doubt Bruce was a one-off. He had experienced jungle warfare doing his National Service in Zimbabwe. He was always liable to go off the edge of reality, like at the match we drew at Manchester City, when he emerged for the game wearing a painted Zulu mask after damaging a cheekbone. You could hardly expect a character as outward going as Bruce to wear an ordinary mask. He was a lovely crackpot who was liable to do anything and everything against convention. But he never stopped diving into the flying boots. He never gave me less than his very best and I knew, and will always maintain, that Bruce Grobbelaar never deliberately threw in a goal to win money for himself. He was naive and brash and he bragged about things a lot, but being paid for tipping is a whole world away from throwing matches. I still think the world of him but towards the end of his career at Southampton he began to do too many ridiculous things. It was no surprise to see him out on the right wing, the goalkeeper, trying to dribble someone. He did that once too often and I ran out of patience with him and put Dave Beasant back in goal.

Dave did not have Bruce's flair but he was reliable and had been around a lot, being well remembered for the penalty save he made at Wembley when the underdogs of Wimbledon's 'Crazy Gang' defeated Liverpool 1–0 in the 1988 FA Cup Final. Picking him ahead of Bruce was the right move. He helped to bring us some defensive stability and we went on to complete a creditable season, finishing in tenth position in the year, the highest position for many years. Blackburn Rovers were champions.

It was a lofty position for Southampton. Everybody was excited. I still had another year on my contract and I went to see the chairman, Askham, imagining there would be an extension. He offered me a further one-year deal, but when I asked about my staff he said he didn't think they would be getting anything.

He said they were all growing old together, which hurt me. They were my people and I wanted something for them. I agreed to meet him to solve this thorny issue when I returned from holiday. He gave me an increase to £72,000 with bonuses. I was disappointed after what we had achieved. I said I would go home and think about it. Money had become a matter of pride by this time, after what I knew I had done. I felt I should be on similar salaries to the top men in the league. Lesley shared my disbelief that they were being so parsimonious. We went away on holiday to Spain, putting the disappointment behind us, but saying we would bring the matter to a head on our return.

At worst I would accept what was on offer, and before we left I told the press that I had been delighted to accept the offer of a new contract and looked forward to a bright future. Everyone just assumed that all was well and that I would sign and be at The Dell for the usual pre-season routine. I was thinking along those lines myself. Still, it was time to relax in the Spanish sun after an enjoyable but hard season. It was around 4.30 in the afternoon and we were at our apartment, thinking about going for a siesta before getting changed for the night out.

The phone rang and I picked it up to hear Guy Askham addressing me. Chairmen often call managers on holiday but I was not expecting this one. Real drama was about to unfold and initially not much of it was to my liking. Lesley and I had earlier been sitting by the pool contemplating just how content our lives had become. We were living in a house we adored, we were close to the kids and we were among some of our oldest, best-loved friends.

Then I was listening to Askham saying: 'Alan, I am just ringing to let you know that Francis Lee has been on the phone to me this afternoon asking for permission to speak to you with regard to the manager's job at Manchester City.'

I just said: 'And?'

He added: 'And, I gave it to him.'

Whether he heard me or not he confirmed that he had granted Francis that chance to talk to me. I was utterly shattered. I asked Askham what on earth was going on. I said I had a year left on my contract and he had just offered me another year and that I could not believe what I was hearing. By now Lesley was aware of what was happening and she was visibly upset. We both thought we had finished with home upheavals. He said he believed people go to work wherever they wanted, whatever that was supposed to mean. I told him I was very disappointed and that I would think about what he had said and be in touch the following morning.

When I put the phone down I was in an absolute daze. Suddenly I began to see certain signs that perhaps I should have spotted earlier. Why was he not giving new contracts to the staff who had worked so hard for the club? Maybe the offer of an extra £12,000 a year to me was meant to be so derisory that I would turn it down and be off. The Southampton decision makers clearly did not know me. I was enjoying the work and would have taken the new contract anyway.

Then the telephone rang again and it was Francis, a friend of many years in club and international football. We were both Bolton Wanderers lads and had gone on to be teammates in the 1970 England World Cup side.

Francis said he could not believe how willing Askham had been to allow him to talk to me. It was beginning to add up in my head that perhaps the Southampton chairman didn't really want me at the club. Francis suggested I pack a few things and fly from Spain to Manchester to talk to him. I told him I didn't want to leave Hampshire. We were all settled. I loved the place, and I was putting a decent Premier League side together.

Then Francis said that whatever my wages were at Southampton I could have them times four at Manchester City. That meant going from a club where I felt I was unwanted on £72,000 a year to a chairman who needed me for £288,000 a year. I repeated what he had said about the salary and he said: 'Yes, now will you fly over?'

I said I would discuss it with Lesley and call him back. I told her the move to Manchester was probably on and like me she was not so sure but Askham had virtually made my position at The Dell untenable. How could he give another club permission to take me away? He should have been fighting tooth and nail to keep me at The Dell, where we had been growing in strength and stature. I could not fathom his reasons for almost helping me out of the door.

As usual, Lesley was an absolute tower of strength. She and the children have grown up with the vagaries of football management and all the buying and selling of houses, packing and unpacking, finding new schools and so on. By this time, of course, we were on our own, Lesley and I.

I went to see Francis and I talked completely from my heart when I told him I didn't want to be there. I was settled happily in the Southampton area and didn't fully understand what I was doing in Manchester. When I stopped to think it was because the chairman of South-ampton for some reason seemed no longer to want me.

I listened to Francis and the more he talked about Manchester City, a club that as a player he had helped through the glory years of Malcolm Allison and Joe Mercer, and as I thought of the money involved, it seemed the challenge might be right. I also knew I had better players and a better team at Southampton, but Francis's talk was seductive.

I signed for Francis Lee as much as anyone, and as it turned out the money was more than I was earning at Southampton, although it wasn't as much as I was expecting. I waited until the following morning before I actually put pen to paper. I didn't sleep a wink that night as my mind turned over every possible scenario.

I had breakfast with Francis and told him I wanted him to listen in while I telephoned Askham to give him my decision, and to ask for any reasons he might have for allowing me to move to another club when we had been doing so well ourselves. I told Askham that before I signed anything I needed my head to be absolutely clear why he was allowing Francis Lee to speak to me when I was under contract to Southampton.

He replied that according to his way of thinking, anybody should be allowed to speak to another party in the cause of bettering themselves in life, and that was why he had given Francis permission to speak to me. In fairness to Askham, he added that he knew the people of South-ampton thought the world of me but giving Francis, or anyone else, the go-ahead to talk to me was the way he would be with anyone. I asked him if there was anything else he wanted to say before I gave Francis, who was standing just a yard away from me, my decision. Francis must have been thinking I was looking to provide Askham with an opportunity to keep me at Southampton. I would probably have said that I was on my way back but he just said: 'If you go to Manchester City I want to wish you the best of luck.' I said my goodbye to him and put the phone down.

Next I wanted to speak to Lawrie McMenemy but he wasn't about at The Dell, so I was put through to the boot-room and spoke to Lew Chatterley, who asked me what was going on. I told him of my disbelief at the events of the last thirty-six hours or so and said I just had to talk to Lawrie. They found him and he came to the phone. I wanted to hear from Lawrie what the whole episode was about, but all he could come up with was that everybody knew about the chairman's way of doing things but all he had been able to talk about that particular morning, when my career was in the balance, was the two ducks he had never seen before that had landed on his pond.

I said I knew exactly what Askham was like and that they would not be seeing me again. I was signing for Manchester City. I had to go back to Spain to resume our holidays because I was being cast as some kind of Judas. The papers slated me, the poison-pen letters had started arriving and our girls, Keely and Mandy, were copping abuse from all sorts of people.

When we returned from Spain and I realized how one-sided the arguments had been, I decided it was time to tell my version of events. I summoned the papers, local radio and television to give my story. Andy Steggles, a TV reporter, was one of my staunchest supporters.

I told them everything. I did not feel stitched up but let down, especially when I heard they were negotiating a takeover and felt they needed a top, high-profile manager. What had I done wrong? I had helped to bring some good times to The Dell. The fact that they were talking about bringing a high-profile manager to the club was an insult in itself. Graeme Souness was the man they wanted, and to tide things over until his arrival they made Dave Merrington manager for a year.

Merrington was soon gone and Souness came in with trumpets blazing. He almost led them to relegation. I had wanted to give so much more of myself to Southampton. What could I do for the blue half of Manchester?

13

MY MISTAKE

When I left Southampton after the last match of the season and finishing a creditable tenth, my only concern, believe it or not, was that I could not prise the lid off the office teapot. Lesley and friends were waiting for me. There was a mood of celebration in the air but I was determined not to be beaten by this awkward lid that was jammed on so I decided to take it home with me and bring it back in full working order next time I returned to the office. There was to be no next time. I was on my way to Manchester with something of a heavy heart. That let-down feeling was to grow over the next thirteen months that I was at Manchester City.

My mood was not helped by the news that South-ampton, who seemed to have been keen to push me out of the door, had claimed compensation. As I settled in at Manchester I had the awful, doom-laden feeling that I was making a big mistake leaving behind the idyllic lifestyle that Hampshire had provided, with all the neigh-bourliness of friends and with family in close contact. If Lesley felt the same way she tried not to show it and went about looking for a house in the Alderley Edge area of north Cheshire. Jimmy stayed down south studying for his coaching certificates.

My apprehension about Manchester City was not misplaced. Going there, whatever the salary and however close my friendship and respect for Manchester City, was the biggest mistake of my life. What finally drove me, I suppose, was the need to be wanted, and I had that sense of rejection by Southampton. Everybody wants to be liked. If they do a good job they need the appreciation of those they have worked for. A pat on the back can work wonders for a man's morale and confidence, but that had not been forthcoming from Guy Askham or any of the men in power at The Dell and that was why, reluctantly, I made my way north.

My images of Manchester City had usually been shaped by the flamboyant style of Malcolm Allison's teams in the past. He had always talked them up and I knew they had supporters who were among the most loyal in the country. They were forever, it seemed, in the shadow of Manchester United, who won trophies on a regular basis, filled their ground and took record amounts of money for merchandise that sold all over the world.

Now I was about to come face to face with the plight of Manchester City in 1995. My first mistake was going to the club completely blind to the precarious financial state of the place. I should have made more inquiries, but Franny was someone I had known since we were lads and I probably allowed that friendship to obscure the reality.

It was amateurish of me, but my mind was screwed up

by the Southampton treatment. Had I known the state of Manchester City, with a huge staff and wage bill and minimum quality, I would have stayed in the south whether or not with the Saints of The Dell. I spoke to Franny about the players and about his own aims, but he had not been there very long himself.

Before I knew it I was in a light blue and white training strip, sending them out on a run at a training ground near the M62 although Platt Lane, not far from Maine Road, was the normal place for them to train. I watched them returning and it seemed to me like there were hundreds of them coming over the hill. Hundreds is an exaggeration but the squad was massive. For the first time in my life I didn't sit a new set of players down and give them the 'Alan Ball expects' routine. This time I didn't tell them about me. I elected to go through them, slowly but surely one to one. That took some time and it soon confirmed in my mind that I was dealing with quantity rather than quality.

For the first time I sensed the wind of change that was beginning to blow through English football. There were bigger cars parked outside the club. The club had a contract with a supplier to provide Scorpios for the players, but they were neither flash enough nor good enough for some of them. It made me realize that this kind of thing measured up to the trappings of a big city club. That did not bother me too much but there was an air, an atmosphere about the place that I didn't like. Maybe I was the one out of step coming from a small but well-run club, Southampton, but there was without doubt an atmosphere at Manchester City that I was not keen on. Was it smugness on behalf of well-paid players? Were the footballers just happy to take their wages and saunter on enjoying their fat contracts? I suspected something like that because I saw few signs of willingness and ambition. A rot had set in and it was up to me to lift them from their lethargy. Instinct told me something was not right in the dressing room. I could smell it. When I came to sit down with Francis and looked at the contracts he laughed at my reaction.

There were players on long contracts at enormous salaries, the like of which I had never seen before. It did not take long for the weight of City's awful state to register with me. I could see why they had enormous debts and the bottom line was mismanagement. On many an occasion, as yet another revelation came to light, I asked myself what I had done to deserve inheriting such a mess.

I put all that to the back of my mind as pre-season approached. I decided I would get them as fit as possible and take it from there after a series of friendlies.

That was how I had approached previous seasons, but I wonder now if I should have had a big clear-out of the backroom staff and brought in my own people, who could share my plight and knew the way I worked. I had relied on those in place at Southampton and decided that as I felt I could work with anyone I would rely on those already in place. They did not let me down. In fact I had nothing but support from Tony Book, Colin Bell, Asa Hartford, Les Chapman and Roy Bailey, the physio who had become a reliable fixture at the club. I made just a couple of changes. At first the only addition was Alex Stepney, the former Manchester United goalkeeper who had been in the 1970 World Cup squad. Chapman left and then I brought in Kevin Bond as reserve team coach. Kevin's dad, John, had been manager at Maine Road in the early Eighties. Jimmy Frizzell and that great old-timer Ken Barnes remained immensely loyal.

They were good, honest people, as was everybody on the staff, especially my secretary, Julia Pringle, who kept things ticking over and always made sure I was in the picture of whatever was going on. If I was unhappy with the atmosphere in the dressing room, I have to balance that by saying the club itself was a warm, caring and helpful place where everybody was made welcome. We found the supporters to be the same. In fact one of the first decisions I made with Lesley was that we should go around the supporters' clubs, talking to them and letting them know what I had in mind for the future. From my first days in management I realized the value of keeping the spectators in the picture.

I found those who followed Manchester City to be absolutely passionate about their team and they had groups of supporters dotted all over the country. It was a genuine love affair with them. In all my travelling throughout the game I had never met supporters as steeped in their club as those who followed City. Their keenness was a constant factor and it cheered me no end. We had a couple of open days and it struck me that the kids who were there had probably been indoctrinated from birth. In Manchester there was no such thing as a City supporter turning his back and going to support United. That was unthinkable treachery. Their blood was light blue and they sang about their Blue Moon. When things weren't going right that became 'Always Look on the Bright Side of Life'.

I began my life in Manchester by saying that I intended to give them a team to be proud of, but in the end it wasn't to be. I tried my socks off. I took some stick, and some people tried to make me feel I was to blame for everything that had happened to the club, but there were many reasons why we didn't hit it off and some of them were major.

As I settled in, talking to Francis about where we were going, it was blatantly obvious that we were overstaffed with overpaid players on long contracts. That really was not my problem, but I had inherited it and had to do something about it. While I was contemplating who might have to go, Francis told me he was very close to completing the signing of George Kinkladze from the Georgia side Tblisi. Francis had seen him play against Wales in the previous season and had been bowled over by the lad's talent as Georgia won 5–0. Francis raved about how Kinkladze had run the show from midfield. He said he was well down the road in negotiations to sign him. How did I feel about the deal? I was comfortable with that but felt that I needed to look at him myself. Was there a videotape available that I could see?

They produced one and I was so impressed that I rang Francis and told him to carry on and sign the lad before somebody else nipped in and took him. It was our first signing and I looked forward to working with him. He arrived and at first the signs were not good. He spoke very little English, had nowhere to stay and kept getting lost in Manchester on his way from the digs we found for him to the training ground. We had to mollycoddle him, make sure everything was all right. Everybody on the staff seemed to want to help him and he needed them. He took time to settle in, but as he grew more familiar with the set-up his talent rose to the surface. He was pure class, as good a player as I had ever worked with, but he found the physical side hard. He was on the frail side but he had a glorious touch. With the ball at his feet he was a magician.

We had a decent pre-season planned, playing some matches in Scotland, culminating in a 5–0 defeat at Hearts. The travelling supporters gathered what I already knew. We were short of good players and even though we had injuries prospects for any success in the Premier League looked bleak. I knew that I had never looked at an opening fixture, at home to Tottenham as it happened, so ill-prepared. Goalkeeper Andy Dibble had been hurt in the last pre-season friendly and Tony Coton had a long-term injury.

On the Thursday, forty-eight hours before the big kick-off, I brought in defender Kit Symons from Portsmouth and a goalkeeper I knew nothing about but who had been recommended, Eike Immel, came in from Germany. We needed a goalkeeper urgently because Tony Coton had not recovered from a difficult operation in the summer. We drew 1–1 with Spurs with a goal from Uwe Rosler after being one down at half time, but I shudder even now when I look at the run of results that followed. We lost nine and drew two of our next eleven matches before scraping a 1–0 win against Bolton at home on 4 November. We were rock bottom of the league and the restlessness about the place was increasing. All season we struggled amid the misery of the relegation zone.

That miserable start had been our undoing. We went down with thirty-eight points. If we had shaped as well in those first twelve matches as we did in the last twenty-four we would have finished halfway. People were not interested in 'ifs' and 'maybes', and neither was I.

In truth it was the shocking start to the season that did us. I had never seen a team in so much disarray as ours was when we approached those early games. The dressing room was not right. There were factions. There were grumblers and grousers and powerful voices on big money that they did not deserve. Any manager will tell you that if the dressing room is not right then you've got problems. Mine came in capital letters and pound signs. There were some dominating people in that Manchester City dressing room. Disruption was likely at any time. They were not my players, but a collection made up mainly of people brought in by previous managers Brian Horton and Peter Reid. A lot of them were making excuses for themselves, especially when I began to work a system around Kinkladze.

He was a player who was difficult to place in a system,

but I decided on three at the back, four in the middle, two up front and Kinkladze floating. There was a hint of rebellion from the regulars. They didn't like the change and they complained that Kinkladze was not interested in the donkey work of tracking back whenever we lost possession. They said he didn't work as hard as the rest of them. They were using the change as an excuse.

There had to be a crunch and it came in the second round of the Coca-Cola Cup at Wycombe Wanderers just before we started winning a few games. I had put up with some of the attitudes for a while and knew the time had come to make some positive moves. I was ready to sort the wheat from the chaff and I was aware that there was plenty of the latter. It was 0–0 at half-time.

We had been shocking. I pulled Terry Phelan, who I felt was letting down the side, and I dug out Keith Curle, who was allowing Phelan to get away with not coming in behind him to cover. As a senior player, Curle should have been doing something about it rather than me having to wait until half-time. I realized Phelan was looking after himself and doing little more than going through the motions of defending. I turned on Phelan and said that I didn't know if he thought he was kidding me but I knew the game and I could see what was going on.

It was the first time they had seen the really angry side of me and at full time it culminated in such a row that we were almost fighting. I was backed by Asa Hartford and knew that the time had arrived when I let them all know exactly how I felt about them.

I told them that the way they had started the season, and now this particular game, had made me doubly sure that they didn't fancy me in the job and had given me the thumbs down in the dressing room. I told them in the richest language that I was on the case and if it took fights in the dressing room there would be fights in the dressing room. They were not going to get away with it and I was going to completely nail them. I am not sure if my fire ignited them but it was a turning point in their performances and those two, Phelan and Curle, knew I was really after them.

There were some unusual goings on. Rosler could be difficult, with a mind of his own, but off the pitch he was a great lad. I was talking to the players in the privacy of the dressing room after a match very early in the season when a steward came in with a tape of the game and walked across and gave it to Rosler. I was annoyed and intrigued and asked what was going on. The steward said that after every home game he produced a tape for Rosler. I told him that in future he should knock first or wait until he was invited in. It was all strange and then Rosler told me that after every match he sent a tape back to his agent in Germany so that he could look at it and then they would talk about Rosler's performance. Different, I thought, but another example of the way Premier League players were going, doing their own thing. I told him he should want to impress me, not his agent. It was part of a dressing room that lacked any real camaraderie or the collective spirit that bonds most good teams.

There were a couple of lads who took my fancy. They

were local boys who had come up through the ranks and felt for City the way few of the others did. Garry Flitcroft and Steve Lomas were fabulous boys untainted by the cynicism of some of the older players. Ian Brightwell and Richard Edghill, a defender who suffered with injuries, were two more who believed in the club and ran their legs off fighting to make City a good team again.

I did Tony Coton a huge favour after he had been injured and helped him on his way to Manchester United but he never showed any real appreciation, I thought. He was one of the loud voices in the dressing room that had seen three managers in four years. Perhaps they thought they had heard it all before. There were too many people in the squad who were not giving full value. I am not saying Coton was one of them but he had suffered a bad injury and I said if he could sort himself out, give himself one more go, I would try to help him. He went to Manchester United and sat on the bench for a year as cover for Peter Schmeichel, and now he is back at Old Trafford working with Tim Howard, Roy Carroll and their young goalkeepers.

I would have liked Coton to have expressed some gratitude to me but it turned out the other way, as if I was trying to freeze him and others out. The supporters picked up on that, making me the villain of the issue.

The impression given to the public was that everyone in the dressing room had complete commitment to Manchester City and I was some kind of interloper who had come in to a job of work without much fervour. Nothing could have been further from the truth. A lot of those players could not wait to get out. The likes of Paul Walsh and Coton could not wait to get away, believing they could pick up money elsewhere. A few of them were coming to the ends of their contracts and were looking for a final financial hit.

I bumped into Walsh at a charity golf event recently. We are old pals now and we talked about the Manchester City days. He had gone to Portsmouth in a swap for Gerry Creaney, which suited him because he wanted to return south. He liked the Portsmouth area and still lives down that way. It seems strange today to realize that I had some problems with him. He was not alone. There was always an undercurrent of discontent in that City dressing room. Niall Quinn was probably the brightest and most contentious of them all, a kind of self-elected spokesman who was never afraid to air an opinion. He was an influential figure with a long contract and had his share of injuries, but I had no doubt that he was a genuine figure who never gave anything but honesty on and off the pitch.

As we were relegated I felt I had brought them around to my way of thinking. We won two and drew one of our last three games, but that early-season fecklessness had done us. There were other things that were not right at Manchester City, and the training complex at Platt Lane was one of them. Training there equated to zoo-time.

Very little could be done in private because it was in a built-up area not far from Maine Road and every man and his dog could see what was happening. The supporters seemed to own the place. They came and went as they wanted, tapping on the shoulder with advice, telling me who should be playing and who shouldn't. There was discomfort among the players, who were like prize exhibits because everything they did in training was scrutinized by these people from either inside or outside the high mesh fence. It was a stupid situation, with the supporters letting rip with their thoughts and feelings. Training was watched every single minute of the day. It was hard to get through any quality work. There could be no secrets and any arguments were pounced on and spun through the rumour mill, so that a debate about the length of stud could become a full-scale near punch-up in the pubs afterwards. You never knew who was watching so that you could not hide injuries, work on special free-kick routines or pick a team in peace.

For all that, the warmth and generosity of spirit that tended to put City in a special category in the football world was continually coming to the surface. One example involved a very promising young player, Paul Lake, a left-sided youngster who would probably have gone all the way to the very top. He was from the Flitcroft, Lomas and Brightwell generation of players and was keeping pace with their progress, if not ahead of them, when he was struck down with the knee injury that finished him.

The club decided, in a typical gesture to soften the blow to Lake's career, to have a year of fund-raising meals, starting at the Midland Hotel (later the Crowne Plaza) in the centre of Manchester. There was not a spare seat in the place. They could probably have fitted in

307

hundreds more had the room been big enough. Everybody wanted to make a contribution to help soften the blow and provide Paul with something he could use as an investment.

Francis Lee made a powerful speech of welcome and revealed that City would help Paul to train as a physiotherapist and that his future at the club was secure. The feel-good factor grew during the meal and Quinn rose to speak on behalf of the players and made a wonderful contribution to the occasion when he said that as it was to be a testimonial for Paul, he and his wife had decided that for twelve months Paul would be given a quarter share of the four racehorses the Quinns had in training, which meant the winnings would go to the lad. I looked along the table to Francis Lee, who had owned and trained horses and ran the Stanneylands Stud, and he just looked up to the ceiling as though bowled over by Quinn's generosity.

Somehow it all summed up the contrariness of the club. On one side there was a tremendous warmth. On the other there was a headlong, ultimately damaging rush to provide long contracts and signing-on fees.

The club was trapped in a financial straitjacket but I made some changes. I bought Nigel Clough from Liverpool for £1 million and I let others go. By March of that relegation season we were five places from the bottom and I was becoming fairly certain that we would beat the drop. I had been voted Manager of the Month for November when we were undefeated after recording our first win of the season. But transfer deadline day in March 1996 brought serious worries.

On the day before the deadline I received a call from Francis Lee and made a note of the call. I always logged telephone calls so that when I reported conversations I could be sure of the date and if it was something important like a query about a player I would always ring Francis and tell him about the call.

This time Francis was ringing me to ask if there had been any inquiries from Blackburn Rovers about Flitcroft. I said there had been a couple of calls from Ray Harford at the beginning of the season but nothing since. Then Francis dropped the ·bombshell. It was something I did not want to hear and certainly was reluctant to act upon.

He said: 'Ring him back and say the goalposts have changed.'

I was furious. I realized I was in a situation that was not of my making and certainly not what I wanted. I sensed that the club's finest playing asset, my absolute diamond in the dressing room, was to become the centre of intense speculation and that I could even lose him.

Before I rang anyone I had to argue my case with Francis. There seemed no logic, I said, in parting with my captain. Selling him was just unthinkable. He was crucial to City's progress. I could feel the anguish in my voice. It was as though I could not believe what I was hearing and I told Francis that any sale of Garry Flitcroft was just not on.

Francis listened and then he delivered the chilling

words: 'I need three and a half million by Friday or the bank will foreclose on us. He's got to go. He is the most saleable player we've got. Ring them and see if you can start something.'

I said to myself that I should have checked on Manchester City's financial standing properly before I took the job. Now I was in it the whole dark scene was unfolding before me. I had too many players and a discontented dressing room, and I was having to part with the one player who had the ability to unite the club, the team and the crowd and he was having to be sacrificed because City had been so badly managed from top to bottom in the past.

Sitting there, thinking, I knew that defiance of the chairman was not an option, so I picked up the phone and slowly pushed the buttons that would get me back to Ray Harford, a man I really cared for and who sadly died from the dreaded cancer in 2002. He listened to my reluctance to sell and asked me how much we wanted for the player. I told him the price would be £3.5 million and then he surprised me by asking me about the lad's qualities. I am sure he knew them all and that he, as well as his scouts and assistants, had seen enough of Flitcroft to know all about him. When I totted up Flitcroft's assets it surprised me even more that we were letting him go. I told Harford that Garry was the kind of lad you could go to war with – an enthusiastic trainer, a faultless character who would do anything for you, play anywhere you want and play his heart out, and that is what Harford would be getting for his money. He said he would get back to me. I knew a deal would be done and that I would be losing Maine Road's finest.

I rang Francis Lee with one of my main concerns about handling the sale with the fans if and when it came off. I was off-loading a favourite; the club would have avoided closure, but I would have no money for a replacement because that was required to save Manchester City. I consoled myself with my belief that this would be one deal the chairman would have to explain away because the supporters would surely think there was something rotten in the fact that we were selling our star at a time when we were scuffling against the relegation drop. Surely, I reasoned to myself, the fans would realize that this was none of my doing.

About half an hour after I had told Ray Harford the price he rang back and said he had spoken to Jack Walker, Blackburn's rich benefactor and chairman, who had agreed to the deal, with half the money to be paid straightaway and the rest to be handed over monthly over a year, which was the normal way of doing things at that time.

Fine, said I, believing that Francis would be pleased with that, and Ray asked me what had brought about the change that had made Flitcroft suddenly available.

I was reluctant to tell him because I reckoned he might be back for some of the others with cut-price offers that Francis might find hard to refuse. I rang Francis and told him we had the deal. He sounded pleased but about twenty minutes later he rang me back and asked me to go over with him the conversation I'd had with Harford so that he could call Walker to sort it out.

Francis's voice took on a serious tone of disapproval when I told him it was the usual half down and the rest in instalments over a year. I could tell he was angry and straightaway he was on the offensive, saying nobody did deals like that and that he had insisted on £3.5 million in one hit. I argued that nobody did straight deals like that any more, but Francis insisted I rang Harford back and said one payment or the deal was not on.

Off I went again, calling Harford, explaining Francis's position and feeling glad that I had not told him of City's near bankruptcy. I was hoping that Ray would say that we should accept Blackburn's offer. I didn't mind because it would mean I could keep the player if there was to be no budging on Blackburn's part. It was not in my interest, as manager of a struggling team, for the transfer to go ahead. Now it was Ray Harford's turn to call me after talking to Jack Walker and Blackburn's new stance was one payment of £2.8 million or the original £3.5 million on the half down, half on the drip method of payment. I reported back to Francis and suggested he call Blackburn himself, which he did.

He came back to me and just said the deal had been concluded. He never told me the terms but I suspect Manchester City took a straight £2.8 million for Flitcroft. They were desperate for money. I called Flitcroft into the office and I saw a mirror of myself when Harry Catterick called me in at Everton to say he was selling me, like a piece of flesh with a number eight on it, to Arsenal.

Flitcroft looked at me and there was sadness in his eyes. He told me he didn't want to go. City were his club. He was absolutely gutted. I told him I sympathized; after all, I had been in the same position. He was a lovely lad and I wished him well and told him that if he played for Blackburn as he had done for me he would not go wrong and would rise in the game. He had the perfect attitude and has blossomed into one of the Premier League's outstanding midfield players.

As he left the office I knew what he was going through. It was hard for him to try to understand and at that point he was not thinking of moving to a club that had won the championship and had a new stadium and star players such as Alan Shearer, Colin Hendry and Chris Sutton. His heart was at Manchester City.

He was no sooner out of the office and on his way to becoming a Blackburn player when the press got hold of him and he fed them the line, unwittingly or not, that he could not understand the manager letting him go. They pounced on it and when I was asked about it I thought I was taking a sensible line by saying that I didn't really want to comment other than it was a good deal and a good price for a young player who had not played for England.

The fountain of all things to do with City and United was the *Manchester Evening News*. They had a writer called Paul Hince who had once been on City's books. Some people thought that, despite some first-team appearances, there was a residue of bitterness emanating from his pen. His article, centred on me, after the sale of Flitcroft, read like a diatribe from Mr Angry of Moss Side as he questioned my judgement.

My role after the sale, in saying very little, had been to protect the chairman and his board. I could have expressed the disappointment I felt at *having* to sell Flitcroft but I kept quiet, honestly believing that the perceptive supporters would put two and two together and realize that the sale was unavoidable because of the financial mess the club was in. But no questions were asked and that was the only time I felt let down by Francis.

He could have spelled out honestly that the club was virtually insolvent and that the sale of Garry Flitcroft had been absolutely necessary to the survival of their team. Surely it must have been obvious why he had been sold and just as clear that I would positively not want him to go. I was given no protection by Francis, which meant I carried the can. Hince could also have been more supportive for the club in its plight. Instead he went for my jugular. I honestly believe that was the beginning of the end for me in Manchester.

We cracked on without Flitcroft watched by an often hostile crowd. It was always going to be difficult and we arrived at the last match of the season, at home to Liverpool, knowing we had to win. It didn't matter what the others did. It seemed, as we approached that match, that this was the biggest hole I had ever been in. I had dug teams out of a few, at Colchester and Southampton, for instance, but this was an abyss. I was down on the touchline. As Liverpool went two up at half-time with goals by Ian Rush it was like watching the slow death of Manchester City.

It was an altogether mad afternoon. Kit Symons got us a goal back and then Uwe Rosler slotted a penalty. We were at two apiece when a spectator close to the tunnel shouted that Southampton, who were also candidates to go down with the already relegated Queens Park Rangers and Bolton Wanderers, had conceded a goal in the 89th minute. It meant that a draw would have been good enough to keep us up. We had the ball, so I told Steve Lomas to take it to the corner flag to kill time. He was doing that when I heard that the Southampton goal had been disallowed. I found myself running down the track trying to get another message across and no doubt looking an absolute fool.

That is something they bring up in Manchester almost every time my name is mentioned. It was ridiculous. Did people think I would be telling them to play keep-ball in the corner at 2–2 if I knew we still needed to win the match? Of course not. But for the misinformation, I would have been throwing everyone forward. I made the wrong kind of headlines, naturally.

My instinct told me that the noose was tightening, especially as the financial man in the background, David Bernstein, was taking a greater interest towards the end of the season. Francis Lee's dream of taking the club back to those days he shared with Malcolm Allison and Joe

Mercer seemed increasingly likely to be unfulfilled. I went to a board meeting halfway through the summer. The overwhelming feeling was one of desolation. We had nearly escaped the drop, finishing on the same number of points as Coventry City and Southampton, but we had scored just thirty-three goals all season and that was the difference between them and us. Had we escaped it would have been like getting out of Alcatraz. We had tried. Fans and players had given their all at the end but it came far too late.

The reality was that the club was going nowhere at the time. Only those in the inner sanctum of the board-room knew the extent of the club's debts. At that summer board meeting I formed the impression that David Bernstein was setting me up for a fall. I was given firm instructions that all the big earners had to go, at cut-price deals if necessary. He was a financial expert and said that we just could not sustain such expense in the First Division. It was ruthless. Peter Beagrie went to Everton, Keith Curle to Wolves. Garry Flitcroft and Tony Coton had already gone, Terry Phelan and Niall Quinn both left. I told Curle I would be relieving him of his captain's duties and that we were circulating his name to other clubs. That's the way it was with most of them as I pulled the players into the office one by one.

I hated what I was doing; bringing all this bad news to these players, telling them that there was no alternative to departure and that it was my job to shove them out of the door. All the time the Manchester City supporters must have wondered what was going on as one after another the players began to leave. As far as the public was concerned, I never said a thing; I kept my peace with Bernstein. I was doing my job for the club but it was a horrible time upsetting people, showing them the way out when I would honestly have liked most of them to stay.

Not many of them were keen on moving, which was understandable given the contracts they were on. It made no difference when I mentioned the difficult time I was having, but I guess that was understandable, too. Quinn's departure was not smooth. He had a seriously lucrative contract that was due to run until 1998. I knew that Peter Reid at Sunderland was interested in taking Quinn and waited for his call, but I knew big Quinny to be another player unlikely to want to surrender what he had in his City contract. July had arrived and almost all of the big-money boys had moved on except Quinn. We were playing a friendly in Athlone, Ireland, and won 3–2. Rosler was one of those still at the club and he scored one of the goals while Quinn got the other two.

We won another match against Cork 3–1 and I could see that Quinn would be a natural scorer and winner in the First Division, but I also knew he was one of those who had to go. I sat him down and said, no argument, you've got to go and you will have to take what you can. He was adamant, in that disarming way of his, that he had a fantastic contract and felt like seeing it through and had no intention of going anywhere.

Quinn was difficult. He said he was sitting still. I said he was on his bike. I felt like the succession of Leeds managers, David O'Leary, Terry Venables and Peter Reid in the early 2000 years, probably felt when they had to get rid of their top players such as Rio Ferdinand and Jonathan Woodgate. The multi-millions they brought in barely touched the ever-increasing debt.

I was almost giving them away. Quinn eventually went for £350,000 to Sunderland, when he came to an agreement with Peter Reid. I thought he was probably worth £2.5 million but we just had to get some cash. I managed to sign Paul Dickov from Arsenal for £750,000, which may sound surprising in view of City's parlous state at the bank but it was spread over a long period and contained clauses about the number of appearances and goals scored.

A striker was an absolute necessity, but the thing that hurt me then and hurts me to this day is that the Manchester City supporters will never forgive me for what they see as my dismantling of their club. People from that area have told me that time and again and I just want to say to them that they simply wouldn't have enough time to listen to me explain fully what went on there. Almost throughout the entire thirteen months of my stay there I felt helpless. Nobody above me was prepared to put the supporters in the picture so that they knew the full situation. If only they had known of the strictures I was operating under. There was no way I could tell them off my own bat. It was a chairman's responsibility but there were no explanations and the *Manchester Evening News* never let up in what I sensed was an orchestrated campaign to get rid of me.

Nor was Francis Lee, a man who had done so much for City, allowed to escape the wrath of the people. Both of us took more stick than was justified. Those directors who had presided over years of their own feeble misman-agement should have been the ones to carry the blame. Francis was not there as an official much longer than me. As Manchester City went to play in the depths of the Second Division I was the complete scapegoat for all that had gone wrong and the reasons generally given were about the players I had culled. Nobody ever told them that I was operating under orders from above. I knew I was heading for the sack but the final match was as cruel as they come.

I am not complaining, because I have been around long enough to know that there are no niceties from supporters when things are going seriously wrong. My final match was at Stoke, a place with few fond memories after my stint there, but we were drawing 0–0 and then gave away two schoolboy howler goals due to mistakes committed by our central defender Alan Kernaghan.

It was a miserable day. I could not believe what I was seeing. The fans were letting me know how they felt, which meant they were in an ugly mood. I followed the players in at half-time and looked for Kernaghan to ask him what was going on. The lads said he was in with the doctor, which was a surprise. It seemed that as a diabetic he had got his insulin doses wrong and was almost having fits with his sugar levels being low. What could I do? What could I say? I was simply bemused that even something like that could go wrong. I had just bought

Paul Dickov and sent him on in place of Rosler, who was something of a crowd favourite. I was about to move Rosler out of the club and on his way as per instructions. That substitution decision only helped to increase the levels of hate and although we pulled a goal back to lose 2–1, I could hear the Stoke fans joining in with City and their cries of 'Ball out.'

The weekend was miserable and on Monday morning, Francis rang me and asked me to go round to his house. I half expected to find gallows erected in his considerable garden, although I realized that if I was to be sacked it was as a result of a knee-jerk reaction because they had just allowed me to buy Dickov.

Franny was there with secretary Bernard Halford and came straight to the point, as he always would: 'Look, mate, I've got to tell you that it can't go on.' I listened and some of the fight drained out of me as I told him, fine. By this time I had not really had enough but I had taken so much on my shoulders; I had fielded so much flak. I had upset so many players; I had done so much of the board's dirty work that I was in danger of being bowed by worry.

Possibly because I understood them, the traumatic times the players were having was weighing heavily on me. I knew how hard it was for them with their young families, having to relocate with all the anxieties of moving house and finding new schools. My own frustration was born of the fact that I wanted to keep many of the players because I knew they could get us out of the Second Division and back towards the Premier League.

But my biggest gripe was that nobody had taken it upon themselves to give the supporters the clearest picture possible about the shambolic finances and the instructions given to me to offload players who were popular in the stands. I told Francis of my feelings on these issues in that I was not getting the proper backing. He listened; he even listened when I suggested he open a bottle of champagne, which he duly did. Then I advised him to face the fans and face the facts. I said that until he spelled out the exact situation the club would struggle. It was only in that area that I felt Francis had let me down.

My fondness for Francis is undiminished. He was good for the club. The gossip on the streets was that he interfered, picked the team and gave them pep talks in the dressing room before matches. None of it was true. He certainly came into the dressing room before matches but it was only to wish everyone the best of luck. He was a football man and he had valid opinions, which I always respected. I stayed with him a long time that night.

There were times when I believed I did not deserve to be in the role of Manchester City's patsy. It surprised me that more of the spectators did not stop and think about the situation. Had they done so they would have realized that I must have been operating under instructions. On paper I am the man who took them down while selling their best players. That is a hell of a statement to live with and it is quite unfair.

As had happened in the past I said to Lesley that we should go to Spain to get away from it all and recover from the curse of Manchester City. Off we flew with plenty of thinking time and the occasional glass of Rioja. There is an inevitable empty feeling when you lose your job in football, as well as a need to restore the battered feelings. I sat there for the first few days analysing every decision I had taken on my own. The enforced selling I could do nothing about but I have never been shy about owning up to mistakes I might have made along the way. Going to Manchester in the first place was the first calamitous move, but there were one or two others that I admitted to myself and shared with Lesley. Bringing in Gerry Creaney was a bad blooper although he came in the deal that saw Paul Walsh go south. Creaney was a disappointment to me. I thought he was a boat-rocker and I didn't think he was doing it on the pitch for me, either.

That and a few things came back to me as I sat in Spain and reflected. I was as close to having a broken heart over football as it was possible to be. I knew where I had gone wrong and should have nipped some of the problems early. I should have stood my ground on deadline day.

Days in the sun helped the healing and soon it was time to go back to Manchester and our house near Alderley Edge, a lovely village. There were not many friendly faces about because I was still cast as the villain in the minds of half of Manchester, but at a time when I needed friendly faces there were some there. Among them were Paul and Anne Phillips and the couple who ran the Plough and Flail pub just down the road, and Mike and Glenys Byrne. Alan and Trish Barker were always good company as well.

The game had hurt me again. I had been hurt at Portsmouth by Jim Gregory, there was pain at the end of events at Stoke and now I was suffering from what had happened at Manchester City. There were good, fun times, too, and one night after we had beaten Coventry City in a cup replay will always be in my memory.

We ended up having an impromptu party in the boardroom long after everyone else had gone home. Francis was doing his party piece, the old Stanley Holloway monologue 'Albert and the Lion', and almost everyone else there did a turn. Francis, who tended to take over on these occasions, was a splendid host. We often went out for dinner together and there was always an enormous amount of laughter, which was a perfect antidote to the cares and woes of the football club. Impromptu parties were all part of the fun. Sometimes we would have splendid Sunday lunches with Colin Barlow and his wife Eunice, who became good friends.

That was me finished, though, and Francis, who seemed to be running things despite Bernstein having the title, was very honourable over the contract situation and paid me out in full promptly and to the last penny, confirming what I had always thought about him despite the hiccup over the Flitcroft transfer. We stayed in Alderley Edge for quite a while because we liked the area and I had started to do some after-dinner speaking. I had a format that was tried and trusted. After all, I had seen all sides of football in my roller-coaster career as a player and manager.

I was picking up the threads of my life as well as I could, although it seemed that every time I went out of the door I was confronted by the whiff of Manchester City failure. I was enjoying the after-dinner routine and the personal appearances. My golf was improving and it dawned on me slowly that I really was finished with football. I didn't want to be hurt any more. I had seen an unhealthy wind of change whistling through the game, especially in the Premier League. It was getting worse. The attitudes of footballers had changed with the big money and the leeching agents.

Managers who normally dealt directly with players now had to speak through the Mr Ten Per Cent (or even more). Respect for authority was disappearing. The more perks the players received, the more they wanted. I saw football as not being as healthy in the modern era as it had been in the past.

One day, after much contemplation, I mentioned to Lesley that perhaps the time had come when we should start to enjoy some of the things in life that we had never been able to find time for before.

A winter holiday in Barbados seemed a good way to start spoiling ourselves. But I had not heard the last of what some folk like to call the Beautiful Game.

14

BARBADOS SURPRISE

Football was no longer our preoccupation as we flew off for our winter holiday on the Caribbean island of Barbados. To go away to the sun with no worries about points or players was a unique experience for Lesley and me. I knew that racing people, especially the trainers of flat horses, loved their Barbadian breaks with the warm blue waters, constant sunshine and those spectacular rum punches. We were there for the whole of January in 1998 after I lost my job at Manchester City in August 1997. It was all gloriously relaxing. We swam, we ate alfresco and we had wonderful balmy evenings. At the hotel there was a bar that you swam to and that, of course, was a novelty I could not resist. We were going to enjoy our Saturdays in particular, thinking of all those cold, noisy grounds with managers twitching and the results of the games taking on life or death meanings for some of them. On more than one occasion I raised a glass among the bronzed bodies and said: 'This is the life.'

One afternoon, after a fantastic time alternating between splashing in the pool and gliding up to the bar, I decided I needed a siesta and left Lesley with her cocktail while I went to the room. As I walked in I noticed the little red message light flashing on the telephone. Puzzled, because not many people knew where we were, I picked up the phone and the operator said there was a message for me. It was just a telephone number in America with a request to call it. I dialled the number without a clue about who might be answering it at the other end. The number bore no resemblance to any I had picked up from friendships made when playing in the United States.

When I got through the voice at the other end announced simply: 'Brian Howe.' I knew instantly that it was the lead singer of the rock band Bad Company. He was a fully paid-up Portsmouth supporter. He asked me how long I was spending in Barbados. We had another week to go and I was beginning to think that perhaps he was going to pop down from the States to spend a little break with us. The call was much more businesslike than that.

He said he wanted me to take over as manager of Portsmouth again as soon as I was back in England because he was planning to buy the club off the Gregory family. By this time Jim had handed over the chairmanship to his son Martin. Brian told me they were having financial problems and were bottom of the league. It sounded a very familiar scene to me. Brian said that the club would be taken over by him along with a pal, Vince Wollanin, and they felt I was the only person to get Pompey out of trouble.

He was very persuasive, saying the Portsmouth people still loved me to death, that they would all be behind me and that I had the experience and know-how to get the club moving again with a lift from the bottom of the First Division. This was the last kind of call I was expecting to receive. I went back to the bar and told Lesley what had happened. I needed a stiff drink. I knew, of course, that Pompey were in trouble, and I could not wait to get my hands on a newspaper that might be carrying the league tables. They were seven points adrift at the bottom, as good as dead and buried in January with nineteen matches to go.

My first reaction was to sense that it was a complete no-win situation as far as I was concerned, but for the football man who had given it all up in favour of a new lifestyle that involved winter sun, there was still that lingering urge to be among footballers and the banter of the dressing room. Perhaps Lesley sensed this in me because she said she still felt I had some unfinished business to attend to. She believed I might like to take the job through to the end of the season to see if I could get them out of their plight. My initial reaction was that only a miracle could save them. The task looked impossible, but she was almost pushing me into it saying that if I did save them I would, indeed, have proved myself as something of a miracle worker. My mind was spinning this way and that. I could not decide although inevitably, I suppose, I could not resist the smell of the liniment and the roar of the crowd.

In the end I rang Brian and said I would take on the challenge. Brian said the deal with the Gregorys would probably be done in Paris. It hadn't happened yet, so would I mind hanging on? No problem, but I made a point of saying that I would prefer to take the job just until the end of the season at first. We flew back from Barbados to see that Portsmouth had lost another game and that Terry Venables, who had been installed as chairman, had resigned along with the Pompey coach, Terry Fenwick.

I also had a call from Terry Brady, a Portsmouth director, who said he was ringing at the behest of Martin Gregory who wanted me to go back as manager. He said it looked as though they were about to be taken over by some people based in America, presumably Brian Howe and his cohorts, but they were not sure of the immediate future except that they were desperate for a manager. I certainly drove from Alderley Edge to watch Sheffield United, Portsmouth's future opponents, play at Ipswich, but I had not agreed to be manager. I had made up my mind that I could not work for Martin Gregory because I had found his father to be a loathsome individual. I decided I would go back to look after Portsmouth for Brian Howe but not for a Gregory.

I only made that trip to Ipswich after Brian Howe told me that he and his colleagues were ninety-nine per cent certain that they would be the next owners of Portsmouth, and that was good enough for me if it meant the complete severance of the Gregory regime. After the match at Ipswich I headed straight for Portsmouth to stay the weekend with Terry Hussey, my lifelong friend. The news had been leaked that I was coming back, a news item that the fans clung to, apparently, after Pompey lost another Saturday match. A press conference was fixed for Monday morning.

Talk about the good old days! Familiar faces were aplenty as TV and radio reporters lined up with the newspapermen. The fans were out, too, with many a Pompey scarf being waved in the air. I answered all the usual questions and promised to do my best to keep the club in the division. It seemed I hardly had time to catch my breath when I was sitting behind my old desk once again. I was back and began to wonder where Brian had got to, because I hadn't seen him or his partner, Vince Wollanin, and had convinced myself that they were my new bosses. After five minutes casting my eyes around the office, peeping in the drawers and all the usual familiarization routines, the door opened and Martin Gregory walked in.

Alarm bells were ringing in my head when he said the press conference had gone well. Then he thanked me for coming back to the club and said he had come to talk to me about my terms. I was not impressed and let him know my feelings. I told him I had not come to manage Portsmouth under his chairmanship but that I was there to work for Brian and his partner, who had assured me that they were ninety-nine per cent certain to take over.

He told me he had turned them down. Now I was in a mess. It had been announced that I was the new manager but here I was facing the prospect of working with the son of the father I despised. Needing some thinking time, and aware of how I had been banging on at the press conference and to the fans, I decided I would

329

take the players training. An atmosphere had been created around the club, which meant that everyone was in an upbeat mood. In a way I was taking charge over Gregory because I jumped up, told him I was taking training, that I would probably take the job until the end of the season and that I would tell him what I wanted, wage-wise, when I returned at lunchtime. As I drove to meet the players I had very mixed feelings. Part of me wanted another crack at football management, which was what I was being offered, but I was also aware of my lack of trust in the Gregory family, whose company I had not enjoyed in a previous stint as manager. I had a lot to think about but once I found myself among the players, the football man in me seemed to take over, although I was anxious to get Brian Howe on the phone to find out what was happening. He told me it was impossible to do the deal with Martin Gregory. I decided I would still take the job, at least until the end of the season.

These were my exact words to the players as I walked into the room where they were waiting for instructions. I said: 'Will you all sit down, please. You have got this club into the biggest mess I've seen in my life. We've got to get out of it now and we've got sixteen games left.'

One of them interrupted, saying there were more matches to be played. I cut him short, saying: 'No, there aren't because you are three matches adrift so you can forget those three. You've got sixteen matches to get us out of trouble, and I don't just mean getting off the bottom, I mean getting out of the bottom three. We are going to do it one way and we are going to do it

330

together. I am going to tell you how we will get out of trouble and how you will stay in this football team. And when we are out of trouble how you will stay and play for me. That is what I demand.'

Then I gave them the 'Alan Ball expects' rigmarole, which I had neglected to preach at Manchester City, and then I trained them. I made it lighthearted with plenty of ball work. They needed to be enjoying themselves because, for whatever reason, there is no fun when you are points adrift at the bottom of your division. It was good to see them smiling. When it was all over I told them we would have something of the same the following day, and then I went back to the ground to sit down with Martin Gregory and Terry Brady. It was my turn to go straight to the point in the negotiations. I told them that I would take the job but that I wanted £1,000 a week in expenses, not wages. I would be flying up and down to Manchester, where we still had the house at Alderley Edge. I told them I didn't want a club car as I would use my own where necessary, but if I kept them up I would want a £25,000 payment.

My feeling, you see, was that above all I wanted to help Portsmouth in their dreadful situation and the £25,000 was what I felt the bonus should be. When you think about it now, in today's terms, that figure in 1998 was not much more than a pittance. I was doing it for Portsmouth and the people and club alone because I did not want to work for that family. I loved the place. I wanted to pull them out of the mire. I was gambling on £25,000 to keep them up.

It was all so strange. On the Saturday, driving from that match at Ipswich, the radio had Brian Howe announcing that I would be Portsmouth's next manager. There was also a rumour that Portsmouth had signed Steve Claridge, once a Pompey apprentice, from Leicester City. It was 24 January and two days later I was there working not for Brian Howe, but for Martin Gregory. Claridge signed two weeks later.

On 31 January we drew at home, 1–1, with Sheffield United. Then we lost at Nottingham Forest and went down 3–1 at Crewe. The signs were not good and I remember talking to Alan Knight, the goalkeeper, a man you would trust with your life and who bled for Pompey. I said I believed he was no longer enjoying his life at the club. I wasn't annoyed with him but I could tell that the situation was getting to him. We went three down against Crewe and the whole outlook was miserable. It stank of rank failure.

What could I do? I looked at the players and at that stage I could see no way out. Then, from nowhere, came the thud–thud–thud of a drumbeat. The Pompey supporters took it up. It was like a heartbeat growing stronger with the noise growing from the crowd. They never stopped, the Pompey Chimes and the drumbeat together, and we scored and hit the post and missed narrowly. We were alive again. The fans were showing the players that the club's heart was sound.

Never in my life did I think that the thump of a drum would give me such encouragement, but we were marching to the beat and in the last fifteen minutes our football was tremendous. I knew I had something to work on and those spectators, I realized, were as vital to our chances of salvation as were the players on the pitch. As the game ended I went to the end where most of our fans were gathered and I applauded them for their efforts, which may not have been very musical but I knew I could use them to Portsmouth's advantage.

I told the newspapers about the inspiration of the crowd and how they could help the team by being like a twelfth man on the field, how when we thought it had stopped at Crewe, they started up again and how supporting a team when the prospects are absolutely stone dead was important. It had worked for us at Crewe and I pleaded with them to make it work again. I told them that there was a heartbeat to our club and they must not let it die. Tomorrow, I said, we have a home game. We must not lose and you fans can win it for us. It was a Tuesday night at Fratton Park. A gale was howling up the Solent with more wind and rain than anyone liked to see. The fans and the players never stopped for a second. They were magnificent. Claridge scored his first goal for his hometown club after fifteen minutes, a header at the Fratton End, against Stockport County.

The opposition fought, as Gary Megson's teams always did, to the very last whistle, but we hung on to win 1–0 and again much of the credit went to those vociferous fans of ours who probably received a soaking for their efforts.

We were still bottom of the league but there was a feeling in the dressing room and in the stands that we were beginning to move well. There remained a long way to go but the signs were looking good.

That win over Stockport became a crucial landmark in the season. All around Fratton Park and on away grounds Pompey hearts were beating in time with the drum and getting louder all the time. We took 3,000 fans to Reading and won 1–0 in the last five minutes. Belief in survival was growing. We went to West Brom and won 3–0 and then took on Tranmere at home and won by a goal. That was four wins in succession and we were on our way. The Tranmere win took us out of the bottom three. We drew 0–0 with Middlesbrough and lost at Sunderland but there remained a Roy of the Rovers belief about the place. But then we lost 1–0 at Charlton and there was something of a blip in the optimism as we became odds on to go down.

Two matches were left and the truth was that we needed six points out of six to stay up. More than 14,000 people turned up on the Wednesday night to see us beat Huddersfield, which we did, and the season came to a climax on the last match of the season with a trip to Bradford City. We beat them 3–1 which meant we had won our last two games to finish fifth from bottom. It is almost impossible to describe the elation I felt over a job well done. It was as though hard work and determination had created the miracle. Ironically, Stoke and Manchester City went down.

The long coach journey back from Bradford was a marathon celebration. The players had done their job and I had done mine. I could not help smiling to myself when

I thought again of my 'Alan Ball expects' moment. On the way home to Portsmouth I left the coach at Oxford. The lads must have seen my departure as a signal to really go to town with the partying because between Oxford and Portsmouth they were in such riotous form that we received a bill for £3,500 from the coach company for damages caused to the interior of the bus. The players had to pay for it out of their wages.

My personal satisfaction was that I had pulled it off and that took away what small sense of failure I felt about events at Manchester City. There was still a long way to go. Portsmouth were in administration and clearly any notion of Brian Howe taking over had long disappeared.

We had another year in administration. It was difficult. Under Martin Gregory I didn't receive my £25,000 and one of the most enjoyable days came in July 1999 when it was announced that the Gregorys were leaving the club. It did not surprise me that there was a £1.9 million loss. I spent most of that summer arguing about a contract while seeking my £25,000. After all, I had kept them up. But then came the good news that Milan Mandaric, who is still chairman – and owner – was coming in to buy Portsmouth.

In some ways I hoped it would end the wrangling I had to endure following the departure of Venables and Fenwick. Before that, though, there was that 1998–9 season. We had saved the club and now was the time to consolidate. It was almost impossible. In my heart I was back in love with the game. I had done so well I was beginning to think I was immortal. All the pain of

Manchester City had, I thought, gone away, and I was enjoying the euphoria of the crowd. To have left them then, although I realized there was no money and there would be tough times down the road, was not an option. I would keep going at least until they found a new buyer. I knew it would not be long because Portsmouth is a club rich in tradition and a rich part of the fabric of British football.

We had our pre-season with one or two worrying similarities to the Manchester experience. In the hands of the administrators I had to sell good players. The money situation was tight and Venables had brought in five Australians with two of them, Craig Foster and John Aliosi, on long contracts at big money. I had to tell them that the club could not afford to keep them and that they would have to go. There was a furious row between Foster and me. He was the Australian captain but I ended up giving him a free transfer just to get him off the wage bill. I was cutting the squad as finely as I could. Aliosi was our biggest asset, our best player, and I needed him. I had a torrid row with Gregory about the sale of Aliosi. It was a real toe-to-toe, no-holds-barred, stand-up row. Typical blustering Gregory, I thought. At that point I decided to take things into my own hands.

I was driving to work one morning when Gordon Strachan, then the manager of Coventry City, telephoned me. He said he wanted a centre forward because the lads he was playing hadn't a clue about scoring goals. I asked him if I was right in thinking he was inquiring about Aliosi. He conceded that the two lads who were scoring the most goals in the division were Lee Hughes of West Brom and Aliosi and said yes, tell me about him.

As usual in these cases I was as forthright and honest as I could be. I told Strachan that if he was looking to build off him, forget it. He cannot bring anybody into play, is no good at linking up. He can't really play with his back to goal. He is a runner in behind people. He's quick, he's left footed and he has a knack in and around the box of finding the net, which he does regularly. He is not the bravest in the all-round aspects of the game.

Strachan's answer came quickly: 'Fine. What are you asking for him?'

My response was just as swift. I said I wanted a million pounds and no less, plus another half million based on goals scored and appearances made. Even then, I said, you are getting him cheaply, because he is among the top scorers in the league. He agreed, telling me that West Brom were asking £5.5 million for Hughes, who had scored three goals fewer than Aliosi and was a bit older.

If it sounded as though I was giving him away I told Gordon of our financial woes and that the money from the sale would help the club and me even if I happened to be cutting my own throat in letting him go. I reported back to Terry Brady who, thank God, was the only one with me through this terrible time. He said he would speak to the chairman, who was still Gregory, although I had virtually ceased to have contact with him, and Strachan went off to speak to his chairman.

Terry Brady said he would also contact Aliosi and tell him of the intentions to sell and added that the deal looked like good business as far as he was concerned. Strachan rang me back a day later and straightaway I could hear the discomfort in his voice. He told me the deal had been done between the two chairmen, Martin Gregory and Bryan Richardson, and the fee was £690,000 with no add-ons.

I thanked Strachan for letting me know and realized in my own mind that I was unlikely to see any of the money for replacements. I was in the role of Billy Muggins again. The deal had been done behind my back and I was helpless. You didn't have to put two and two together to deduce what had happened, but now I had lost my best striker and the money had gone into the big, black hole of debt. The fans were probably more distraught than anyone, but this time they seemed to understand the club's poverty. Fund-raising became an issue in everyone's minds. Lesley and I went on sponsored walks and at one point the fans went round the town carrying a coffin. It had on it 'Portsmouth FC Rest in Peace', and wherever they went people threw money into the coffin. I had never seen anything like it in my life, but by now the men in grey suits were all over Fratton Park trying to unravel years of financial mystery and intrigue.

I had to watch them sacking people who had been at the club for years. Cleaning ladies, office staff. Many of them were in tears and all I could do was stand and watch them, put my arm around them, try to offer words of consolation. Everybody knew it was nobody's fault, but the person who was getting most of the flak was Terry Venables, who had left Portsmouth in that hideous state of seven points adrift when I came back to the place in January 1998.

Usually I just got on with my job, doing what I did best on the training ground and out on the pitch, but now I felt embroiled in it all. I wanted to see things through to the end so that the day would come when I could leave them feeling healthy. That seemed something far away in the distance, almost unreachable as I took a drop in money. They wanted to sack my staff, Keith Waldron, Kevin Bond, Ted McDougall, Neil McNab and our Jimmy, who was with the youths. I brought Jimmy in to work with McNab on the youth side. He was doing a good job and learning his trade. He played a couple of matches in the reserves as a non-contract player but, as with the rest of the staff, he knew he was vulnerable.

Initially they all took pay cuts. It was easy for the men in suits to illustrate to me where the mistakes had been made over the years. The levels of incompetence and mismanagement that had gone on with those involved in the balance sheet of running the club were frightening.

While I was paring the playing staff and the expense right down to the bone I was learning some invaluable lessons, mainly on how not to run a football club. At first we were losing £30,000 a week but with prudent cuts – and some not so prudent – we got it down to £3,500 a week. We were having to make savings that had never bothered me before at any football club. The lads had to buy their own boots, their own studs and their own strappings. When we went away on long trips overnight we had to take cash and pay in advance, otherwise there was no room at the inn. The pre-match meals were the cheapest we could afford, usually one egg on toast. The coach firms had to be paid in cash in advance, otherwise they would not take us anywhere, and often we used buses without card tables because we had to take whatever the bus company gave us. No one could ever accuse any of that season's players of being prima donnas.

Somehow the difficulties brought us closer together in that 1998–9 season. We were down to about seventeen players but they were all heart. We won games people expected us to lose because of the desire that was within the players.

There were no slackers. Everybody gave their all. The fact that we stayed in the division was the impetus for Mandaric to come in and buy us in May 1999 for a figure that was generally touted at around £4.6 million.

We finished in nineteenth position and clinched our place in the First Division for another year with some memorably spirited performances. Soon after the season had ended we decided to go for a few days to Killarney, Lesley and I. On the way to the airport we heard the news that Mandaric was poised to buy, and soon there was the official announcement that the Gregorys were no longer involved. Their era was over. I had been aware that David Deacon, a previous chairman's son, was involved with Mandaric, along with Bob McNab, the former Arsenal fullback who had been coaching in the States, where Mandaric had owned a club, San Jose, for whom George Best had played. The pair had become good friends. It was good to hear that the administrators, Tom Burton and John Ariel, had announced 'an agreement to secure the future of Portsmouth Football Club'.

I was delighted that the club was going to be rescued. The situation was dire and I did not believe that we could have hung on for another season. I was not bothered who bought the club but knew it was essential that someone should come in. David Deacon telephoned me in Ireland and asked if I would like to speak to the chairman. We had a brief, friendly chat and I said I would fly back as soon as I possibly could and would meet him at the Post House Hotel.

We had a very long chat and I liked him instantly as a person, and still do, but in some respects I misread what he had in mind for Portsmouth. That was my fault. Although he was a powerful and successful businessman he had never lived in England and was not familiar with English culture or the way English football operated. He was a football man all right, for as well as San Jose he also owned the Belgian club Charleroi, and had played quite a bit in his time. He was a Serbian-American and probably knew little about Portsmouth until he heard of the club's financial problems and fancied a piece of some interesting action if he could clear the debts. My first impressions when we sat down were that he was ambitious. He gave the impression of being a strong man. He sounded very supportive of me and said he had watched from afar and was fulsome in his praise of what I had done over the previous eighteen months.

Mandaric assured me everything was fine about my

contract. He paid me the £25,000 that Martin Gregory had failed to deliver. It was a terrific meeting and I thought it was fantastic that I could now get on with building a good football club. I did not realize that he wanted instant success.

I was looking three years down the line, getting things in order properly. I could restart the youth policy, which had been run down. I could regenerate the scouting system, which had also been hit by the administrators. Previously there had been a network of people all over the country looking out for talent.

Mandaric was agreeable when I went to him with my budget proposals. I wanted budgets for scouting, youth development, buying players and so on and he said my ideas were marvellous. He agreed with me when I said I was going to get a group of players in around the twenty to twenty-two age group and mould them, teach them over a couple of years, so that we would have the players to take us through the division and further and who would be able to handle themselves well in the Premier League. I said I wouldn't milk him for millions but that we would get there with good, young talent. We would build up slowly without him having to fork out millions of pounds.

That was where I read him wrong. Big spending appealed to him. I was going the softly-softly way when he wanted the headlong rush into the transfer market throwing the big bucks around.

My thinking was that I would build constructively, giving him time to get his feet under the table, and then

PLAYING EXTRA TIME

have a look at the ground, which was badly in need of either refurbishment or rebuilding, while I was laying down proper foundations on the playing side. Sadly, I lasted only a few months with him. We were just below halfway in the First Division, which would have been all right for my first year, but he was an impatient man. Everything had to be done in a hurry. It was all black and white. There were no grey areas. He had driven himself to the top in big business, where he was a winner. And like all winners he was a bad loser. A shocking loser, in fact, even worse than me. We lost 3–0 in a pre-season friendly at Dorchester and we didn't get to bed until 3.30 in the morning because he could not stomach the defeat. If we hadn't taken his tie and shoelaces off him I think he might have hanged himself. He could neither understand nor accept my theories about pre-season friendlies, which were finding out missions with players who were still reaching full fitness. He went on at Kevin Bond and myself, criticizing the selection, the tactics and the players we had brought in.

In defeat, nothing was ever right. If we lost a match at Fratton Park he would keep us there until midnight so that the groundsman was hanging about waiting to lock up. We had a poor run of results leading to a 1–0 defeat at Sheffield United. We had lost a few matches by the odd goal and I knew he was getting restless; the end came for me after that Sheffield game. I was out on 9 December 1999. He was quite polite about it when he asked me to a meeting and afterwards he spoke at a press conference. This is, verbatim, what he said:

343

This is not the most pleasant time of my football business life, but a man's gotta do what a man's gotta do. This club really does not belong to me. This club belongs to thousands of loyal supporters in the city of Portsmouth and the region and I happen to be a temporary caretaker for them. When I say temporary, I mean it has seen 100 years of history already and I will not be here in 100 years' time. I just hope I will be a small part of a very rich history of this club. But I don't want to play the part where I took the club down to the Second Division.

I have a tremendous respect for Alan Ball as a person and as a football man but things don't always happen like you want them to.

If somebody had told me six months ago when I took over this club I would have told them today would not be possible because we would do things properly and professionally and I believe we did not do things properly off the field especially. The major thing that hasn't happened yet is a good football team and we don't have that today.

I believe we have a lot of good players but we don't have the team yet. Therefore whatever happened this morning had to happen. We have to motivate players to give their best because if they had we wouldn't be where we are today.

It was a slightly upsetting statement because I felt we were getting there – although clearly not quickly enough for the owner who may well have reached the top of the business ladder but didn't realize that football often requires patience. I had a very small squad and we had been hit by a run of injuries. I lost my central defenders, Jason Cundy and Adrian Whitbread, through injury. My goalkeeper, Aaron Flahavan, was having blackouts on the pitch and he was out for a long time, and then our bright young striker, Rory Allen, suffered a badly broken ankle. It upset me, too, that no sooner was I out of the door than I was followed by Kevin Bond, Ted McDougall and our Jimmy. He'd been with me at Exeter, Southampton and Portsmouth and now he was seeing the harsh realities of football. He did not go to another club but kept in touch with the game working on sports issues with a London firm of lawyers.

There was a moderately worrying development before I left the club when he brought in Bob McNab, who had lived in the United States for twenty years. His presence had me worrying about what was being said in the background and I wondered if he had been lined up for my job weeks before. He took the team for the first match after I departed. McNab had been Mandaric's friend and football adviser in America and I saw the danger signs when he first appeared as the chairman's guest. I knew McNab as a man of opinions who fancied himself as a judge and as a tactician. He was the man behind the signing of a defender, Jason Crowe, from Arsenal.

It transpired that Bob had been keeping his hand in at coaching at Arsenal and had been impressed by the youngster, who was going to find it hard to break into the first team there. Mandaric told me all this and said we had been able to buy him. The fee was around £180,000, not a million as was reported. This lad just turned up at training, having been foisted upon me. The deal had absolutely nothing to do with me, the manager. When I went to watch an Arsenal reserve team game soon afterwards I asked them how long Bob McNab had spent with them and they told me it was one week.

It was around that point, I suppose, that I knew I was leaving, and as I went I had time to reflect on the ways of Milan Mandaric who, I must stress, has always had the success of Portsmouth Football Club at heart. It was not easy for him to see me that December morning in 1999 and tell me my time was over. He began by saying that I had done a fantastic job and that but for my efforts the club could have disappeared altogether. He said, however, that he thought I had gone as far as I could with the team. He wanted to move on. He said my contract would be terminated but that he would make sure I was paid in full. Indeed I was, and I will always be grateful for his honesty. We remain friends and there is a warm welcome whenever I go to Fratton Park these days.

In seeking that elusive quality, success, he was the proverbial bull in a china shop. After Bob McNab's one-match caretaker role, the club went through a run of managers in a matter of months. There was Tony Pulis, Steve Claridge and Graham Rix before the chairman went for Harry Redknapp, who had seen some heady days as a player and manager at West Ham. We are all different and Harry had his own style. He was something of a quick–fix merchant, a show me the money and I'll get the job done kind of man.

He received the money and brought in another wise old bird, Jim 'Bald Eagle' Smith, as his assistant and they plundered the market to put together a team that took Portsmouth back to the Premiership. They manipulated the loan system and flooded Fratton Park with foreigners, and the spectators have been having a ball.

The drum still beats and Mandaric continues to talk about turning the ground around and creating a 35,000–seater stadium. You can only applaud the application of a man who is driving on, rubbing shoulders with the Manchester Uniteds and Arsenals, and wish Pompey well. There should be no more empty coffins being paraded through the streets as begging bowls.

It is hard to imagine championship champagne being quaffed down by the Solent but the old city has every reason to be thankful for Milan Mandaric.

15

FIGHTING ON

Cancer haunts and stalks. It is with you twenty-four hours a day, seven days a week, and affects every aspect of life. For the last two and a half years I have watched our eldest daughter, Mandy, and Lesley battle the cursed disease.

Mandy was first to find that dreaded telltale lump in her breast. At the same time, Lesley was aware of a pain in her groin. At first she dismissed it as something or nothing. It was the beginning of her ovarian cancer. Very soon I was watching Lesley go with Mandy for her chemotherapy and then sit for five hours the next day having her own treatment. Their inner strength constantly amazed me.

Mandy's chemo worked. After the long months of anguish she was cleared, though the check-ups go on. She is fit. So much so that in March 2003 she ran the London Marathon with Jimmy in aid of the Bobby Moore Fund for Cancer Research. For Lesley, the fight for quality of life went on. She had chemotherapy, radiotherapy, special treatments and diets and operations. Still, a smile was never far away.

Believe me, Lesley was braver than any footballer I

have ever played against. However, there were sad reminders of her plight every day. We always used to walk the dogs together, the black Labrador called Louis and Teddy, her little white Maltese, on the beach by the Hamble estuary every morning. Then I began taking them on my own.

Lesley deserved to live and it is difficult for me to think of anything else, but these are difficult times. Every day I realize just how much she did for me. As with all footballers, the clubs mollycoddled me. Everything was taken care of: tickets, hotels, transport, all sorted. They even kept your passport and gave it back to you for checking through controls. You were carried everywhere.

All of a sudden you are out of football. Even having been around the world a few times, I still felt lost at airports. Mundane procedures such as checking in were new to me. Lesley did all that and I followed her until I became confident enough to do it myself. I thought everything in our lives had been arranged.

I'd had great times. There were times when I had lots of money and occasions when funds were low. But I have done sufficiently well to be able to look at our house in a lovely part of Hampshire, the village of Warsash, and conclude that there could be nowhere better to live together.

Lesley always had energy to burn. Even when the prognosis was poor, when we knew the cancer appeared relentless in its progress, she tried to get the most out of life for as long as possible. She insisted she was feeling relatively fit early in 2003 and announced that it was time to do some travelling, so we booked a trip that we hoped would be rewarding, stimulating and fun. We were not wrong on any of those counts.

After spending Christmas Day in the warmth of all our family we flew out of Heathrow on Boxing Day with an exciting itinerary ahead of us. The first leg took us to Bangkok, and then we flew on to the restful Thailand resort of Ko Sumui, where we spent three relaxing days. It was a wonderful way of breaking our journey to the next destination, the spectacular Australian city of Sydney. We stayed with our dear friends Peter and Jill Hensman.

The New Year celebrations, on a yacht in the harbour, were breathtaking as we watched the fireworks shooting from the famous Harbour Bridge and marvelled at the Opera House silhouetted against the night sky with rockets, flares and cascading stars everywhere.

With all that fresh in our minds we flew up to Surfer's Paradise, where we stayed at the Glades Golf Resort for five days before meeting up with our friends Terry and Jean Hopley and my ex-World Cup teammate Geoff (sorry, Sir Geoff) Hurst and his wife, Judith. We had four idyllic weeks sharing a house at Sanctuary Cove, a desti-nation as blissful as it sounds. During our last week in Australia we flew to the Whitsunday Islands on the Great Barrier Reef and had four truly fantastic days on Hayman Island.

The whole experience was perfect. It was a dream holiday and we flew home enriched by the experience. We were feeling well and happy and the buoyancy stayed with us so that a few days later we were off to Portugal, where I was to play in the Jimmy Tarbuck Golf Classic. Jimmy, a Liverpudlian who is one of Britain's best-known comedians, is as funny off the stage as he is on it. With him a great time is guaranteed. With Jimmy and his wife, Pauline, and friends Steve and Fran Roots, it was a fun-filled time.

Everything was going well but, always at the back of my mind, I knew it couldn't last. We both prayed that Lesley would at least stay well until our daughter Keely's wedding. She reached that goal and was the driving force behind the organization of Jimmy's wedding to Lesley. Yet another illustration of her strength.

We had our World Cup reunion with a great turn-out of the lads at Rhinefields, in the New Forest. Lesley had done most of the arrangements and I felt tremendously proud of her, as it was a huge success. I could also tell that she was not as well as she would have me believe.

She was tiring easily. There was a lot of pain, and we became convinced that the chemo wasn't working. We decided to see Professor Martin Gore at the Royal Marsden Hospital in London. We went in hope; with Lesley there was always optimism. Things were always half full, never half empty. Maybe Professor Gore would know of some new treatments or trials that she could consider.

After a long debate with him that day, he suggested some experimental and some conventional treatments. There was another chemo that he could try. We knew that it was starting to become desperate. I could sense that Lesley was beginning to lose faith in conventional chemo methods. She was questioning things. There were doubts in her mind and she was anxious to look elsewhere.

We were due to go on a family holiday to Spain, and we all met at Southampton Airport, Mandy, Dave, Louie, Jimmy and his girlfriend Lesley and baby Lacey, Lesley and me. Keely was flying out a few days later to get a tan ahead of the wedding. We all stayed in accommodation organized by one of her best friends, Anne Phelps, who lives in Puerto Banus.

Again I had that deep-down feeling that this trip might not go as well as expected. A few days into the holiday it was obvious to us all that Lesley was struggling. Her tummy had swollen so much that she looked eight months pregnant. This was as a result of the cancer seedlings in her stomach producing fluids known as ascites. The rate of production was alarming and we had to come home as her condition worsened. We went to the Royal Marsden where they drained an astonishing seven litres from her. She had five sessions where they stuck a tube into her tummy. It was terribly painful but, as usual, she bore it without a murmur. The procedure also drained away the muscle from her body with a severity that made her look extremely gaunt and left her feeling very weak.

Around this time, poring over the Internet and reading every book available, we began to look more and more seriously into the possibilities of alternative remedies. We were searching for something that would prevent or slow down the ascites and shrink the cancer. Lesley hit on a website that talked about the Ukraine method, which had been having good results in Austria. It is a natural, non-toxic approach.

We gave it every chance. Three times a week she went off to the Dove clinic to have her treatment. She changed her whole diet. She had her juices every morning and a vitamin intake to boost the immune system. We did everything possible and kept our fingers crossed. With her new diet she was able to end 2003 brighter, perkier, busy and enjoying herself. She was going shopping. She took the kids out and went to see a show. At times Lesley seemed unstoppable. When I came home one day just before Christmas 2003 she announced that she had booked a day trip to Lapland so that little Louie and Laccy, our grandchildren, could see Santa Claus. The power of speech just about failed me for a moment. A couple of days later we set off, Lesley, Mandy, me and the little ones. It was one of our best days ever even though it was a twenty-three-hour trip. The day will never be forgotten.

She was also interested in more surgery. Her philosophy was that if you could get rid of a large percentage of the cancer you would have more time to live with what was left.

All the time I was setting her targets. Another goal was reached when Keely gave birth to little Jimmy. Another trip to the Caribbean, for instance. It was a continuing scrap, marking our goals and moving from one to the next. The new treatment was helping her along the way. Some of the details have been pooh-poohed by conventional-thinking people but Lesley tried it and felt much better.

She began thinking about holidays whereas beforehand she had thought such pleasures had ended. She stopped murmuring phrases such as: 'I'm not going to see Barbados again, the blue sky and the sea.'

I remember sitting at the kitchen table one day. She was at the sink doing something when suddenly there was a deafening bang. I jumped up from reading the *Racing Post* and saw she had hit the wall with a saucepan and was repeating: 'I am not going to die. I am not going to die.' I got up and held her. This was Lesley Ball in fighting mood.

I never knew what I was going to get with her. She was strong, she was a battler. There were times when her spirit was simply unbelievable. We fought this thing with all our might.

People may be surprised to know that there have been plenty of smiles along with the dark days. I know how to use the vacuum cleaner now. I know how to shop. I know how to seek out bargains at the supermarket and I don't care who sees me. I was brought up as a typical, macho Lancashire lad by a father who considered it soppy if you went shopping or held somebody's hand. That was women's work. I now know how to operate the dishwasher, but hadn't a clue until Lesley fell ill. She used to spoil me. Mind you, the first time I used it I didn't take the wrapper off the tablet, much to everyone's delight.

I come from a long line of men who went out to work, brought home the money that provided food for the table and put their feet up before going to the pub to meet their mates. I was no different. I am no New Age man. My role was to provide a house, food and clothes. That was the way I lived my life and Lesley, being a northern girl, was used to that and demanded nothing more.

She laughed at me because I had to adapt. I had to change light bulbs and put washing into the machine. I had to learn what the knobs represented. I never knew my pin number for the hole-in-the-wall cash dispenser. Lesley paid every bill that came into the house. Financial matters used to baffle me. It was a foreign language although I can work out a Yankee racing bet in seconds. I am getting to grips with the other stuff.

When we moved home, which was twenty-four times in thirty years, I would invariably leave Lesley packing boxes and arrive at the new address to find her unpacking with the kids having to help out.

I was having to deal with everything as Lesley sometimes struggled with her illness. It was a long fight and one, to borrow boxing terminology, that I was in without the gloves on and my hands tied. The cancer was always at the back of my mind no matter how hard I tried to relieve myself of its implications. You asked questions of yourself. How brave would I be in her situation? How would I cope with my hair falling out, losing weight, going so gaunt in the face that people would look at me and think that I was wasting away?

I always used to tell Lesley that she had a great bum, but she came out of the shower one morning and said: 'You are not ever to look at my bum again because it's gone.' That gave us a great laugh. Then came the tears of realization.

No man could have had a better wife, no children a better mother. Because I was always away on tour she brought them up almost single-handed. She taught them manners and morals and worried about them. Any problem and they rang her, not me. She exuded wisdom and advice. I have been the provider and they appreciate that. I have also impressed on them the loyalty they must have to their partners. They've got to make their marriages work and they are doing so.

We have a friend whose wife was diagnosed with cancer and Lesley was counselling her even though she was struggling herself. She has learned so much from Stephanie Moore, whose husband, Bobby, died of cancer at the age of fifty-one. He was a marvellous man, gone in his prime, an impressive and proud Englishman and World Cup captain.

Lesley met and learned from professors and from books and was always a fantastic woman who did so much for people. Everyone loved and understood her. Soon after her cancer was diagnosed I was supposed to play in a golf charity day organized by Frank McLintock, my old Arsenal captain, at South Herts Golf Club, which is where the team met for lunch before home games at Highbury.

I rang Frank to tell him that I would not be able to make it but I could not tell him the nature of the problem. Lesley heard me and said: 'Go, play your golf, clear your mind a bit and have some time with your mates. I'll be all right.'

That reflected her perennial mood.

16

INTO THE DISTANCE

Most mornings you will find me walking the dogs along the beach near our house in the pretty Hampshire village of Warsash, which lies just across the Solent from the Isle of Wight. This is when I do my thinking. It is a time to reflect and a time to look forward and most of my thoughts are devoted to Lesley and the fight against her illness.

The life we had together, the ups and downs, the laughter and the hard times, the loyalty of friends: all of those things come together in a wonderful kaleidoscope of memory and gratitude. We knew when we found our house in 1998 that this was the place for us. After the nomadic life of a footballer and manager, trailing his family and his belongings to all ends of the country, and beyond, this truly was home. There was an intangible, welcoming warmth about it and after living in twenty-four different houses throughout my career this one seemed as if it was telling us that it was time to stop the wandering. This was permanent.

Behind us lay a trail of experiences that took us around the world from Lancashire to Hampshire, via Hong Kong, Australia, America and all parts of England.

There was no argument about the future. Finally, I accepted in my heart that my managerial career was over and with that acknowledgement came a huge sense of relief. It had been a long and fascinating road, with the inevitable humps and hollows, but it had brought me back to a part of the world that I knew and loved. We had wonderful friends here; the Jolly Farmer pub with its collection of characters and a whimsical Irish landlord was just up the road. Above all, though, was the nearness of our children and grandchildren.

Family ties were always important to us. Mandy, Keely and Jimmy are all within fifteen minutes of our house with their partners and children. We have some wonderful Sunday lunches when we all get together, Mandy and Dave with impish Louie, Keely and John with another little 'Bally' called Jimmy, and Jimmy himself with his Lesley and their twinkling starlet, Lacey. All three of our kids appreciate the values of loyalty and honour within their own marriages.

As a youngster, Mandy loved to spend her time with horses, show-jumping and so on. She could find happiness in mucking-out but eventually trained as a nanny before going into hairdressing. Keely had a good career as a dancer, working alongside Jim Davidson and Freddie Starr on the West End stage before taking her talents on to the entertainment side of the cruise liners. She had such balance and movement.

I would have loved our Jimmy to have made it as a footballer but it didn't work out. He did everything possible but just lacked that bit of natural ability that separates the top players from the rest. He could have managed in the lower leagues and non-league. He had reserve team games at Southampton but was probably anticipating my words when I told him: 'Son, you are not going to be good enough for this and with your name it is going to be doubly hard. I suggest we look elsewhere.'

He said he wanted to stay in football so we decided he should take all his coaching badges. Although I had released him as a player I had watched him work as a coach and asked him to take on a job with the young Portsmouth players, believing he could make a natural progression from there. I believe there is a part to play for a young coach in the football club academics. Jimmy, as well as being a good coach, was of the same generation and could relate to the pressures and temptations facing young players. Unfortunately, when I left Portsmouth, he had to go as well. He has always been a grand lad and not an ounce of bother.

Inevitably, as soon as I was an ex-manager, people were asking me about the next job. I could comfortably and confidently tell them there wouldn't be one. I know people say never say never but my assurance is 100 per cent. There will be no going back. I am finished with the sharp end of the business but I will always be there if anyone needs advice. I would even go and help someone should the call come, but have my name on a door some-where? Absolutely, positively, no.

There is no doubt that I still have boundless energy though I will be sixty in 2005, but my reasons for not wanting to run a club are simple. The game, as I grew to know and love it, I feel has gone into decline. Priorities have become so warped that it seems to me the game is being run by the players with their wage demands and their agents. The only time the players should be in charge is on the pitch. I always remember my father drumming into me the fact that no player is bigger than the club. When I look at players manipulating things to their own ends I am not sure that applies any more.

The traditional values that were the cornerstones of the football upbringing of the Charltons, Bobby Moore, Nobby Stiles, Ray Wilson and the rest of us in that generation have been eroded. Those were the pie-and-pint days and everything was relative.

A few years ago I could not imagine life without a job in football, but everything is fine and I am still in touch. Television, mainly Sky, has brought the game into our homes. Everything about the sport is closer to us. I am involved with the Saturday afternoon show of Radio Solent and go to a match now and again, usually Portsmouth or Southampton. I must be one of the very few people in the area who wants both teams to do well because the Saints and Pompey camps are strictly divided. My own experiences at those clubs were roller-coaster affairs, but these days I look upon them both with affection.

Call me an old grump, if you like, but I am not as convinced about the quality of the Premier League as some people are. I admit to being something of a traditionalist and believe that the qualities of the players in the

Sixties and Seventies, most of them British, were as good if not better than those of the players around today. You have to remember that Sky TV has programmes to sell. They are constantly packaged in euphoria, with all the trumpeting a kind of propaganda to impress on the people that everything in the game is brilliant. The top three – and as I write they happen to be Arsenal, Chelsea and Manchester United – have something special, but outside those three there is a lot of mediocrity in which twenty-two players, all as fit as fleas, charge around making mistakes. The introduction of dozens of foreigners is a worrying trend that could damage the whole foundation of the English game.

As well as that, the PLC boys have come in from the city looking for instant rich pickings. Football isn't like that. Most businesses are built over a period of time. It's like erecting a house. You need solid foundations and careful building, and then eventually you can put the roof on it and own something solid that lasts for decades. Football should be like that but it isn't. Managers have to be today people. They have bosses who demand success straightaway, when the classic example of building a club, rather than throwing in a team at short notice, is Manchester United. Sir Alex Ferguson said, when he took over at Old Trafford, that his long-term plan was to recreate the Busby Babes, that generation of young players brought through with amazing vision by the late Sir Matt Busby as long ago as the Fifties.

Some people became impatient with Ferguson, but he delivered and the proof of his policy can be seen in the likes of David Beckham, Paul Scholes, Nicky Butt and the Neville brothers, Gary and Phil, among others. Fergie has also been judicious in the transfer market, but the bottom line of Manchester United's continuing, trophy-winning success is the belief in youth development. Even he, though, has in recent years been compelled to follow the do-it-today syndrome with some of his purchases.

Too many managers now are not allowed that luxury as they set out their blueprint for progress. Life expectancy of a manager used to be three or four years, but in these days of high expectancy a man's future can be decided over three or four games. These days the essential requirements of a manager, apart from coaching qualifications, appear to be a tin hat and a survival kit.

Too many clubs are existing without looking to the future and I believe that some of the blame lies with the managers. Many of them are not thinking of building a club from the academy upwards but are pursuing a path that means if they can survive three years they will leave as millionaires. They hang on but not for the right reasons.

As another thought which might help the promotion of younger players, I would bring in a rule that says two of the five substitutes must be under twenty-one. It would give youth a chance. You need hungry fighters. Too many of the millionaire footballers make their own conditions, and as soon as you have players who have become complacent you have an animal that is unpredictable. Players such as Paul Scholes of Manchester United, who is the perfect example of commitment and honesty on the pitch, are too often in the minority.

Agents have also become a problem for the game. They come in to negotiate on behalf of the players but will have nothing to do with performance-related contracts. My contracts were on performances all the time based on appearances, goals scored, league position, crowd figures and so on.

I once tried to sign a player for Portsmouth and met the lad and his agent. They wanted £200,000 a year for the player, from which the agent would take his fifteen per cent.

I said: 'Right, there's the cake. I will give him £100,000 a year but if he scores me fifteen goals I will give him another £25,000. If he plays thirty games and doesn't get fifteen goals I will still give him £25,000. If he gets those goals and plays those games and we get to the play-offs, I'll give him £50,000. If we get promoted I'll give him another £50,000. That, to me, adds up to £250,000. I am giving you the opportunity of getting £250,000 a year.'

The agent said: 'No, we can't have that.'

Turning to the player I said: 'There you are. He doesn't fancy you getting that £250,000. He wants to guarantee £200,000 and he's got his fifteen per cent. He can sign, rub his hands and disappear.'

This is the kind of thing that is happening all the time these days. The agent did not want to take a chance on losing some of his percentage. Agents will not have performance-related contracts. The deal was not done.

I don't want to get the harp out and rhapsodize about 'the old days' but it somehow seemed a lot healthier then and I use my granddad as an example. He worked down the pit all week, in the dark, breathing in the lung-damaging dust, and emerged black as pitch after every shift. Come Saturday I would get the number forty-two bus from Walkden to wait for him in Bolton. It was his day off, the time when he smiled with his eyes and there was a definite spring in his step. Win, lose or draw we would walk home with fish and chips out of the paper. He would have two pints, never any more because he had the pit the following day. He supported his team because Saturday was the most wonderful day of the week.

He was not unduly bothered about the result. It was a day out to be enjoyed. That is what they should be doing now. Football watching should be a recreational thing. It has changed out of all recognition and really upsets me when I see pictures of fans, their faces contorted with hate, screaming at opposition players.

But I have experienced good times in the game too. Even in football, when you are struggling, there are people willing to help you in the most amazing ways. At one stage when I was managing Exeter City I was so short of players that out of sheer desperation I rang Sir Alex Ferguson at Manchester United in 1993 and asked him, rather forlornly, if there was any young player I might be able to take on loan. He told me he would think about it and the next thing I knew this young lad turned up with his boots.

It was Simon Davies, and we could see right from the start that he was a class player. Manchester United paid his wages all the time he was with us. A year after leaving us he was to be seen by millions scoring a goal against Barcelona in the Champions League.

On another occasion, in 1987, I had a similar shortage at Portsmouth and rang George Graham, who was managing Arsenal, on the off chance that he might be able to help me over my predicament. George sent me Michael Thomas, who did us an excellent job and went back to Highbury to establish himself as a regular first-teamer. He also won England caps as a driving midfield player.

At other times I could call a club and ask to speak to the manager and the call was not even returned. Alex and George demonstrated how football should be when you need help.

These are the kind of things I remember as I wander along the shore in all weathers looking at that historic stretch of water on which the fleet sailed out to war. Lesley did not walk with me in those last days. She stayed at home, or too often in hospital, to fight the cancerous demons that never quelled her spirit.

When you are out in the solitude with the wind and the rain and the dogs for company all manner of thoughts enter your mind. One morning I was pondering on the unfairness of it all and felt like ringing George Best after hearing that he had been drinking again, abusing his liver transplant.

If I had seen him I definitely would have had something to say to him. I would have said: 'George, there is somebody here who is desperate to live, who would do anything, or give anything, to live and you are going the other way.'

I might also tell him about the time she went very quiet and I said to her gently, something like, 'What's the matter, love?'

She said slowly and deliberately that life would go on without her being there, that the grandchildren would grow up and forget about her and that she hated the thought that it might happen that way. I tried to tell her that was nothing like how it would be and that the treatments would work. That was when she sighed and said they weren't working.

I promised we would continue to search the world. We would do everything possible. Money would be no object in the quest to find something that was good for ovarian cancer. As I lay looking at the ceiling, my arm around her, searching for words of comfort, she said: 'I don't want to wither away. I don't want to look old. I'll have to lock myself away. I don't want people to see me as I am.'

She had these 'Why me?' days and you sometimes became slightly cross with her and for her. You wanted to fight but all you could do was hold her and say: 'Believe me, darling, you'll come out of this.'

That's not enough, though. You thought of the money, the beautiful home, the cars, the wonderful children and gorgeous grandchildren and everything else. But you were helpless.

My life became caring for her, making sure she

enjoyed the things that were left. We wanted another Caribbean holiday, more trips to Spain for the winter sun and hundreds more Sunday gatherings with Mandy, Keely and Jimmy and their spouses and children.

A constant theme was the support of so many friends, who were always on the telephone offering the words of encouragement that meant so much to Lesley. She would hate for me to miss anyone out and Anne and Paul Phillips, who seem to have been friends for as long as I can recall, Jim and Anita Smith from Blackpool, Julie, who was our nanny when the kids were very small, Chris Newton, Lesley's brother, Terry and Janet Hussey, Sir Geoff and Judith Hurst, and Jimmy Tarbuck are all golden people.

For many, many years I was a driven man. Succeeding at football was my obsession. I made it and have come away with a torrent of memories and two decorations that are prized beyond any price. To receive a World Cup medal from the Queen in 1966 and then, thirty-four years later in the spring of millennium year, to visit Buckingham Palace to accept the MBE from Her Majesty were experiences almost beyond reality.

Lesley was with me. I needed her there as I needed her all my life. She was my friend, lover, wife and guardian angel. Who knows where my life might have wandered had it not been for her mental strength and loyal devotion. As the mother of three great children, she took the credit for making them the way they are.

She fought her illness with resolution and without complaint. Whatever I said, the words sounded empty. I told her she'd be OK and that I would always be there for her, but you can only say that so many times. You couldn't answer her questions about the illness and why it happened to her. Why? I asked myself the same thing all the time.

This remarkable woman elected to have a pioneering operation in the North Hampshire Hospital, Basingstoke. She found out about the operation when she was again studying world-wide websites and happened upon Paul Sugarbaker, who has an oncology centre in the United States and was involved in ovarian operations there.

Lesley was searching, looking for something positive to stay alive at the time. Further research told her that Mr Sugarbaker had two associate colleagues, Brendan Moran and Tom Cecil, specialist consultant surgeons who were based in Basingstoke and studied under Sugarbaker. They agreed to operate if Lesley was up for it.

A five-hour operation to remove some of the cancer and wash away what was left of it took place. They reckoned to have got eighty per cent of it. When I went to see her after the operation I received the shock of my life. She was in the intensive care unit, white as the sheets, totally immobile, bleepers going and tubes everywhere. I marvelled at her bravery. She was searching for a life and was prepared to go to any length.

I just wanted her home to have some quality time without the ascites, the cancer seedlings which caused her so much discomfort when they swelled her abdomen. We knew the operation was not going to cure her but she wanted to be a pioneer, to have a go at something that might in the future help others. She realized she was going into the unknown. There have been very, very few of these types of operation performed and with Lesley they went further than they ever did before.

All she wanted was to be able to see the grandchildren and to be able to enjoy them. We hoped to give her that. How brave is a woman who undertakes a massive five- to six-hour operation knowing it is not going to cure her? We went for a short walk down the hospital corridor when we got her up for the first time. It was one of the most satisfying moments I had had for a long, long time. How many times am I allowed to say that she is amazingly brave?

After six weeks in hospital she was not making the recovery they wanted. She was having her good days but the main part of the tumour was round the bowel and that was not allowing her to function properly. When she was eating food there would be a build-up because nothing was passing through and she would have really sick days. It was making her weaker and affecting her positive attitude. She stopped saying things such as: 'I'm getting better now. I'll push on from here.'

These setbacks brought her down and because she wasn't able to take the food that would have kept her strength up they put her on a self-feeding device, a drip. Lesley thought this was a backward step. They rested her tummy and then tried to let her feed herself and we were able to bring her home. Unfortunately, the build-up was there again and, just as we were back home with the family around for Sunday lunch again, the intense pain returned and I had to rush her back to hospital after a few precious days.

That was another dark day in our lives. I was beginning to think this thing would never end, wondering whether this poor lass was ever going to find some relief. Back at the hospital they gave her painkillers and settled her down. She had a barium meal, something that shows the dye moving through your system, and that worked, if slowly. Mr Moran and Mr Cecil said they could operate again to make the bowel work sufficiently well to enable her to eat.

Lesley was up for it, of course, and talking about it with thoughts of lengthening her life and putting weight on. It was a typical response from her but I was in a state of anxiety. I did not believe she was strong enough. She had been through so much but as she said to me, 'I'm here for the long haul. I've started out on this route and I am going to go all the way with it.'

We asked if we could bring her home for a day. It was a beautiful, sunny spring day, Sunday 2 May 2004. There were bright flowers everywhere. The birds were singing, the hanging baskets were overflowing with colourful life and we had all the family around us. It was great for the little ones to see their Nana without tubes and drips attached to her. She laughed a lot that day.

I took her back to hospital that night in readiness for her second operation the following day. Deep down, I was filled with trepidation. But Lesley was determined. She would have tackled anything if she thought it might make her feel better.

As I watched her after the operation I sensed that she was growing weaker. The old sparkle was not there. It looked to me as if her body was not strong enough to keep her up to the mental fight. There was an infection, the wound wasn't healing and she was on antibiotics and morphine.

I saw her for hours every day. The worry was intense. Then I was faced with a dilemma. On the Thursday there was to be an Everton reunion dinner at Goodison Park. The supporters had voted me into the club's greatest all-time eleven and there was to be a presentation on the pitch at the last home game of the season, against Bolton Wanderers on the Saturday.

I told Lesley that I would not go, in order to be with her, but that if I felt I must I would leave the match at half-time to drive back to the hospital. She simply said, quietly: 'It is Everton. You must go with your people.' That said everything about her. She was thinking of me when she was very, very weak.

The children visited her all the time I was away but when I arrived back on Saturday night and stayed late I could see she was not improving. She had no strength although she was nibbling at bits of things such as mashed potato and yoghurt. That static state went on all week and on the Friday I was due to play golf with the Country Gentlemen's Association (I am captain of the golf section) at the Berkshire, one of the most attractive places on any golf calendar. Again, she told me not to worry and that she would see me the following day.

I went and played and was walking up the twelfth

when I saw a buggy pull up alongside the green. A chap stepped out with a mobile phone and I knew immediately that there was a problem. It was a man with the impressive name of Rory Storming-Darling, a member of the CGA. He handed me the phone and said: 'It's William.'

William Harrison-Allan is a fellow member, an old friend and my partner in a horse we own called Pick Up Sticks, trained by Mick Channon. I was almost already in a daze as I heard William say: 'Alan, Jimmy has just been in touch. Drop everything and go to the hospital. Lesley has gone into a coma this morning.'

I flew and once more I was heading down the M3 with those same feelings I had in 2001 when we first heard about Mandy's cancer. I wanted to be there instantly, but at the same time I was consumed by dread. When I arrived a nurse came to meet me and said: 'Lesley has gone into a coma. She is in no pain. We think she will be able to hear you if you want to say something.'

She was lying there peacefully and I just said: 'Lesley, it's Alan.' Her eyes opened briefly. I am convinced she knew I was there. I asked everyone to leave and I spoke to her, very privately, for three or four minutes. I said all the important things about my love for her. She was breathing very heavily but as I spoke she was nodding slightly and I could see the flicker in her eyes. Then she just lapsed into the deepness again. They were regulating the morphine, assuring the gathering family that she was in no pain.

Our three children, Mandy, Keely and Jimmy, had arrived at her bedside before me. Her brother, Chris, came soon after. We knew she was dying. Her body had started to shut down. It was just a matter of waiting, really. It was an agonizing time but, although this can hardly be described as a plus, cancer gives you time to plan. Lesley, in the months before her illness took its drastic turn, had planned what she wanted in death: the funeral, the children and grandchildren, the pensions and what she wanted for the family house and me. It's not like a sudden heart attack and 'what do I do now?'

That particular Saturday, 15 May, in that tiny room, watching her take one laboured breath after another, enabled us all to come to terms with the reality that we were about to lose the most special person in our lives and that we needed to get our grief out together.

We sat around the bed to the point where our children were asking her to go, to be released from this thing, to join her mum and dad in heaven. 'You've suffered enough. We don't want to see you like this, Mum,' one of them said.

She died at 2.40 on Sunday morning. I was alone with her. The kids had gone for a walk and a breath of fresh air, Chris had gone for a lie-down in the resting rooms they have at the hospital. They had all been having rest shifts, having been at the hospital for what was a long, long time watching someone they knew was going to die.

As I sat there her breathing became very laboured. At one point I felt like having a little snooze myself but, thankfully, dismissed the notion. Her breathing became slower. Then she took two long breaths with a long exhalation and she was gone. I shouted for the nurse to get the kids and Chris. We shared our grief. Our hearts poured.

And as I looked at Lesley I saw her as I did the day I married her thirty-seven years earlier. She appeared more like the girl I married than at any time since our wedding day. She was absolutely beautiful.

We thanked the staff and we left the hospital in a convoy. Lesley had said that we should get the funeral formalities over as soon as we could. The service at Southampton Crematorium was beautiful in its simplicity. A measure of Lesley's popularity in and out of the football world could be seen in the hundreds of friends who packed the chapel so that there was standing room only for many of them, including several of my colleagues from the 1966 World Cup final.

At the beginning of the service, with the coffin covered in white flowers lying on the catafalque, the silence was broken by the gentle guitar of the James Taylor song 'You've Got a Friend'. For many, it was an emotional moment. For me, too, it was a reminder of one of the favourite songs of our younger days.

We had chosen some of Lesley's favourite music to punctuate the service. Bette Midler's version of the Len-non–McCartney song 'In My Life' said so much about Lesley's outlook, and no one could fail to be moved by Eva Cassidy, a cancer victim herself, singing 'Somewhere Over the Rainbow'. At the close there was Take That's 'A Million Love Songs', which was special to her because as soon as we walked into our favourite bar in Marbella, Andy, the resident pianist, would strike up with it.

The chosen hymns had a special poignancy, too. When Lesley was a little girl she always watched the FA Cup final on television with her grandma and together they would join in the singing of 'Abide with Me'. Her gran was a keen Bolton Wanderers supporter and on one occasion, when they won the trophy in 1958, they stopped the coach outside Scalper Jack's, as Lesley's barber-father was known, and showed the old lady the trophy. 'Jerusalem' has always been special to us. Lesley always sang it lustily whenever the band played it at the end of racing at Royal Ascot.

After the service we all went back to the Nook and Cranny, the restaurant close to our house in Warsash. There we reminisced with old friends. The warmth of everyone was moving. It was also a time for reflection. We had spent a lifetime together, Lesley and I, and the last three years had been almost surreal.

There were days when we thought she would win and others when we thought she wouldn't. There were highs and there were low moments when everything seemed hopeless. Lesley was the eternal battler, seeking that quest for just more time.

Sadly it wasn't to be. But I still have my happy memories of her and of my life in football of which she played such an important part.

When I think of Lesley, I realize that football, the game which was my lifelong fixation, is, after all, only a game.

INDEX

INDEX

INDEX

INDEX

Max (dog) 193
Mee, Bertie 107, 108
Megson, Gary 333
Mercer, Joe 171, 291, 315–16
Merrington, Dave 274, 277, 280, 294
Mexico 47, 89, 92–101
Mexico City 100
Middlesbrough 185, 246–7, 334
Midler, Bette 374
Mill Reef 114, 125
Miller, Kevin 256–7
Mills, Mick 238–9, 240–2, 251
Millwall 209
Milne, Gordon 41, 87
Minett, Jason 262
Money Fields 197
Monkou, Kenny 285, 286
Moore, Bobby 35, 37, 44, 45, 56, 59, 63–5, 66, 89, 101, 127, 162–5, 360
death 59, 165, 356
stolen bracelet affair 90–3
Moore, Stephanie 162, 164–5, 356
Moore, Tina 128, 162, 164–5
Moores, John 29, 111–12
Moran, Brendan 368, 370
Moran, Paul 225
Moran, Ronnie 24
Moran, Steve 136, 258
Morgan, Nicky 190
Morris, Colin 151
Morrisey, Johnny 77, 83
Mortimore, John 281
Muggeridge, Frank 141, 159
Muller, Gerd 99
Mullery, Alan 90, 92, 96, 98

Nantwich Town 71
Neasom, Mike 181
Neill, Terry 127, 129–32
Neill, Warren 219
Nelson, Paul 145–6
Neville, Gary and Phil 362
New York 158–9, 173–5
New York Cosmos 144, 148–9
Newcastle United 266, 267, 268, 270, 283
Newmarket 125
Newton, Chris 367, 372, 374
Newton, Hilda 32, 121–2, 145
Newton, Jack 32, 145, 375
Newton, Keith 41, 89, 96, 108
Nicholl, Chris 136, 138
Nield, Maurice 243, 244
Noakes, George 15
North Hampshire Hospital, Basingstoke 368–9
Northern Ireland 39, 267
Norway 42
Norwich City 276
Nottingham Forest 116, 179, 188, 189, 332

O'Callaghan, Kevin 187, 190, 195, 209
O'Connell, Brendan 178
O'Farrell, Frank 107
Oldham Athletic 191, 195, 206, 207
O'Leary, David 130, 318
Orient 138
Osgood, Peter 90, 136, 138, 140, 142, 196, 217, 218–19, 226
Oswestry 9, 11, 28
Overath, Wolfgang 98

INDEX

INDEX